For Bridie

SKINT ESTATE

**NOTES
FROM THE
POVERTY
LINE**

CASH CARRAWAY

EBURY
PRESS

Ebury Press, an imprint of Ebury Publishing
20 Vauxhall Bridge Road
London SW1V 2SA

3 5 7 9 10 8 6 4 2

Ebury Press is part of the Penguin Random House group of companies
whose addresses can be found at global.penguinrandomhouse.com

Penguin
Random House
UK

First published by Ebury Press in 2019
This edition published in 2020

www.penguin.co.uk

A CIP catalogue record for this book is available from
the British Library

ISBN 9781529103380

Author photograph: Michael Wharley

Typeset in 10.24 pt/16.7 pt ITC Galliard Pro
by Integra Software Services Pvt. Ltd, Pondicherry

Printed and bound in Great Britain by Clays Ltd, Elcograf S.p.A.

*This book is a based on the life, experiences and recollections
of the author. In some cases names of people, places, dates,
sequences or the detail of events have been changed to protect
the privacy of others.*

CONTENTS

AUTHOR'S NOTE:

The words written on these pages were not intended to be read in silence. So please say them out loud whenever you can – preferably to someone who doesn't want to hear them.

Some names, places and times have been changed to protect the guilty.

PROLOGUE

I WRITE THIS SLUMPED on my cream pleather sofa. My fat, tattooed arm wobbling as it scribbles down memories in between greedy mouthfuls of pasta (that – isn't – gluten – free), and a Richmond menthol gritted between my disgusting rotting Jeremy-Kyle-guest-style teeth. And I'm just about to pop down to the local Chicken Cottage to grab my daughter a bargain bucket of crushed battery-hen vessels and connective tissues because I can't be arsed to cook. You all *know* where this is headed – first stop Chicken Cottage, final destination Irvine Welsh degenerate, there is no doubt that I'm leading my kid down the grim path to heroin addiction.

A *lot* of my free time (which *is* a lot of the time) is spent mooching about my estate hoping that a Channel 5 producer will discover me and turn me into the next 'White Dee'. Later on tonight, I shall leave my child alone as she sinks into a fitful sleep, constantly disturbed by the cries of 'Hey, guys!' as her favourite YouTubers spin like a disco ball at an all-you-can-drink nightclub across her iPad – the closest thing she has to a family. But I'll be out there, on the town. In a vest top tightly clinging to my Lambrini curves bingeing on depravity with other women – like – me down the local Wetherspoons, before getting my fanny serviced after closing time in an alleyway by a manual labourer.

I am a *terrible*, scrounging, despicable little woman – when I celebrate my birthday at the Harvester, I visit the salad bar an *unacceptable* amount of times. I misuse food banks (because – who – doesn't – like – free – food?) yet I own two iPhone Xs and three Orla Kiely cushions. I'm so disgusting that I've never even been to Center Parcs. My eight-year-old daughter has water fights on the estate with the other kids purely to entertain the local paedos who gather en masse with their horny eyes and fat dogs (who – run – around – leashless) but at least it keeps her out of my hair for a few hours whilst I'm living a champagne lifestyle courtesy of the taxpayer.

Where's the dad?! – I make you want to write forty times over in the *Daily Mail* comments section.

(*There is no dad. The dad didn't stick around. Couldn't – even – keep – a – man.*)

And whilst it is true that my daughter's biological father doesn't feature in her life, I am not a walking talking *Take a Break* magazine article. I am not a stain on society. Or a statistic of shame. I am not a *burden* on the state (there is no such thing as a burden within a welfare state). And I am not the solo creator of a future stain. That is just the mainstream media's targeted witch-hunt against women like me.

Perceptions created by sneering producers at Channel 5 and privileged men of the right-wing press who will utter any old drivel for a chance at a viral tweet. A witch-hunt intended to inject anti-female propaganda into our already divided communities, to demonise and shame and to keep women in check. Portraying 'working-class woman' without nuance in order to keep us trapped in our little poverty porn boxes to be observed like a freakish curiosity from 1834.

I am one of 2 million demonised single women in the UK banished from the sisterhood of posing against Insta-perfect urban walls in gentrified areas because we can't afford to cook Deliciously Ella on Agas. Women like *me* – we don't have husbands and we most certainly don't have wine o'clock – *we have borderline alcoholism*. We don't have Farrow & Ball No. 26 'Down Pipe' adorning our living-room walls, we have standard magnolia woodchip in the squalid little council flats we shamefully refer to as 'home'. Because that's what we *deserve*. Magnolia, woodchip and shame. We haven't worked hard enough, we just don't deserve it, we – just – haven't – put – the – work – in. And you *do* get what you deserve in life, that's an actual fact. You work *bloody* hard, and you get back what you put in. That's the popular perception, isn't it? And I've written this book to show you the flip side of these perceptions. The unheard voice, that thanks to this caricatured and vilified portrayal has led to a cycle of disregard, humiliation and misunderstanding. Because I've worked *bloody* hard yet I've lived below the poverty line since 2010 when I found myself pregnant and alone. Over 8 million other hardworking people (in *actual* employment, according to government figures) in the UK have been living similar, unstable and impoverished lives too. Does anyone really *deserve* that? These words of mine are here to attempt to break that belief system and answer that question.

It's May 2010 and I'm heavily pregnant. The grubby sofa in the communal area of the women's refuge is stained with the period blood and sweat of a domestic violence victim's past. There are eight of us women squeezed onto and around it. David Cameron is moving into Downing Street, but before he wheels in his suitcase and obedient Boden wife, he stops outside to give a quick generic speech about fairness and family values. He forces self-assurance but is clearly broken – here stands a man who had always dreamed of power yet gained it in the most un-triumphant of ways. He's like the guy who got the girl but only after guilting her into submission by threatening to jump in front of a train if she continued to reject him. I sigh, and I tut, and I think I probably shout at the screen, much to the disdain of the women in the room. An old South African woman tells me to calm down or I'll harm my baby, 'Your baby is feeling your anger,' she says.

So, I shut up and watch in silence like the others, but something within me has definitely changed.

This is the very moment where the story begins. This story of motherhood, survival and poverty. For the first time in my life I have something to live for. To fight for. I remember the start of this story vividly, everything so clear, jolting me into the lucidity of an out-of-body experience. It's one of those stories that becomes more significant to me with each retelling.

It's like remembering the band who were playing in the Uber the first time you shared an awkward kiss with the person who turned out to be the love of your life. It's that *one* line in that book you read that made you quit your demoralising job on the spot, so you could travel round India or *somewhere* for six months. It's the realisation that hits mid-altercation with the stranger on the bus shifting your world view forever. For me, *this* is that argument. Right there in the refuge, pregnant and alone. This is the moment that gave me a purpose in life.

Here is the moment: David Cameron is giving his speech and I am terrified and … disappointed. I didn't want him as our prime minister, and I hadn't even been given the right to make that known. I'm shouting at the TV, but no one is listening. I'm wrapped in a blanket and chain-eating orange Calippos because my baby is making me crave ice – which I later discover is because my iron levels are as depleted as my spirit. And apparently eating ice helps – who knew? The other women in the room don't seem to share my concerns. They say things like 'our vote wouldn't have made a difference anyway' and 'all political parties are the same'. They say '*nothing* is going to change'. They say 'everything always stays the same'. Everything always stays the same for women like us. And it does, I say – *until it doesn't*. Until one morning you wake up and realise you have zero autonomy over your life and something has to change. And *this* is when and where I realised that.

This is the *very* start of the story.

And I am not a natural political creature, certainly not at this moment in this refuge. I am apathetic and don't consider myself smart enough to tackle politics. Politics is something for other people to get to grips with, more educated people, those who follow traditional career paths and have normative families and ambitions. Not people like me who can't seem to make sense of it all; who, when getting into a debate with a pompous man with a voice *loud* enough to make the things he's saying sound plausible, clam up and just nod in agreement. Plus, I have a common South East London accent and people are always telling me that I sound 'thick'.

Women like me don't do politics. The aggressive accent of Penge doesn't seem apt for creating change or stirring revolution. I watch the news but don't really listen. I have a tattoo that reads 'Intellectual Hooligan' in response to reading Albert Camus' *The Rebel* but I don't quite understand the point I was trying to make by permanently engraving my arm – apart from the fact I almost immediately regret my actions. I demonstrated against the illegal war in Iraq because I consider myself a pacifist but also so I could get drunk with my friends afterwards. Up until this moment in the refuge I had been lost in a sea of nihilism. Nothing means nothing to me. Took jobs that didn't lead to careers. Was offered opportunities but ruined them all. Played in bands. Wrote plays that no one watched. Lived in filthy overcrowded house shares, communes and caravans with ... strange men. Took a lot of drugs. But *now*, with the birth of my child imminent, the televised eviction of Gordon Brown from Downing Street gave me a shunt of realisation: that it was important to at least *start* to care.

I suddenly wanted to be political – whatever *that* means. Us women in the refuge, we weren't allowed to vote in the General Election due to living in a secret, safe, yet temporary address that could only be identified on legal documents as a PO BOX and it suddenly became important to me to have a voice.

I knew things were about to get very dark. Not just for me and my future child but for millions of others. Here I was, about to graduate from a women's refuge into life as a single mum with no family to back me up and I knew, even then, that when you're placed at the very bottom of society the last thing you need is a Tory government holding you down in an economic gang rape that makes the poor and vulnerable the scapegoat for society's decline. And with mine and the other refuge women's voices kept off the ballot we had no choice but to put our faith in society – with Cameron shuffling into Number Ten I didn't much trust 'the voting public'. I think the real question a General Election asks isn't what party you are traditionally expected to stand behind, but rather: Do you want to vote for equality and fairness? Do you consider the lives of the voiceless and the vulnerable? Or do you just vote for your own selfish needs? For your mortgage rates, your cars, your business revenue – voting to keep hold of as much of your money as possible. Or to put it simply, a General Election asks the question: Are you a decent human?

My vote and my voice were stolen during that election and I vowed I would never let that happen again. However, instead of being able to assert my new-found appetite for class equality, as I attempted to start my new life with my baby, an acute laryngeal cancer grew against my vocal cords, growing stronger and more deadly with each austerity measure designed to ensure the working class were made to pay for the actions of greedy bankers: the benefit cap, housing benefit cuts, zero hours, rising rents, one attack after the other – austerity is terminal and wanton. As the cancer grew bigger and stronger I discovered there was no way back from this socioeconomic terrorism against the vulnerable.

Cut to June 2017 and we're standing in West London watching the season finale of austerity.

We watch it burn. My daughter and me. We're just watching it burn. Smoke filling the remaining space inside our rotting necks. In a series of events far too tragic to be described as poetic, seven years on from leaving the refuge my daughter and I find ourselves living in yet another women's hostel just around the corner from Grenfell Tower. The resting place of deprivation. A cruel statue that celebrates the life of incessant silent struggle before it is brutally erased in smoke, destroying all evidence.

'Will we get burned too, because we're poor, Mummy?' she asks.

I don't know. I don't know if we are next. I honestly do not know ...

This is a book about my life as a working-class woman in modern Britain. This is a book about trying to find your voice as a marginalised citizen who has been thrown into a pit and buried deep by society's stigma. Consider my personal stories and sordid experiences as gonzo from the gutter. An antidote to right-wing media portrayals and poverty porn spunked across our screens from Channel 5 ... You might not *like* what you read, and you might not like the way I write it; my glibness and causticity makes me incredibly unlikeable at times. I am not detached nor a slave to stats. This is not worthy journalism written to instil fleeting empathy into a middle-class readership and to be garnished with awards. This is my reality. I – am – angry. And you'll mutter – 'she's got a chip on her shoulder', because you won't find me gushing gratefully, 'Thank you, thank you for giving a woman like me the *opportunity* to write a book, thank you. Thank you for *allowing* me to share my story' – the way women like me are supposed to. I act like it's my right to speak up, a behaviour deemed transgressive for a working-class woman, and in turn certain people will find that offensive. *And* I sometimes say and do terrible things because I am a fully complete human. I say stupid things, behave in ways I regret. I fail. I make mistakes. But I want you to know that my intention is to do something good – I want people to know what life is really like below the poverty line in modern Britain, the reality behind the readily available yet *ignored* statistics.

Stats that people can find but seem to ignore

Statistic: 68 per cent of single mothers are in work yet are more likely to be stuck in low-paid roles than any other worker.

Another stat: Over 14 million people live below the poverty line.

More stats: 75 per cent of people living below the poverty line are in work.

More stats: 1 in 3 single-parent families live in poverty.

One more stat: Child poverty is predicted to rise from 37 per cent to 62 per cent under a Conservative government.

But this is *not* a book about statistics.

I've written down some things that happened to me whilst living my life of poverty, loneliness and violence amongst a grim landscape of temporary housing, forced self-employment, sex work and food banks. I think these stories speak louder than stats. Living a life shrouded in failure and desperation paints a more realistic picture of society than a percentage or a pie chart. I know what it really means to fuck up and be fucked over and I've written all that down too. And there is *so* much to say about failure. And the shame of living with your mistakes and accepting failure.

I've written about my encounters of oppression, which I experience far less than most yet far more than many in our seemingly broken and unequal world. And I've written about my friendships, survival techniques, hope and the unbreakable bond between a mother and her child, because, although I am the narrator of these stories, my daughter very much emerges as the protagonist. Because what I've *mainly* written about is love, and the things that women like me do for the love of their child in a society designed to break them.

A hundred years ago, 'hysterical' women like me would have been carted off down the asylum to give birth to my shame away from the prying eyes of society, but we now live in a world with newspapers dedicated to slamming our 'reckless' lifestyle choices. And in response I guess I've written up some of my little sordid stories in an attempt to cobble together a loose yet accessible manifesto for change. Why is it easier for the middle classes and the media to blame working-class mothers for moral decline and cast us as villains – the creators of hooligans and murderers than for them to take a hard look at the failings of a government who bow to the rigid constraints of a patriarchal structure that perpetuates misogyny? It seems like an impossible prison for marginalised women to break free from.

This is about what life is really like for a woman raising her voice from the gutter, and the consequences of daring to speak out.

1
EVICTED

NAMASTE IS SMEARED IN shit across the toilet cubicle mirror.

It's the first day of my new life. I'm low on cash so I'm searching for the cheapest way back home to London. And it's lucky we're being dragged out bleary eyed into the early days of the year because most of the staff are still on their holidays – they've left the barriers wide open, and I just walk on through. Just *walk on through*. And nobody checks me – but just to be safe I'm riding home in the train toilet, in case any jobsworth ticket guards are on the prowl. But my phone is ringing and I reject the call because it's Gary – *metrosexual Bill Sykes with terrible tribal tattoos* – who up until an hour ago was my boyfriend, who I'd been staying with in this dismal place called Grantham – in his childhood bedroom with his lower-middle-class (yet aspirational, yet slightly backward) parents – before he'd served me with a *very* threatening eviction notice. So, I pack my entire life into my Herschel rucksack, throw on an old pair of Tom Ford sunglasses to hide the bruise which by now is spreading all the way down to my jaw. So now Kirsty – *best friend since art school but she fell into 9 to 5* – is worried about me (because – I – left – her – a – voicemail – dramatically – sobbing – like – always) and now she's ringing my Nokia.

My eye is snapped black shut. And I am pissing on a stick. I let Kirsty go to voicemail, she'll call again, she always does. I'm angling my arse to hover lightly above the fresh faeces gifted by the previous cubicle occupant, which has been carefully buttered across the entirety of the seat. It's someone from Retford I reckon, because it's still steaming, it's such a Retford thing to do, this shit is fresh, *so* Retford, so fresh like someone birthed it a mere 20 minutes ago in Retford. We're pulling out of G-Town. And Kirsty's ringing again but she's *relentless* like that, so I put her on loudspeaker and she doesn't utter a word for at least a minute as she listens to me piss and then she asks me if I'm really *that* lacking in manners to be using the toilet whilst I'm supposed to be talking to her, but she doesn't wait for an answer because now she's telling me she's been Googling homemade abortions.

'Do you remember dark black Davinia?' she asks.

I don't remember.

'Dark black Davinia. You hung around with her all the time. She was one of your crazy stripper friends from The Aquarius Club.'

I don't really remember, I say; plus I'm only half listening because I'm trying to catch my reflection through the gaps in the NAMASTE, but I can only make out my lips which are busted and keep bleeding.

Kirsty keeps talking ... You *do* remember. She did Runway in Milan. *Vogue.* You resented her. Pinnacle of *your* modelling career was applying for *FHM*'s High Street Honeys; you pulled out saying you didn't trust anything voted on by the public. Speaking of voting – when you get where you're going – register, yeah? People I once thought decent are backing Cameron. Others are getting behind that Lib Dem. What's his name? Doesn't matter. A vote for him ensures a Conservative victory. I'm scared. We'll be living a 1980s throwback: National Front, they'll rise. Another Hillsborough. Another working-class massacre fuelled by corruption. And we're only ever one Tory government away from an IRA comeback. *You* said that. You were joking but it's true. Isn't it? Cash, are you even listening...?

I'm listening, and I sigh; it's 2010, Kirsty. Nobody is worried about the IRA anymore. You're paranoid. People will never forget what Thatcher did. The Tories are NEVER going to get back in. Never.

NAMASTE bounces in front of my face to the rhythm of the train, which in juxtaposition to the toilet seat I find to be a very positive sentiment but—

My aim is off.

It's all over the place.

Every violent jerk towards Peterborough results in my hot heavy urine spurting onto the floor. Kirsty is *still* on loudspeaker and she's *still* Googling because I can hear her fat fingers typing as she asks – 'You don't remember dark black Davinia?'

I vaguely remember. I vaguely remember Davinia. I say.

'She did the reality show and it ruined her life, so she moved to Stockholm with that ugly rich man,' Kirsty reminds me. 'We booked the room at the Dorchester, so she could do the abortion,' Kirsty reminds me. My piss seeps through the holes in my Converse.

'She was five months gone and the doctors said she was too late to have the procedure legally, so she paid for that suite at the Dorchester, and me and you went along in support of her ... *and* to have that relaxing spa weekend.' Now my piss is spraying off the plastic bowl, rebounding onto my thigh and I realise that by the time I make it to King's Cross there'll be a huge wet patch on the crotch of my skinny stonewashed jeans.

My – piss – as – directionless – as – my – life.

'I'm Googling now but nothing is coming up. Do you remember what she used?' Kirsty is frantic. On the frosted window – the word #BLESSED. It's from a different set of bowels. I can tell because the hue is different, it's darker and it's dry. Like it's been there for some time. 'I think it's something to do with vitamin C. You overdose on vitamin C and it triggers a miscarriage. You need a fuck load of it though. Or did she use vitamin B? Was it vitamin B? I know it's a vitamin ...'
I think about ending the call because I'm taking pregnancy tests to kill time and I need to concentrate on my aim because my piss is everywhere and the next person who uses this toilet

will think there's been some kind of massacre in here because I've just spat out about a pint of thick blood from my gums into the sink.

Kirsty reminds me – 'And then she smoked all your PCP and you were angry at her for *that* and by the time she bled it all out over the fluffy towels you were planning to steal you totally lost it. You weren't very sympathetic towards her ...'

I really don't remember. But I believe her – I *can* be horrible like that, protecting myself under the guise of savagery like some Pinter bitch.

This is my second test within the hour-long journey. But a few lucky drips of urine hit the stick and a pair of blue lines emerge with speed. I put the phone down on Kirsty.

Definitely with child.

Almost certain of it.

Almost – because I'd bulk stolen 20 multipacks from Poundland a couple of days back and with this being my tenth test in 48 hours I'm either *very* pregnant or those cheap stolen tests are big-time liars. Kirsty calls back, again, she's back on loudspeaker again.

'How do you feel about all *this*?' she asks.

I feel fucking great, I tell her. I tell her that this is the happiest moment of my life. This is where things finally start to turn around. I tell her that *this* is everything I've ever wanted.

And it is.

Kirsty says: 'You're in shock. I'll find out which vitamin it is. And I can't afford the Dorchester, but we'll find a nice little hotel out in the countryside somewhere, get rid of it there, somewhere quiet, nice girlie weekend.'

And that's when I tell her I'm hashtag Blessed. I read it from the stinking shit-covered window. I'm so happy. #BLESSED.

'You're talking utter shit. I'll find us a hotel,' she says. That's when I put the phone down again.

(We've stopped at Peterborough.)

I'm covered in piss and blood and most likely some stranger's shit, but this is all I've ever wanted – all I've ever wanted is a family. My own family. Of course, I thought it would be different, didn't think I'd be doing it alone. No one plans to run away with the clothes on her back and a bag containing 40 stolen pregnancy tests. I take the opportunity of my two still minutes in Peterborough to pull up my knickers and rinse the blood right out of my mouth. Of course, I'd have loved to have done the 'big reveal' to a partner who loved me, done things the socially acceptable way, like the other women do; bowed up the positive result in a nice glitter wrap from Paperchase and presented it as a gift. Bought a card that said 'Dad' and watched with contentment as his confusion turned to a delightful surprise. Presented him with a football kit by his team of choice in newborn-baby size. That kind of thing. But Gary *definitely* wouldn't have been into all that.

I told him he was going to be a father over our third plate of Pizza Hut buffet.

Flash back 1 hour. And he's taking his time to chew the unnecessarily thick slice of meat feast that they serve up in those places. No one likes their pizza that deep but even after I deliver the news we move onto our fourth plate because I take buffets really seriously and it's important to get your money's worth regardless of how sick you get later, and then he lifts up his watery steroid-filled arm and simply points to the black eye he'd given me for Christmas.

In all fairness, he'd also given me a box of Milk Tray. But the injury had a more personal touch, handmade presents are always more memorable, aren't they?

The point to my eye? That's my eviction notice.

No – actual – words – required.

He takes a long swig of refillable Coke Zero which he swills around his mouth and, after a quick visit to the Ice Cream Factory, he is finally ready to speak with words.

ABORT IT. OR I'LL ABORT IT FOR YOU.

Cut to me paying the bill and by then I'd say he'd made his position on fatherhood pretty clear.

He went back to work, I packed up my life.

Threw £2 in coppers into my rucksack, a change of knickers, my laptop and 40 stolen pregnancy tests.

Starting again.

I've started again like 50 times now and I'm only 29.

I know the drill.

My mum threw me out at 16 and I've been facing evictions ever since.

But this time it means something.

Ten positive tests. That means *something*.

This time is different.

I grab some toilet roll and attempt to scrub off the NAMASTE, so I can smile into the mirror.

But my reflection won't give me the response I want: Try to smile with a broken cheekbone and your whole face might just cave in.

I take a second to breathe it all in.

The first day of my new life.

'Mother died today. Or maybe it was yesterday. I can't be sure' – are the opening lines to Camus' novel *L'Étranger*, but also the words I utter whenever anyone asks about Mum. For the past 11 years I've been killing her off every few months. Consider it a perk of estrangement; you ever need a few weeks off work or want to avoid a hen do with ten annoying semi-strangers in Valencia or something like that, then just tell them that Mother has died.

Mother deaths are the worst of the deaths and people will be very kind to you.

There was the tragic car crash in France. The heart attack. The haemorrhage. The Rod-Hull-style roof-fall. The rapid AIDS demise. The suicide. The brutal murder in Nigeria.

Tips for killing off your estranged mum: Don't prolong it with an illness, colleagues ask questions. It needs to be sudden. *Don't* do a cancer. I made *that* mistake back in the early days. The thing with a cancer is that everyone has been affected and someone will corner you in the office kitchen and the next thing you know you'll be holding them in your arms as they sob about their kid sister dying from leukaemia back in 1992. Or they'll want to talk to you about treatments, which means you'll have to do your research. You don't need that. Make her die with minimal effort. Go with sudden death. Make it outrageous so people feel awkward. Throw in an unusual location to set the scene. Go with murdered prostitute, that's my *favourite* of the mum deaths.

Make your mother a murdered prostitute and your boss isn't going to ask any questions.

Anyway, Mum's not dead. I know this because I'm meeting her at King's Cross. We haven't seen each other in over ten years and, despite not being the type of person to believe in fate or synchronicity, I do find it poetic justice that I should return to her with a black eye. I was 18 and she smashed in my face with her Hoover (she has terrible OCD and all of her violent acts towards me always involved a cleaning product of some kind) and I haven't seen her since. Full circle. Same eye – she even got me in the same eye as Gary did! At least it means she'll recognise me.

It's thanks to Mum I learned how to live life on the run. I was 15 when I started planning my getaway. Whilst my friends took Saturday jobs at the Bakers Oven enabling them to buy ten B&H and the cover charge to Popscene down the Astoria on a Friday night, I took an after-school job on the door of a Soho clip joint. I needed proper money to ensure a safe getaway. My role at the clip joint was to lead horny men downstairs to the 'club' under the premise of having sex with them – only once they'd get downstairs they'd find a couple of gangsters waiting to steal the contents of their wallet, of which I'd be given a cut. I did whatever I had to do to save up for that first month's rent and deposit in preparation for when Mum finally chucked me out, which turns out was my sixteenth-birthday present from her – a gift with a personal touch. We do speak from time to time. Always hoping she'll change. Make a desperate phone call every few years or so. When I'm lost, or high, or drunk. Usually all three. Those dark moments when everyone craves their mother, even if she is the mother who once tried to strangle you with the washing line. She's always so superior on the phone:

'I've been expecting your call,' she says.

She says *that* because she's got 'the gift'. That's what she calls it. Her and my uncle Colm take their psychic show around the spiritual churches of Greater Manchester, preying on lonely middle-aged women whose husbands have gone away. Filling them with hope via her lies. Like me, she'll say whatever she needs to get what she wants. That's the *only* trait we share. And that's why I don't feel guilty about the amount of times I've killed her.

We meet outside the WHSmith. She doesn't get close, always a full metre away, and she doesn't mention the black eye. It's like it's always been a part of me.

Listen, I don't want to admit any of this. I don't want you to *know* any of this. I told you that you'd find me disgusting because I do terrible things but I'm merely providing context. And all this stuff happened to me on the first day of my new start. Happily pregnant, yet alone. And *nobody* wants to admit hiding from a ticket guard in a shit-smeared train toilet or wants to reveal to the world that they're the kind of person who gets a week off work by pretending their own mother has died of AIDS. Or that you're pregnant by an intellectually inferior man who broke your face into pieces. Or that you stole 20 multipack pregnancy tests. Nobody wants to admit to being poor and alone. And it's painful to write it down because the memories are squeezing my skull and the fact is that my truth looks pathetic typed up on the page. Victimy. Because pain is hack, isn't it? Most stories of abuse follow a similar trajectory. But this is the truth. And maybe it will help you to understand why women like me live the way we do.

I am filled with shame, you should know that. Not because of the things I've done, I do what I have to do, I always will. But – ashamed my foray into motherhood doesn't fit into the socially acceptable narrative of nurture and financial security. And because of this I will forever remain an outsider. *L'Étranger.*

Would have loved to live life like all those other women do; a Victorian conversion in Crouch End with a man who has bad taste in music and questionable right-wing voting habits (which – I'd – ignore – for – the – sake – of – financial stability). Own a selection of Sweaty Betty maternity bras. Show off my Tiffany ring push present. Expose my floorboards, dabble in yoga. Brunch at Banners. Slightly embarrass my husband at dinner parties by getting drunk in front of his friends and gently revealing my snowflake leftie views. That kind of thing.

Vaguely unhappy like everyone else, but sometimes verging on happy because I'd have a driving licence and would aspire to buy a Land Rover.

But my reality is sordid. It's disgusting. Utter filth.

I've never even had a driving lesson.

Christmas Eve 2009 and me and Gary are getting ready to attend a fancy-dress party in Newark-on-Trent. The theme is serial killers and we are going as Rose and Fred West. We've opted for a version of the Wests in their younger more attractive period and my hair is styled into some kind of 1970s feather cut. From a shop called Party Poopers I've selected Gary a curly wig, some handyman overalls and a prop drill (that looks like it could carve through concrete walls). I'm wearing a vintage floral dress and Deirdre Rachid-style spectacles.

This is eight days before my first stolen pregnancy test. This is ten days before the Pizza Hut buffet. Ten whole days before the train toilet cubicle situation. I do not yet know the fate awaiting me.

So, we're walking Gary's Pomeranian, Nick Clegg, through the park dressed as two of Britain's most notorious serial killers when he accuses me of sleeping with my ex whilst I'd been back in London a few days earlier.

'Are you in character?' I ask.

What?

'Are you asking me this question as Fred West or as Gary? Because it's a *very* Fred West type of question . . .' I laugh.

That pissed him off. He hates it when I've been back home in London. He says I come back walking taller, talking louder, getting swaggerous, too confident. It's like my city gives me power.

But there I am smiling at him like some cocky Rose West after getting away with it for 20 years.

That's when his headbutt comes out of nowhere.

That's when I hear my face crack.

It's like my nose is being forced inside my skull, but I check, and it's still on the outside. It's the first thing I check as I wake up face down in a puddle.

All I hear are the footsteps of him and Nick Clegg running off down the alleyway.

And I'm out again. Not sure for how long.

The next thing I see is Gary's father.

He's holding a bag of frozen peas above my face. He lifts me out of the puddle and gently places the cold to my eye. Then he puts his mouth to my ear.

'If you go to the police, we'll say you're lying.'

The bruising came up almost immediately.

In the taxi on the way to the party I joke –

'I imagine Fred gave Rose many a black eye over the years.'

Gary agrees.

'We look authentic, mate,' he says with a supportive hand squeeze.

We won the prize for best-dressed serial killer couple.

Merry Christmas.

Eight days later and I'm pissing on my first positive stick of 2010.

… You might not know how to leave. You might have nowhere to go. But when a man offers you a bespoke abortion over a Pizza Hut buffet then it's time to start plotting your next escape.

That was when I decided to revive Mother and phone her.

'I've been expecting your call,' she said.

When I get off the train at King's Cross and jump the barriers, I spend 30p of my coppers to enter the pristine station toilets, so I can do another test. I'll present it as a gift to Mother, I decide. Grandmother. My aim is back on form and the lines emerge fast and positive. Behind the dark sunglasses and the rigid moody pout my face has been broken into, I am smiling. In front of a clean full-length mirror I stick out my pregnant tummy. It looks like I've just eaten four full plates of buffet. But it's in there. The baby is in there. The family I have always wanted. It's in there. The new start.

The last of the new starts.

'Here, Mum, look.' I reach out to hand her the positive test.

'Get your filthy piss away from me,' she shouts.

I wish she really was dead, I think. I wish I didn't have to pretend she's dead.

We walk around Camden for a while, but she doesn't mention the baby, or acknowledge she's going to be a grandma. She doesn't ask where I'm staying or where I'm going. I walk her back to the station and she doesn't give me the hug I've been waiting 29 years for. And she doesn't look back and wave from the ticket barrier, like I hoped she would. Even though I waited and watched the train pull out.

That's the last time I ever saw her.

That night I check into a women's refuge and accept that I'm going to be starting my new life alone.

I'll be alright. I always am.

The first day of *our* new life.

2

NOTES FROM: A SAFE HOUSE

AN OLD TRASHY BLONDE South African with infected lip fillers is shouting stuff about the devil. She is banging on my bedroom door, convinced a demon lives within me. She says it's evil, and it's eating at my soul and its body is deformed and its mind is *twisted*. She is talking about my foetus. She'd mentioned me to the pastor at her church and he replied that my melancholy and constant swearing and disdain towards the world had already harmed my baby. If I allow it to fully form then I'll have a disabled one on my hands she reckons. She's screaming all this outside my door.

'Let the devil free,' she cries.

Eventually a support worker drags her to the top of the house where her screams transform into a soothing rhythm. I was yet to receive any congratulations and was getting used to these unorthodox reactions to my pregnancy by now.

From my room in the refuge I'd just posted a picture of my 12-week scan on Facebook. You can announce at 12 weeks, it's the *thing* to do. It was beautiful. The scan. The radiographer had captured its feet in the air mid-kick and its hands dangling arrogantly like it was smoking a ciggy right there inside my womb; its heavy skull looking dazed into the blackness of my insides – and it's safe, and apparently, according to the doctor, it's very healthy. No deformities. No disabilities.

That was when I received the shopping list via Messenger from Davinia. Hadn't heard from her in years – since our unconventional spa weekend at the Dorchester – and things were frosty to say the least and she doesn't ask how I am.

It reads: three bottles of wine, vitamin C tablets, powdered cinnamon, chamomile oil, laxatives and a packet of aspirin.

She follows it up a few minutes later with a list of bullet points:

- Dissolve ten vitamin C tablets into a bottle of wine
- Wash down 15 laxatives with the entire bottle
- Run a hot bath infused with chamomile oil (Note: you might want to boil the kettle and a few pans if the water pressure is low – it needs to be scalding!)
- Pour yourself another glass of wine, add a generous dash of powdered cinnamon and … relax.
- Pop a couple of aspirin. You'll bleed it out within an hour. Don't use your best (stolen) towels.
- Polish off the rest of the wine to knock yourself out.

Then one last message: You've got this, babe. Kiss.

Kirsty had tracked down Davinia in Stockholm where she now lived with her rich ugly husband who she had settled for in exchange for stability because she has a family a bit like mine. The abortion recipe is hers and Kirsty's *gift* to me.

Kirsty means well, she sort of loves me yet resents me in only the way that female friends can; she thinks I'm a proper loser but admires how I refuse to give up. She just doesn't understand me. She comes from a stable loving family and has always had somewhere to go at Christmas. The worst thing that has *ever* happened in her life was when her dad got caught having an affair with his PA, and after five years of therapy she *still* isn't over it. I'm basically her friend because my life is more of a mess than hers. My fuck-ups make her feel good about the fact she gave up on her dreams. She has a 9 to 5 and a mortgage and a boring balding boyfriend called Mark who works in Graphic Design. She should be the one having a child, not me.

Anyway, she wasn't the only one with doubts. My baby scan sat there on the screen for just over an hour before even one person dared to like it (and it wasn't even a face I recognised, just some random who'd added me after a squat rave back in 2005) but *no one* commented.

Then a girl who I hadn't heard from since our teenage years in youth theatre sent me a private message. She was blind in one eye and her hands severely deformed into claws – although we had never discussed why. She did a really good job of 'hiding her disabilities' (her words) but I always admired how whenever we evaded train fares and got caught by guard she would amp up her difficult hand situation, making such a meal of trying to get into her bag to find her non-existent ticket that the guard would feel sympathy towards her and just let it go. I on the other hand – functioning hands and ticketless – always landed a hefty fine or court appearance.

My pregnancy announcement had inspired my old friend to reveal the reasons behind her deformities. Turns out her mother hadn't wanted her and had drunk a bottle of gin before attempting to remove her with a metal coat hanger.

As far as her mum had been aware it had done the trick – and she was surprised when her daughter arrived seven months later, underweight, twisted hands and semi-blind.

'If you don't want a deformed child then book yourself in on the NHS, it's still early days,' she wrote.

I replied straight away. Thanks, babe, still doing the drama? No, she said. She'd given up on all that now and was working as a legal secretary. Good money, good husband prospects – her words. Although she dabbled in a bit of am-dram 'to keep her hand in'. *Her* words.

After a short while the comments came flooding in underneath the scan. I was excited to share my news and awaited the dizzy feeling of congratulations.

The first read:

You've got until 24 weeks to have an abortion, but you probably don't want to leave it *that* late ...

And then, below my baby-to-be, began a discussion about a woman's right to choose. Sixty-three of my 117 friends joined in. There were 277 comments in total. Friends of friends who I vaguely remembered dumped their abortion stories on my wall and creepy pseudo-woke men I'd mistakenly snogged at parties years before were keen to declare themselves pro-choice.

Remember it's YOUR body, it's not even a real baby yet.

My girlfriend got rid of hers (before we'd got together) – best thing she ever did, I wouldn't be with her if she had a kid lol!

It's two pills, some cramps and a really heavy period.

My ex-wife had a vacuum suction at 5 months, very traumatic – do you want me to come to clinic with you?

Are you actually keeping it?!

All of this. Underneath a scan of my baby.

I'd wanted to send out cute cards with a due date and a party invitation. I'd wanted to bake a cake with a sponge suitable for a gender reveal. Announce my happiness at family gatherings surrounded by love and joy. Watch everyone raise a glass in mine and my baby's honour. Buy meaningless parenting books written by mum bloggers and up-and-coming TV presenters. Indulge in a belly cast, or at the very least have Henna covering my bulge. Have a supportive man to proudly pat the bump. Do a maternity photoshoot with my husband in a wheat field. Book a babymoon on the Amalfi Coast. Receive a fruit hamper. Feel resentful at interfering in-laws. Post weekly updates on YouTube. Have a baby shower and play pointless party games ...

But because my life didn't flow with convention, everyone assumed I wanted my baby gone.

The social worker offers me a fag. I decline. I'd kicked my 20-a-day habit cold turkey on the day I suspected I was pregnant, and I didn't appreciate the social worker's sneaky little test. We're on the top floor at Barnet Council in an interview room filled with cameras, a tape recorder and a two-way mirror – because if you flee domestic violence whilst pregnant or with your children then you are immediately referred to social services for a risk assessment. They need to know that you are avoiding violence and keeping your child safe. This woman held mine and my child's future in her hands. We stepped out onto the balcony and the social worker lit up.

'Do you want this baby?' she asked, blowing smoke in my face.

Yes. YES.

Of *course* I do.

What a stupid question.

I ran away from him.

And that was that. They discharged my case. At least the social worker believed me.

As I walked back towards West Finchley a girl of around 14 asked me to go into Tesco and buy her a pack of Sovereign. She gave me the money and when I returned with her cigarettes, she offered me one.

'I'm pregnant,' I said.

Then she said congratulations, right outside the Tesco. Someone had *actually* said it. I was beaming all the way back to the refuge. I called Kirsty to let her know social services wouldn't be taking my baby.

Kirsty said, 'You can't trust social services though, look what happened to Baby P.'

What do I know about rejected children?

They grow up half formed.

They grow into rejected men and women.

They spend a lot of time not knowing who they are.

They doubt themselves.

They doubt everyone. They are gullible, and they'll take love from anyone who exploits their loneliness.

Even – for – just – one – night.

When rejected children grow into adults, they lose their minds on Mother's Day, on Father's Day, on Christmas Day – all the *days* supposed to be spent with family, whatever your age.

And you'll always remember your mum's birthday even though you promise yourself that *this* is the year you will forget. You'll change your name by deed poll as soon as you are able, and you won't celebrate your birthday on the day you were born – a protest against the vagina you hopefully destroyed.

And you will ask yourself at *least* once a day – *What makes a mother reject her child?*

Every day.

And talking about it *will* help, but it can never absolve the feeling of rejection, regardless of how many times your GP refers you for CBT.

And at night you'll look through your Internet history and you'll feel ashamed when you see your most searched sentence – *What makes a mother reject her child?*

And you will never know the answer; could it be untreated postnatal depression or is she just a narcissist or was the rejection a reaction to her own past, or maybe I just looked at her funny when I was a toddler … *because that's what she once told me.* But. I honestly do not know.

And it's not knowing that hurts the most.

A sort of ex-boyfriend called Kingsley asked – Have you considered adoption?

The old South African screamed from her bedroom – How does it feel to *harbour* the child of a monster?

An annoying girl in an AA meeting shared at length about her seven drunken miscarriages before turning to me and

25

asking in front of the entire group – What about fostering? Are you going to have *it* fostered?

Then my midwife referred me to a psychologist who worked specifically with parents who reject their children.

I said – I'm 16 weeks pregnant, I haven't rejected my child …

She said – I *know*. But no one would blame you if you did.

I whispered (and I was crying) – *Please* can everyone just STOP this. I want this child so much. I could *never* reject my child. And I am broken and sad and I have no idea how to live from one second to the next but … I ran away so I could keep this baby and I do *not* reject my baby and I *never* will.

But I guess they didn't know about us and the conversations we had late into the night. They didn't know how I'd mutter into the walls of the dark refuge about the life we would lead.

About the home we would live in. And the places we'd go together.

And the love you would always feel, regardless of how hard things could get.

They didn't see the headphones draped on my tummy playing what appeared to be your favourite song 'Octopus's Garden' by the Beatles and how you would dance by my bladder and through your kicks beg me to play it again and again, even though I'd sometimes piss myself.

(And by then I could laugh because my cheekbone had healed.)

Nobody knew about the secret sold-out Suede gig I blagged myself into – so one day I could tell you about how I took you to see my favourite band play before you were even born. And how if you were a boy you were going to be called Brett, after the lead singer. And nobody knew that you forced me to eat Mr Wu buffet every week and orange Calippos for breakfast and greasy fry-ups at Café Renoir in Kentish Town. They didn't know about our strolls down the South Bank and across our favourite bridge – Waterloo, obvs – and how I would sit and read you Hubert Selby Jr on the terrace of Somerset House.

They didn't feel the fear in my heart every time I went to the toilet and was worried that the stress of it all would make you leave too soon; that I couldn't even wipe myself without shaking. And how when there was no blood and I knew that you remained I could function until the next toilet trip.

No – one – knew – that.

They didn't know about those long naps at the top of Parliament Hill in the hot summer where I spent every Monday afternoon sleeping over our city with a small smile on my face as I stroked your bump.

They didn't know that I took a job in a peep show working 13-hour shifts so that I could save £10,000 to get us out of that refuge and set up our new life.

Or how we cycled there every morning from Finchley to Soho and back again late at night without any lights even when you got really heavy and I could barely balance.

3

THE LAST PEEP SHOW IN SOHO

MY PREGNANCY SMELLS OF stale semen.

Poverty always has a smell. And a sound. Right now, the smell is stale semen and the sound is 'Gypsies, Tramps and Thieves' by Cher, which plays on loop throughout my 13-hour shift.

The owner, Vladimir, tells me he chose the song because of its perfect wank tempo.

He'd conducted an experiment after becoming inspired in a branch of McDonald's whilst treating his kids to a Happy Meal. As his children hurriedly stuffed fries into their mouths he looked around noting a direct correlation between the frenetic pace of the music piping into the restaurant and how quickly the customers ate their food and got out. That was when Vladimir hit upon the idea of the perfect peep-show song. He intended to discover the consummate piece of music which encouraged men to prolong their pleasure and stay in the private booth for as long as possible; the longer they maintained their erection, the more money he would make.

One £2-coin buys you 15 seconds of woman and, as the searing chorus quickly hits at just 30 seconds into the track, the familiarity of the song lulls the customer into a gentle sense of security, ensuring they are able to rub one out at leisure whilst enjoying their semi-public display of voyeurism.

During my audition Vladimir tells me that in Russia they have a saying

– Тише едешь, дальше будешь.

It means if you take things slowly you will go further.

And it's clearly a business plan that works, Cher hasn't left the peep-show stereo since 1986 and Vlad is rolling in cash. When I first approach him for a job, he, like all people in business, isn't too keen on employing a pregnant woman, but I eventually seduce him on the idea that public viewings of my constantly changing body will be a source of intrigue for the customers, leading them to return regularly to check in on my progress.

Vlad takes a long hard look at me and through squinted eyes decides I look a little bit like a young Cher, and not only will a pregnant woman add a touch of the exotic to the peep show, he reckons my tragic little story fits perfectly within the narrative of the 2 minute and 36 second pop song.

If you squint hard enough, you can find poetry in the most desperate and dirtiest of situations.

The peep show is a step down for me, I remind Vlad. I used to be one of the highest earners at The Aquarius Club alongside a beautiful former *Vogue* model who danced under the name Isis.

But I'm here now.

I take my place in the booth the following morning, Sellotaping my 12-week scan above the letterbox-sized peephole, just to remind myself why I'm standing here in my ever-tightening dirty bra and knickers. I'm doing this for *us*.

A friend of mine, she has a YouTube channel. Each week unleashing a new video to her subscribers, updating them on the progress of her pregnancy. She's made a very successful career out of sharing her body as she takes her viewers on the intimate journey from conception to pregnancy test and all the way to the birth and beyond.

She says things like 'This week, he is the size of an aubergine!' as she documents her changing shape whilst posing for her audience at the most flattering of angles.

I decide our jobs are practically the same. Pregnant bodies become public bodies regardless of whether we're scrutinised in a live sex show, via social media or just minding your own business on the bus. A moment doesn't pass without a comment on how big we're getting, or how big we're not getting, or how tired we're looking. Then, of course, enter the strangers drenched with concern checking we're getting enough rest and eating right and probes filled with assumptions as they seek confirmation that our husbands are taking good care of us – the answer is always 'Yes, he's just so *wonderful*' because things just get really awkward if you tell the truth, they don't know where to look if you reveal there is no man. And let's

31

not forget the men hollering at us from their vans declaring just how *gutted* they are that another man 'got in there first', but how we're still a 'sort' because we still look 'normal' from behind. So … why *not* make some money out of it? YouTube, peep show, whatever.

It's just that my friend, the one on YouTube, her public performance fits into society's acceptable version of voyeurism; a supportive partner, a mortgage and a peony and geranium Diptyque candle burning brightly by her side.

My pregnancy smells different to hers.

It sticks to my hair and seeps into my skin; I take the scent back with me to the refuge each night and it lingers on my borrowed Primark sheets. No matter how much I shower, the stench of peep-show residue never leaves and I swear I once smelled it pouring from my bleeding gums as I scrubbed my teeth after yet another shift.

I could have applied for a job at a call centre but I'm on a deadline – having just 26 weeks to raise a whole £10,000 if I'm going to ensure that I don't bring my baby 'home' to a refuge or council-imposed bed and breakfast. £10,000 isn't a figure pulled from nowhere – landlords often ask for up to 6 months' rent in advance from single mums, especially those on an unstable income, and as the peep show sits undecidedly within the eyes of the law I'm unable to provide a credible work reference. And sex workers have zero rights when it comes to maternity pay. Plus, I'd left all my belongings behind when I fled Grantham, and Gary was refusing to return them to me. I literally had nothing on my back but the sleazy underwear requirements of the grubby sex space in which I now worked. *And* I needed to buy a pram and a cot and Babygros and all the stuff babies require. But first we needed a home. Ten grand will sort us out. So, between Tuesday and Saturday I cycle from Finchley to Soho and back again after dark without any lights. And back again once it gets light.

There is an urgency to connect. With everyone. With anyone. Now that it is just me and my growing baby, for the first time in my life I can admit that I cannot stand to be alone. I find myself making conversations in supermarket aisles, with my fellow diners at the array of all-you-can-eat buffets I regularly frequent and I even join a life-drawing class for the homeless in Primrose Hill.

I ask people for the time, all – of – the – time.

I request demonstrations at make-up counters without the intention of ever making a purchase. I walk up to women in parks playing with their toddlers and tell them how sweet their kid is. I even ask for directions to places I could walk to blind.

Every second away from the peep show counts and I make use of every minute. If only I'd been this productive before I fell pregnant then I probably wouldn't be in this position. But I'm working hard to make up for lost time.

Despite being agnostic, I attend a church in Kensington known for its congregation of PR girls in pashminas seeking wealthy god-fearing husbands and I enrol on their ten-week Alpha course; by week five I'm on a residential trip to Hampshire and pretending along with everyone else that I'm speaking in tongues. I become a member of a drama group in Kentish Town for women at risk of offending and bag the lead role in their play. I attend AA meetings whenever I get a spare hour, even though the desire to drink is a distant memory. Just so I can share myself with someone. With anyone.

I – need – to – connect – with – everyone.

Late at night, whilst the women in the refuge collectively weep under their duvets in a ritualistic sharing of pain, I force myself to fake sob along rowdily before stalking social media for old school friends, work colleagues and former enemies. There is a need to make amends, make new friends, to tie up loose ends. I am on the cusp of delivering a new life but it sort of feels like the end is looming – not only am I consumed by the fear of death by childbirth (the nightmares awaken me each night) but I'm also mourning the life I never had, because there is no getting it now.

My first 29 years – a hell. A life lived alone. Dragging myself up. Running from Mum to my nana's to taking refuge at schoolfriends' houses and then back 'home' in a cycle of disorder. Before childhood had even ended, dragging my life from place to place – then 43 homes between 16 and 29 – hopping from bed to bed, from trauma to trouble, through a violent landscape of both literal and emotional poverty.

This is my chance to escape all that. If I work *hard*, make that ten grand, then by the time my baby arrives I'll be set up and ready to live life on an equal footing with everyone else. I'll be just like everyone else. And I'll finally have a family.

The shifts in the peep show are taking their toll, the potency of toxic masculinity grinding me down. Standing there exposed, pleasing them as I pose into all the positions men like their women to be fucked in as they wank over my bump. Pissed off that the only way to earn a bonus in this stinking flea-ridden spunk cemetery is entirely dependent on a man's ability to stay hard. Another £2 hits the slot as powerlessness grips me. They have *all* the power. I spend 13 hours a day keeping men happy in the peep show, yet am fearful of a man attacking me and my baby-to-be as we return to the refuge late at night. I carry a pen knife in my cowboy boots should we collide with any rape gimps in the shadows.

It is a shock when I step back into the real world to attend my monthly midwife appointments; around the waiting room are these seemingly kind and attentive men holding their partner's hands. Content to nurture and protect, these are not the men that frequent my world. I've never known or met a man like that. Where did these women find them?

Where did they find these protective men?

I need some protection too.

A man who won't attack me.

So, after years of no contact, I track down my dad.

Around the time my mum chucked me out, Dad left her too. We didn't make a pact or anything like that, but he saw it as an opportunity to make his escape too. I was 16 and moved in with a group of artists and hookers in Dulwich and my 37-year-old dad into a boozy bachelor-pad house share in Beckenham. The first day of his new life.

He'd been abused by my mum just like I had. When I was young she started waking me in the middle of the night with an invitation to attack him. He'd be passed out on the sofa drunk and she'd be shouting instructions on how to beat him. Offering up prizes if I hit him in the right spot:

'Get him in the eye.' – A packet of Opal Fruits.

'Poke his ribs.' – A fish and chip supper.

'Punch his stomach until he is sick.' – A trip to Chessington World of Adventures.

'Kick his kidneys.' – A much desired kiss on the head from Mum.

'Pull what's left of his hair.' – A new My Little Pony lunchbox.

It's confusing being violent to someone you love, yet I daren't disobey her. If I was hitting Dad that meant Mum wasn't hitting me. I'd begin by tentatively attacking him and he'd just take it. But when I'd use the cleaning products on him his glassy eyes would flick open wide and I sensed his disappointment in me.

I'd always adored him. He was funny. Dressed a bit like Billy Joel. Took me to the polling station with him.

Watched everything on telly written by Jimmy McGovern. Demonstrated against the Poll Tax. Refused to be in Penge when the Queen visited. Boycotted the *Sun*. Shunned the stereotype of the working-class man – sure, he played the Pools desperate to win a way out yet took me to art galleries in the school holidays. And he had great taste in music. Introduced me to The Clash and The Pogues. He bought me a cheap guitar when I was five, a book of six-string instructions and made me practise every night. And because he was practically a kid when he became a father to me he was young enough to appreciate Britpop. He'd take me with him to see bands. He let me bunk off school when I was 14 so we could go and watch the first showing of *Trainspotting*. He was just so smart, but like most working-class children born to alcoholic immigrants in the 1960s he left school without qualifications or direction. Took a low-level admin job and remained there forever, bowing to authority and toeing the line until he became reliant on being compliant in the system.

He confided that he'd won a poetry competition as a teenager and it had always been his dream to write. Men like him weren't allowed to write. If you failed the football trial for Charlton, or hadn't shown much interest in criminality and fast tracked into a boxing career, then you took a job on a building site or if you were 'bright' – a derogatory term always used to describe intelligent working-class people – you took a job in low-level admin and *that* was that. You and your future generations forever stuck, banging on the door of the lower middle class, hoping they'd one day let you in. And maybe they'll think about it if you can pull yourself together, 'act appropriately' and play the game, but one mis-step and it's all over.

After school he would come into my room as I practised my guitar and show me pages of lyrics he'd written in the middle of the night. They were either about his abusive father or gave an insight into the horrific relationship he had with my mum. He wanted me to put music to his words and I remember how his language was so vulnerable and raw, to the point where it made me feel a little bit uncomfortable as I read through them. The kind of writing so exposing that people get angry with your vulnerability and inevitably use it to their advantage. His weakness was disgusting to me. Yet the joy in his eyes as I struck three chords and threw a melody over them containing his lyrics . . . He loved it. So proud of me.

But whenever Mum beat me up, which by the time I was a teen was every fucking day, he'd just stand by and watch, never once trying to protect me. I guess he was afraid of her. If she was beating me then she wasn't beating him.

After an incident with a rented industrial carpet steam cleaner, I finally decided to call the police on her, but Dad told me that when the police arrived he'd be backing her up. 'We'll tell them you're mad,' he said. 'Look at all the cuts on your arms, you look like a fat Richey Edwards.' He could be horrible like that. That was when the last drops of respect I had for him trickled away. I have, however, spent my entire life since attempting to replicate that brief moment of pride in his eyes, by being in bands, going anorexic for a while and getting the odd short story published, but nothing ever works.

He started a new life with a wealthy woman and her three young sons – and I really liked them; desperate to be included in their lives, I hoped I'd be taken in too, forever awaiting an invitation for Christmas dinner but he wanted to leave me and Mum in the past. We'd speak from time to time, drift apart for years on end and he could never understand why I'd get so upset when he forgot my birthday.

'Grow up,' he'd say.

Still, I dropped him an email with the good news that he was going to be a grandad and he replied a few months later agreeing to meet for lunch. Throwing a baggy jumper over my peep-show costume, I went to meet him for a jacket potato in Wholefoods on Brewer Street. His greeting polite yet cold, unfalteringly maintaining the somewhat comforting air of disappointment prevalent in all our liaisons since we'd both escaped my mother over a decade ago.

Pleasantries in place, he said he Googled me every now and then; didn't like *any* of my bands or thinness or the things I wrote.

He said: What are all these disgusting stories you write on-line about your life in the gutter?

I just write about what I know.

He said: Have you ever considered being a bit more like Jane Moore?

Who?

He said: Have you ever considered being a bit more like the *Sun* columnist Jane Moore?

No. No I haven't. Wait. You always told me never to read the *Sun*.

He said: Well, I read the *Sun* these days. I really like Jane Moore. If you worked hard you could be just like her.

No I couldn't. Even if I wanted to be. We're from different worlds. Did Jane Moore's Mum make her eat carpet mousse when she got lippy? He said: I don't know about that and neither do you but according to her Wikipedia page she doesn't speak to her dad.

Well that's somthing me and Jane Moore have in common, isn't it? But I could never be like Jane Moore. One mis-step and it's all over – that's what you always said, Dad. Multiple mis-steps with added violent mother and next thing you know you're rolling up to midwife appointments stinking of multiple men's jiz.

He said: That's not true. Anyone can be like Jane Moore.

He'd really changed.

Then out of nowhere he suggested I become a children's television presenter. If I was going to be a mother then I could at least try and be a children's television presenter.

I said: That's ridiculous. I've never even had any interest in that.

He said: It was always your ambition to live in a refuge, work in a peep show and become a single mum, was it?

This was clearly the most disappointed he'd ever been in me. In between mouthfuls of potato and beans he would sigh and mutter, 'Where did I go wrong, eh?'

I am so desperate for that man's approval. Even as I write this I'm seeking his approval, but I know he'll be reading filled with disappointment and shame.

He *will* be reading this now. He'll have bought this book. No, I'll have sent him a copy. Via my agent. Just to prove I'm worth something. So, he'll be reading this now and he'll be shaking his head and *sighing*. The bits that really cheese him off he'll read out to his wife. And he'll laugh mockingly as he speaks the most horrific words out loud. Conflicted by his own emotions; proud his daughter is a published author yet disgusted by the filth she has no choice but to write.

After we'd finished our jacket potatoes, we strolled towards Wardour Street where there was an awkward pause long enough to almost hug outside of Raymond's Revue Bar, but after a while we didn't.

'Good luck with the rest of your pregnancy. See you around?' he offered. See you around. He always says that, and then another couple of years would pass. Sure, Dad.

And then I returned to the peep show to finish my shift.

It could be any time of the night or day, but I know it is somewhere between 10am and midnight because that is when my shift begins and ends. There are no windows and there is no running water. You cannot get a phone signal because we are underground and the management refuses to pay for Wi-Fi. The clock in my claustrophobic 5ft by 6ft sex cell stopped working sometime in the 1970s and, despite Vladimir's obsession with time, watches are banned in the peep show – time is not sexy.

There are always two women on shift and there are four peepholes active at any one time where they can spy on Dasha, Tasha, Tanya, Misha, Masha – a rotating slew of pretty young Polish and Lithuanian women new to London. Or they can spy on me. I am by far the oldest and least attractive and some-times the customers watch me sitting on my stool crying and sometimes they witness me puking into the bin, but my peep-hole is the busiest. I'm a freak show.

Each hour of my shift is counted down according to the voices of the men in the queue outside exchanging their notes for £2 coins from the door girl, Caterina, who keeps hundreds of pounds in change strapped to her body in an apron.

There is little variety in the conversations they offer her, all beginning with the same line, 'Smile, love', which would suggest she is sour-faced and dour but in fact I find her to be entirely the opposite. As a mother herself to three young girls she is gentle with me, bringing me fruit platters and lollies, and every day she shares her top birthing tip with me, the same one every day – 'It's basically like taking a very big constipated shit. It's a tough one, but you squeeze it out eventually,' she utters in her beautifully harsh Polish accent.

The day begins with a group of homeless men who arrive the moment we open, taking sanctuary in the booth like they're at some kind of dirty soup kitchen. Some might say it's a frivolous use of their funds but don't even the homeless *deserve* the warmth of a wank?

'Smile, love.' I can tell that it is 11am, according to the cheeky Chelmsford twang of the fruit and veg market traders. They like to knock one out before the lunchtime rush and then it's back to the grind of selling carrots (always ensure you wash your fruit and veg). 'Smile, love.' It's between midday and 1pm because the giggly hushed voices of young media runners from the local post-production houses echo around the booths. They are very excitable, fresh out of college, indulging in the delights of the dirty mile. 'Smile, love.' Early afternoon introduces groups of horny crackheads who stay hard for *hours*.

Note: If your customer stays past three loops of 'Gypsies, Tramps and Thieves' then we start to make bonus. You always hit bonus with the crackheads, but they make you work hard for it. Bang on the walls screaming very specific instructions through the peephole. The very first time I feel my baby kick is under the gaze of a crackhead. It was in response to the words – TURN AROUND AND SPREAD. I WANT TO SEE THAT BABY'S HEAD. They stay until we close for an hour at 3pm, when the shutters go up because the peep show is located next door to a primary school.

During that hour we turn off 'Gypsies, Tramps and Thieves' and a sense of calm overtakes the sex space. I meditate and practise pregnancy yoga and hear Caterina removing the stash of crumpled sticky tissues from the four booths (which are often knee deep) and she quickly pops the mop around.

That's when the smell really hits.

It is only after I have been there for a couple of months I realise it is the smell of stale semen. We don't have any running water in the building and it dawns on me that Caterina has been using the same filthy grey gunge in the bucket for months. I leave my booth and nip into reception to get confirmation and there she is spreading hundreds and thousands of ancient sperm around the booths again and again. The smell akin to a tray of out-of-date fish having an orgy in the industrial bins at the back of a GUM clinic.

Each day I spray a can of Oust but nothing removes the stench. I like to think that, when the building is inevitably bought up by investors and turned into luxury apartments, its wealthy tenants will be forever haunted by the brazenly abandoned spunk that has seeped deep into the building's bricks and foundations.

4pm to 7pm is often our quietest time and that's when I get to enjoy my pregnancy; making a list of potential names and creating a birth plan. Feeling its butterfly tumbles and hiccups, I talk to my baby providing a running commentary of our strange little life. At my 20-week scan I discover I am having a girl and I Sellotape my new scan above the peephole; directly above the ever-changing sets of eyes that all roll back like death as they cum. As the peephole slams shut I look up at her to remind myself I'm doing this for her.

'Smile, love.' The tourists from suburban Sutton unable to hold their booze are limp dicked by nine. And as we approach closing time we get a few drunk and open-minded couples who fuck against the stud wall that divides us whilst staring at my pregnant belly. And as Cher leaves the stereo for the night a few stragglers wander in after pub closing time for one final stab at intimacy desperately throwing in those coins to watch us change out of our underwear, remove our make-up and into our street clothes before they catch the last Tube home.

It's those customers I relate to most.

On the day of my last ever shift, when the peep show had closed for the school run, Vlad, Caterina and Dasha surprised me with a baby shower. We drank Fanta Fruit Twist in plastic champagne glasses stolen from the clip joint next door and all the girls chipped in to have a cake made from the Slovak bakery on Berwick Street.

It read: Тише едешь, дальше будешь.

'A good lesson for you!' cheered Vladimir.

I felt content for the first time in my pregnancy. Vlad's perfect wank tempo provided a good life mantra. Although he did also tell me that in Russia they have a famous saying that goes: 'If he loves you, he beats you.' So I guess his advice is a bit hit and miss.

When we ripped the cake apart it revealed a light pink sponge – just like my friend had for her gender reveal on her YouTube channel.

Then they blindfolded me and led me to the office. Inside it was rammed with presents and balloons. Turns out my regulars had been dropping off gifts for the last few weeks. Men delivering brand new buggies, their children's barely used sleepsuits, a Moses basket. One man even gifted me his ex-wife's breast pump just before he ejaculated into my booth.

At quarter to four, with a small queue forming outside the peep show as the customers returned to witness my final pregnancy update, Caterina suggests we do an impromptu maternity shoot using the camera on her phone; me and my bump next to a pile of cum tissues. Me and my bump attempting to climb the pole. Me and my bump with the bucket of stale semen. Me and my bump spying through the peephole.

My maternity shoot was different to yours.

The next morning, I don't cycle into Soho. Instead hailing a taxi and dragging my life from the refuge to my new flat where I'll be able to bring my daughter when she is born in the coming weeks. I hand over six months' advance rent to the landlord, ensuring a borrowed roof for her life to begin. The walls are heavy with damp, there is no hiding from the mould and it smells like the budget Butlins chalets where I spent every Whitsun week with Nana as a child – but at least we have a place just for us.

Poverty always has a smell. And a sound. The smell is damp. It's a step up from stale semen.

The sound is the squad of mice clawing all over the kitchen surfaces in the middle of the night.

But I have a home, I can settle here for a while and I'm about to give birth.

The show is over.

4

SYMPHOROPHILIA

WHENEVER I TELL PEOPLE the story of my vagina (which I inevitably do, I always do) I start with this: the smallest tampon.

I start. Then, I throw in a fact.

Before I gave birth, it was a struggle to get the smallest of tampons inside of me. Oh yeah. The *smallest* of the tampons.

Got a bit of a history with tampons. Before I fell pregnant I was a stripper. You strip to make money and you don't let the monthly reminder of your fading fertility put a stop to that. If you find yourself working in a strip club on your period, then you *must* remove the blue string. A stripper will be spreading her legs. Wide. To have the blue string dangling lonely between your thighs would be ... *niche*.

Sure, they'll be plenty of men into that. Women like me get weird requests all the time. Some men will ask you to publicly piss your thong or offer to throw you a little extra cash for passing wind directly in their face whilst grinding to 'Freak Me' by Another Level. And every now and again you *will* come across men desperate to catch a glimpse of your blue string – men seeking a more natural, 'earthy' experience. The type of men who get turned on by blood, odours and episodes of *One Born Every Minute*. And they'll pay you for the pleasure of it, and you'll take the money – but guys like this are not your bread and butter, not in your glitzy chain strip clubs.

To make real money in the strip club you need to be mass market. Think Coldplay. Conventional, dull, yet ultimately solid songwriters. Think of yourself as the Chris Martin of strippers and you're well on the way to being one of the club's top earners.

In fact, while we're at it, it's my one tip for life: If you want to be one of society's 'success' stories, then be as dull as possible. Marry a man in middle management, have a couple of kids, write a PR-friendly mum blog, vote centre-right and join the PTA. Don't – step – out – of – line.

Same rules apply within the sex industry. You want money?

Cut. Off. That. Blue. String.

At The Aquarius Club, before we could hit the stage, all girls were subjected to an inspection from Juliet – a glamorous Spaniard in her late fifties who kept order in the dressing room from 11pm to 6am the next day on an income entirely dependent on house fees from the dancers (which, at £100 per dancer, per night, meant she was doing pretty well). Juliet was our House Mum. The House Mum is the bridge between management and the strippers, and her role was to keep us girls in line.

Club regulations stipulated that vaginas were kept bald and sweet smelling, and Juliet would inspect our fannies with the thoroughness of a chief Gestapo. And although Juliet had a job bordering on the outskirts of acceptability, she *loved* rules, adhering to a gangster-style code of conduct – be loyal to your family but if someone becomes difficult then make them disappear. Basically, if your fanny was out of shape then you'd be looking elsewhere for work.

When our periods came around she would conduct a meticulous tampon spot check; you sit on the sofa and part your legs as wide as they will go, then she'd place her head between your thighs and search for traces of tampon.

Her menstruation minge checks were *legendary*.

After one particularly gruelling inspection where she spent ten minutes shining a pocket torch inside me, she declared my vagina to be the most perfect she'd ever seen. Deserving of a mould providing the template for blow-up dolls all over the globe, to be used enthusiastically before being thrown amongst the debris of sex toys underneath the beds of perverts. To this day it remains the finest compliment I've ever received.

Vaginal inspections were one of the more conventional happenings that I experienced during my stripper years. I mean, the things you witness in strip-club changing rooms; my friend Jenna gluing her *actual* nipple back on with nail polish after a botched boob job in Thailand; a young mum expressing breastmilk and storing it in the beer fridge – to sell to her customers.

A tampon spot check is tame. My strip-club story is vanilla. However, I will warn you now, the story of how I lost my vagina may make you squirm. If you are of a weak disposition, then I suggest you look away now.

I spread my legs so Juliet could take a closer look.

Can you see it? Can you see the tampon? No? Get on that stage, girl.

I was supposed to have a Caesarean. The doctor said they'd be admitting me at 38 weeks and they'd deliver my baby by hand. It was all planned. It was my midwife's suggestion. Marie. She knew about the refuge and social services and the peep show. She knew I had no family. Marie knew it was just me, that I'd be giving birth all alone, so she wrote the words HIGH RISK on my notes.

She even joked, 'You're too small to get a baby out of that thing anyway!'

To be clear: What she meant was that my delicately tight vagina couldn't *possibly* cope with a child's big head emerging from it like a monster.

'I struggle with the smallest tampons,' I murmur self-pityingly.

I have a story about that, I tell her. I tell Marie the story; its 5am and I'm on shift at The Aquarius Club. It's *very* exclusive, I tell her. Very difficult to pass the audition. Celebrities every night, only the best girls in London. And I've been on shift since 6pm. I work hard. I like money. I make money. It had been a good night, over a grand in cash spilling out of my handbag and I'd been so busy that I hadn't had the opportunity to change my tampon – it had been 'up there' for 11 hours straight and it was definitely time to fish it out.

I explain to my midwife about the missing blue string and she nods like she definitely gets it. She smiles politely, like it is a story she has heard a million times. But just in case she hasn't I decide to explain just how difficult it is to remove a string-less tampon that has been living inside of you for half a day.

The trick is, I say, the way you hide the tampon so that you can spread your legs wide for your customers (because let's be honest, regardless of what anyone says your hole is the real window to your soul): you've got to push it up as far as you feel it should go. Keep pushing to the point where you feel it disappear. It has to *feel* like it has disappeared, and it will – especially when it has been in there so long – it's almost like it becomes part of you, y'know? And I'm wearing these long, acrylic nails that Juliet insisted I get because 'house rules', which of course makes everything more difficult: you can't remove contact lenses, you can't type – but men go wild for them, they're just not tampon compatible.

And I cannot free this trapped tiny tampon. It's so small, like the ones they give you at school when you're ten. Like the little tampons virgins wear. The smallest tampon. And I just cannot get anywhere near it – where did it go?! My nails are trying to grab it, but each claw returns empty handed.

After an intense half-hour of rummaging I am defeated, it is officially lost, and I run into the dressing room hysterical and crying and I fall into Juliet's arms.

'I'm dying, I'm actually dying,' I sob.

I let Juliet comfort me for a while. She strokes my hair extensions and wipes away my tears. She tells me that I'm going to be OK and I look deep into her dark eyes and I believe her. If anyone can save me from Toxic Shock Syndrome, it's Juliet.

Juliet could clean up *any* situation.

In barroom brawls she'd pick up both men by their collars and throw them out onto the street. If a customer ODed in the private booth she'd be able to resuscitate them within seconds. If someone accidently offloaded their *load* into your hair (a rarity, yet a very real possibility – all jobs have hazards, and this one was ours), then she'd clean you up and get you back onto that stage as good as new.

She escorted me to the corner of the dressing room and laid me down on the sofa. She plumped up some pillows to make me comfortable and instructed Jenna to fetch her 'special box' from underneath her desk, which contained every cleaning product available in Poundland. I have no idea what she is about to do but Juliet has a solution for everything.

According to Juliet, the best shampoo to rid cum from your hair is Pantene. The best way to remove STDs from a dildo is to soak it for 24 hours in hydrogen peroxide before placing it in a freezer for two hours. Stray semen splash on your dress? All you need is a spray of Astonish Window and Glass (but you must treat the stain within 20 minutes). Fresh anal blood can be removed in an instant by Viakal limescale remover. Scrub your skin with vinegar to cleanse yourself of piss and if someone shits on your dress then throw it in the bin, don't be such a beast.

Tonight, Juliet would be saving my life – and I was in the most capable of hands. She may have just been my House Mum, but in that moment, she was the closest thing to a real mother I'd ever had.

She was constantly talking to me, wiping my brow, telling me I wasn't going to die and then out of nowhere she suddenly slipped her un-gloved glamorous hand into my vagina and delivered the lost tampon like some kind of master midwife saving a mother and child from a difficult birth. As she let go of the tampon she immersed her hands in Cillit Bang.

Jenna with the glued-on nipples screamed, 'It's a healthy blood-soaked tampon!' before throwing it in the face of a security guard.

This *actually* happened, I tell the midwife.

My midwife nods like it's a story she's heard a million times before and makes a few notes before saying, 'I think if you gave birth naturally it would be of great harm to you physically ... and mentally.'

A C-section would be happening at 38 weeks. Done deal.

It was a relief knowing that I would have an element of control over the birth. Everything in my pregnant life was lopsided and ... lonely. The thought of being alone in labour for hours was one of the most terrifying feelings I'd ever encountered – and I'm someone who almost got strangled to death outside the strip club by a customer's jealous girlfriend with some kid's skipping rope. I'd visualised dying during childbirth so many times that it almost felt destined to become a reality, leaving my daughter to fend for herself felt like an apt end to my tragic and dirty little life. The story of a million fallen women before me, sent to their deaths birthing illegitimate kids alone in Victorian workhouses.

Being booked in for a C-section gave me comfort because I had no idea *how* to give birth. I'd been too embarrassed to attend antenatal classes, unable to bear the thought of sitting alongside loved-up, middle-aged, middle-class couples panting together in matching North Face fleeces.

Of course, I knew that a C-section wasn't the easy option, it's a major operation that would require six weeks' recovery. But I wasn't planning on leaving the flat for the first month anyway. I just wanted it to be her and me. For us to get to know each other, to feed and cuddle and sleep. Nothing but her and me.

She would be everything I would need.

And everything was in place. By week 30 I'd already batch-cooked two months' worth of meals to freeze and invested in a stash of reusable nappies. I'd even installed a phone line, so I could work as a telephone psychic in lieu of maternity leave.

I was ready for her.

The month before I lost my vagina something went wrong.

My midwife. She just disappeared – she was taken sick and I was given a replacement. My new midwife was a young, kind, professional woman who had thoroughly read my notes, but she had not been on this journey with me.

To her I was a single mum-to-be, an escapee of domestic violence, someone with a *lot* of problems. And of course, I was all of those things, but I was also a lot more than that; I was scared, I was excited, and I had really interesting stories about strip clubs.

As she examined me, a look of horror crossed her face.

'What's wrong?' I asked.

She didn't answer, she turned and sprinted out of the room.

The new midwife returned with her panicked face and a doctor by her side.

The doctor examined me.

'It's breech,' he said. 'You'll need a Caesarean.'

I told him that I was already booked in for a Caesarean, but my words failed to register with him.

'We'll book you in for a scan and then we'll book you in for a C-section.'

I'm already booked in, I said. But it was like my sound button was muted. It was the first time I realised that people simply don't hear women like me.

As I left the hospital, a man outside Chicken Cottage asked if I had found a baby-daddy yet.

'I'll take on that role! Whoa, you sure look hot pregnant,' he said.

I stopped in my tracks.

'You don't know me. What makes you think I don't have a husband?' I asked.

But he just shrugged and stuffed a handful of nuggets in his mouth.

I was running into these kinds of encounters on a daily basis, from the moment my bump started to show the comments from both strangers and acquaintances began to flow:

Where's the dad?

Do you *know* who the dad is?

Oh, he got his way with you and then left you, did he?

I've always fancied you, but I'd never date you now – someone has already 'ploughed that furrow'.

It'll be difficult to find a man whilst pushing a pram, won't it?

Did you get pregnant in order to get a council house?

The telly break, did it? (I don't even know what that means.)

How will you explain to your child that it wasn't wanted?

Did you miss the abortion cut-off date?

It'll be tough to find someone willing to take on your baggage.

Young girls like you are scrounging off the state – I pay for you!

How will you cope?

You don't seem like a mum.

Jesus *will* forgive you.

Just to be clear, this was 2010 not 1969. We live in a world where one in four women are single mums, it shouldn't be a big deal. I mean, one in four men don't believe that exposing themselves counts as sexual harassment yet these men are not derided as society's scum, they're just allowed to get on with it. Different rules apply.

I had expected pregnancy to change people's perceptions of me for the positive. Hoping that men would be less sexualised towards me and that women would view me as someone nurturing and trustworthy. Like I had finally been given permission to be a *real* woman, to be treated with dignity and respect – but that didn't happen.

It was like I had the words 'single mum' tattooed on my chubby arms. And the world clearly disapproved of my new body art. Even some of my female friends became distant and angry towards me, especially those in their late thirties who were in settled relationships. It was like I was helping myself to something that a woman like me didn't deserve.

My friend Clover told a newly-wed acquaintance that I was pregnant, and her response was, 'I don't want to get involved with any gossip.'

'It's not gossip, it's good news, our friend is having a baby!'

'I don't agree, the child is fatherless. It's gossip,' she said. In 2010.

I decided the best thing to do would be to create a fictional husband from this point on and so I brought my friend Kingsley with me to my final scan.

The doctor took one look at the monitor and declared my baby no longer breech.

'Congratulations, you can give birth naturally.'

But … I'm booked in. I don't want to give birth naturally. Please … My midwife said I *can't* give birth naturally. What about the tampon story?!

The doctor said there was nothing he could do, and he patted Kingsley on the back, 'You'll hold her hand, won't you?'

I was supposed to be having a Caesarean but now I wasn't.

Kingsley had been my sort of boyfriend at university. I say sort of because he's secretly queer in a violent way, like a Tennessee Williams creation. Kingsley is breathtakingly handsome yet incredibly cruel due to being so short. Our 'relationship' ended when he was carted off to Pentonville for physically assaulting me. It was while he was in prison that I ran off with his friend Gary to Grantham.

Like everyone else he disapproved of my pregnancy, but when he offered to be my birth partner I couldn't say no, it meant that when I went into labour I was given the opportunity to walk into the hospital as a respectable mother-to-be.

No one could have guessed I was due to become a single mum. Even the taxi driver was jovial on the way to the hospital – 'Good luck to all three of you!' he shouted from the window as he drove off. Never before had I experienced such positivity towards my pregnancy, unless you count the Chicken Cottage experience.

My new midwife took an instant dislike to Kingsley. Most people did. A quick glance at my notes revealed I had spent the majority of my pregnancy living in a PO Box addressed safehouse and they assumed that he was the man who had put me there, and although he wasn't directly responsible on this occasion I'd been on the run from Kingsley my entire adult life. Kingsley has owned me since I was 18.

'Don't worry, he's not the father! I'm on my own! There is NO father! He's just my friend. This is my friend! I'm all alone, there is NO FATHER!' I said through mouthfuls of Haribo and gas, keen to establish the huge level of loneliness that still remained.

The first ten hours of labour were brilliant. Eating sugar, high on gas and waiting for my new life to come into being. Then I started shitting myself.

I would say that, when I started shitting myself, that was the point when things went downhill. I didn't see the shit and I couldn't feel the shit, but I could definitely *smell* the shit.

I'd shat myself in public just once before.

I've got a story about that. The Aquarius Club insisted that all the girls attended a weekly weigh-in. If we exceeded a certain weight, then we were suspended from work until we lost the pounds. Once I tipped the scale at eight and a half stone and wasn't allowed to work until I lost six pounds. I'm 5'6" by the way. But you strip to make money and you don't let your need for three meals a day put a stop to that, so after a light lunch of tuna salad I swallowed 46 laxatives.

It was whilst walking though Soho with my friend Clover that my stomach suddenly cramped. There was an intense whirring and a desperate need to get to the toilet but there wasn't a toilet, and then ... Well, I found myself shitting against a graffitied urban wall. In the middle of Soho. In the daytime. I mean, the things you see happening against urban walls in Soho; women in Boden dresses being photographed by their husbands, child YouTubers discussing their favourite brands. My urban wall story is dull and unsellable in comparison: I hadn't even had the chance to pull my knickers down or hitch up my skirt before the most painful, stinking, muddy juice publicly escaped my bowels.

Clover, who was standing right next to me, started whispering 'oh my god, oh my god'. And then she laughed. She just exploded with laughter. And then I laughed, because there was nothing else I could do before the next wave of pain and gush of faeces.

If I'm honest, defecating during labour in front of a small audience of Kingsley and a couple of medical professionals didn't really faze me, if anything this was a huge step up since my last public episode.

And from here it all becomes a bit of a blur. This is the point where you can begin to consider me an unreliable narrator because the epidural took away all my fears. Everything was wonderful, despite knowing my baby was in trouble, despite hearing phrases like 'heartbeat slowing' and 'cord wrapped around neck' and despite a whole team of doctors surrounding me with concerned faces. Someone shouted, 'She can't give birth naturally,' and I really wanted to turn around and say 'Well I could have told you *that*,' but there's no time to be glib when your baby's life is on the line.

One of them said, 'We're going to have to cut your vagina! Cash, are you OK with that?'

I say, 'Thank you. Yes! Slice my vagina, slice all of it. My vagina means nothing to me. Just – give – me – my – baby.'

The doctor slices my *small, perfect, sex-toy* vagina and delves inside of me like … a beautiful House Mum retrieving a stringless tampon.

She throws my baby onto my chest – 'It's a girl!' – and … she is just there. She is just *there*. Covered in crust, she is mostly double chin and flecked with blood and her head is all cut up from the ventouse and she is crying on my boobs and she is … beautiful.

She is here, and she is safe, and she is healthy, and I love her.

Life is complete. I love you, I love you, I love you – I keep on saying it. I'm your mummy and I love you, I love you, I love you. I say it until my eyes roll back into my head.

Forty-five minutes later and I come around on a slab in theatre. They are attempting to save my vag. I lost a lot of blood and now they are sewing up the gaping wound. Kingsley is next to me and he is holding Biddy to my face so that I can kiss her.

Fourth-degree tears, they say. In between all the slicing and rummaging they literally ripped me a new one. My vagina and my arse are one hole. One hole!

They tell me I'll be incontinent for the foreseeable. What type of incontinent? *All* the incontinences, they confirm. Oh. They tried their best to stitch it up, but it wasn't really very successful and I'm just … one hole.

I am some kind of J.G. Ballard creation.

Gained a daughter, lost a vagina.

5

DEADBEATS

THE POLICE ARRIVE AT dawn. It's what they call the 'six o'clock knock'.

The aim is to catch you unaware, half asleep, a human at their most fragile; mid-nightmare, semi-erect, stumbling around without your glasses. Even the most hardened of criminals are vulnerable stinking of stale morning breath whilst shivering in a doorway in their Batman underpants. And here they are. The police are here. For me. They're at my fucking door. Treating me to the Full English of dawn raids. Pressing the buzzer long and hard, peering through the windows of my basement flat in search of signs of life. The telly is on, they know we're home. They scream my surname repeatedly through the letterbox. It's clear, they are *here* and they're v. keen to talk to me. So much so it's actually before 6am. The clock above the big screen reads 05.17. The cops, they've got me right where they want me. Their theory being that I'll implicate myself before reality awakens.

But.

As sleep-deprived connoisseurs of twilight television, Biddy and I have been up all night watching *Jeremy Kyle* reruns. She's teething/I'm depressed. The calmingly reassuring phrases of 'put something on the end of it!', 'It's 50/50', and my favourite, 'Where's the Dad?', provide a meditative meta lullaby that soothes working-class babies into the fitful anxious slumber they deserve. The guests on the show somewhat lift my spirits. My life isn't *that* bad – I'm only missing two teeth – a trophy of violence survival now disguised with an NHS bridge, but my smugness dissipates with speed when I realise the feds are at the door.

That – unmistakeable – knock.

First instinct: Hide behind the sofa. I'm not too proud to admit to that. Hide behind the sofa and pretend no one is home. It works for debt collectors and Jehovah's Witnesses, why not the police too? But these guys are going nowhere. I hatch a plan: Strap Biddy on my back and hop out the window – but they'll be on my tail. Where will I go? Who will harbour this mother fugitive? Being on the run gets complicated lugging around nappies and snacks and a breast pump and sterilising equipment. Babies just ain't crime friendly.

I surrender with speed. I'm going to have to hand myself in. I pop my head up from behind the sofa – 'I'm awake. We're awake. We're in here!' I shout. I mean, I've already given them sufficient time to conduct their ritual and they've loved every minute of it, because let me reassure you, my crime is of the petty variety; the Met have sent their youngest and lowest-ranking cops to fetch me and it would have been cruel of me to deprive them of their big moment. But it's done now. The dramatics are over. I'm answering that door – but just as I'm about to stick *Jeremy Kyle* on mute and grab my keys to open up, they kick down my door like it's the finale of a year-long undercover sting to bring down a pae-dophile ring.

I am standing there exposed like Rolf Harris in his Batman boxer shorts and stinking morning breath.

A stand-off in the hallway. A tired mum with a scream-ing baby hanging off her and these two bum-fluffed coppers looking out of their depth. I'm out of mine too, my landlord is going to lose his shit when he sees the smashed-in front door.

'Hey. So, I guess you're here to arrest me?'

Then.

'So, what do I do about childcare in this situation?'

Childcare is a struggle at the best of times. Offers only in the form of empty gestures. Whenever I ask Kirsty to babysit, she invents an emergency therapy session she must attend. And Clover is an academic which means she's always off her face on acid and having sex with her anarchist boyfriend in his squat in Woolwich. And I don't want to ask Kingsley because I want him out of my life once and for all – he's owned me my entire adult life and I don't want him owning my baby too. With these as my only three options, it's meant that Biddy and I haven't spent *any* time apart since she arrived ten months ago.

'Where's the dad?' the younger of the two officers enquires, and my reply is in the form of an awkward giggle that us women often do to keep the peace.

I gesture to the officers an offer of a chair but do not propose a cup of tea because they're *not* my friends. Plus they keep trying to make me chat about the crime I've committed but I've got previous and know to keep the arrest period stoic and my mouth slammed shut until I'm making use of my phone call down the station.

But because I am calm and compliant, they're actually really nice and give me some time to organise childcare. They mind the baby as I take a shower and I make a real effort with my make-up – last time I was arrested I was drunk and crying and had mascara dripping down my cheeks so, when it came to fingerprints and photos, I wasn't looking my best. Now my mantra in life is: Always be improving upon your last mugshot. I make some calls with regard to cell-time babysitting – and as predicted Kirsty has therapy, Clover is on acid and I'm out of options. I call Kingsley (it's either him or social services whilst I'm in custody) and he is round at my place within minutes. He loves a confrontation with the police – 'It's a disgrace you coming around here and arresting an innocent mother! The real criminals are out there. The real criminal is that little baby girl's dad.' Kingsley doesn't know what I've done but he does knows what I'm like so he gives me his look. Kingsley has a look dedicated especially for keeping me in line.

'Don't say a word without a solicitor present.'

My mouth remains shut.

The officers don't shackle me because I'm being 'compliant' and they go on and on about not *knowing* I had a baby. Saying it again and again. No one told us you were a mum. No one told us there was a baby.

As the credits roll on *Jeremy Kyle*, I finally lose my cool.

'It's BECAUSE I have a baby that I'm being arrested!' I snap.

Kingsley shoots me his look *again*. I've never been very good at keeping my mouth shut. Hence why I'm forever ending up in situations like this. Instead of letting things slide I get into a fight like I'm attempting some kind of solo revolution. It never works out well.

From the backseat of the police car I view the debris of the summer riots. CAPITALISM WILL COLLAPSE FROM WITHIN is sprayed in black across the shutters ripped from the looted Carphone Warehouse as the police car drives over a bump of abandoned iPhone 5s. The officer next to me mutters something about the disenfranchised youth, kids without fathers and bringing back National Service, as street cleaners sweep up glass from smashed television screens previously destined to broadcast David Cameron's big post-riots speech – 'Moral collapse. Irresponsibility.

Selfishness. Behaving as if your choices have no consequences. Children without fathers.'

Children. Without. Fathers.

My big post riots speech:

We caused all this. We did. Us single mums. We are nothing but the lazy, worthless, ignominious class – responsible for gang violence, benefit fraud, high taxes and rising unemployment. We congregate at a Pontins in flesh-coloured leggings and ill-fitting pink bras of straps we dare to bare, sluttily drooping down our upper arms and spend whole afternoons in Footlocker browsing discounted trainers. We treat ourselves to plates of meals at Frankie & Benny's, a cheeky Nando's, some jumble sale earrings before feverishly browsing the Argos catalogue – which contains all of our desires. Melanie Phillips asks – Where's the dad?

We should be barred from all supermarkets except Aldi and Lidl and force-fed a diet of UHT milk and corned beef – grub for fallen women choosing to live off the state, this is the food that is 'right' and 'just' – chemicalised milk and tinned slop is more than enough to sustain these vile beasts. Keep us away from Sainsbury's Taste the Difference and the Asda Extra Special range – block us ALL from the premium aisle! To experience microwaveable meals made from the finest of ingredients might make us forget who we really are. Let's never forget who we really are; collectively responsible for the deaths of Baby P, the birth of Robert Thompson and the disappearance of Shannon Matthews. We launched World War II, creators of fascism – after all Hitler was dragged up by a slag of a single mum.

So was Stalin and look at all the trouble he caused. We birthed all those bastards committing moped thefts, those babies on benefits and we instigated domestic violence – Why didn't you leave? Why didn't you stay? What did you do to provoke him? It's our fault either way. Burn the working-class witches! Ban Andrea Dunbar. Ban J.K. Rowling. Ban Jack Monroe. Ban Shelagh Delaney. And continue to fill our Kindles with the stories of upper-middle-class men, because let's not forget that the author most renowned for writing about poverty went – to – fucking – Eton. We are the fallen souls who handcrafted sink estates, skint estates and single-handedly manufactured the future drunks who will piss in the doorways of the closed-down community centres. We don't drink enough water. We never dilute our tropical squash. We love sausage rolls. We are perpetually late getting our kids to school. That's if we can even be bothered to take them in the first place. And we always return our library books late. Richard Littlejohn asks – Where's the dad?

Poundland is burning and Sports Direct mugs are smashed across every UK high street. Stolen widescreens in every room, and we don't even have a TV licence. Vile! Someone send Boris Johnson to Clapham and hand him a fucking broom, let's restore order! Someone come and clean up the disorder us lone women spewed from our dirty cunts filled with the sticky residue of men we were never ever good enough for anyway. Peter Hitchens asks – Where's the dad? Food bank misuse, Little Britain, Broken Britain, White Dee from Benefits Street and Victorian baby farms. Big society? Bollocks. Born out of wedlock? Bring back the 1834 poor law! Starve – them – all. Drug the weakest babies and sling

places I do not recognise during this time in my life and the first thing I do is check whether or not I'm wearing underwear; knickers intact then I've just collapsed somewhere to sleep it off, but if they're missing then someone else is involved and the situation becomes a little tricky. The fireworks knock me out of my blackout; I'm not wearing knickers. Above me a poster pasted to the ceiling reads: ARE YOU SICK AND TIRED OF BEING SICK AND TIRED? Right by my head is a chrome toilet and the very moment I notice it I'm vomiting down the hole. Convenient. With the last heave of poison I notice the blood splattered around the bowl matches the clots on my clothes. Clothes I do not recognise. This cornflower-blue playsuit does not belong to me. What the fuck am I wearing?

The blood is mine. Coming out of me. Gushing from the wound. And *that's* reassuring. I couldn't remember if I had murdered someone or not.

There's a man outside the room and I'm panicking because it's a cheap feeling having sex and not recognising them afterwards and I'm searching for a creative way to discover his name but no one enters the room. Just bright light surrounding a pair of eyes. And as the eyes close with the jangle of keys a little bit of the night returns to me – I'm in a police cell somewhere in Lincolnshire.

Now I remember. I've been arrested for assault and I'm in pain. So much pain. The night returning to me with every contraction.

A contraction: The arresting officer checking me into the cell with the words 'Are you pregnant?' A contraction: Me shouting, 'NOT ANYMORE!' Another contraction: The arrogant officer cuffing me for assault. A contraction: I'm … smashing up the kitchen. A contraction: I'm watching the fireworks out the window. A contraction: I'm downing two bottles of wine. Contraction: Before that was … when the cramps started, and I just *knew* it was over. And even before that, Gary had … tried to push me down the stairs. Before that … A contraction: He'd held me down with the threat of a 'commotio cordis'.

Commotio Cordis.

It's Latin for 'agitation of the heart'.

'You don't need to kill me to agitate my heart,' I said.

The eyes appear at the hole in the door. Again.

'Why do you keep staring at me?' I slur.

You're on suicide watch, the officer tells me. That's why you're in that suit, it's a prison regulation anti-harm suit.

I look to the Alcoholics Anonymous poster again – ARE YOU SICK AND TIRED OF BEING SICK AND TIRED? I don't know. But maybe I do have a problem if the first thing I think when I wake up in a police cell after a night of drinking is – Who did I kill?

I haven't killed anyone tonight but death is pouring out of me.

This is a miscarriage in a police cell.

In Conversation with the Duty Solicitor – Charing Cross Police Station, 10 August 2011

> CASH: It began as a mistake.
>
> SOLICITOR: The harassment?
>
> CASH: The crime.
>
> SOLICITOR: The crime is harassment.

My solicitor. He drops hot coffee down his salmon shirt. After a while he stops screaming.

> SOLICITOR: Go on/
>
> CASH: Went down the registry office. Registered the birth. Signed the certificate on my own. I signed it. Mother, me. Father, blank. And it made me angry. It made me so angry. When you're a single mum you're basically declaring yourself a solo creator of life, right? Saying — I did all this on my own. If *I* didn't register her then I'd be in trouble. But the man can just refuse. The dad just has the right to refuse. If he doesn't want to show up, he can just get on with his life. No repercussions. And it's not right, is it? Do you think that's right?
>
> SOLICITOR: Do *I* think it's right?

My solicitor. He pulls out a pen. It doesn't work. He shrugs.

SOLICITOR: Do I think it's right?

CASH: Do *you* think it's right?

SOLICITOR: Calm down.

CASH: I — am — calm.

SOLICITOR: You're acting hysterical.

CASH: I'm just telling you what happened.

SOLICITOR: You're acting very aggressively.

CASH: *This* is not aggressive.

SOLICITOR: Act like this during the interview and they'll say you're mad.

CASH: I am mad. And I'm ... justifiably angry.

SOLICITOR: Act like this and they'll flag you up to child protection.

CASH: I'm just telling you what happened.

SOLICITOR: And I'm just telling *you* — put one foot wrong and social services get involved.

CASH: That's just what happens to women like me, right?

SOLICITOR: I'm here to help you.

My solicitor. He's wearing a whole can of Lynx. He smells like a room of 13-year-old boys.

SOLICITOR: Go on/

CASH: Well. Say what you like. But. Nothing breaks me. Nothing. Took the pregnancy test with a black eye. Ran to a refuge. Worked in a peep show the whole time I was pregnant. At the very *least* ten thousand men wanked over me. Ten thousand wanks. Maybe more. Nothing breaks me. This situation now, yeah? Me telling you this whole crazy story in a police cell.

It's – just – a – normal – fucking – day – for – me.

SOLICITOR: Nothing breaks you.

My solicitor. He is chewing four whole pieces of Hubba Bubba. Maybe more.

SOLICITOR: Go on/

CASH: Don't you think it's disgusting though?

SOLICITOR: Ten thousand wanks? Yeah, it's disgusting.

CASH: Not the wanks. *Not* – the – wanks.

SOLICITOR: What are you talking about?

CASH: That a woman, she has to sign a document that forever reads – 'Your child does not have a dad.'

SOLICITOR: You're upset about that?

CASH: Yeah, I'm upset about that. That a father doesn't have to sign. It just gets left blank. Father unknown.

SOLICITOR: Do you know who the dad is?

CASH: Of course, I know. Why did you ask that?

SOLICITOR: Father, blank.

CASH: That's socio-economic profiling that is.

SOLICITOR: What is?

CASH: That. Assuming I don't know who the dad is.

SOLICITOR: Well, where *is* the dad?

My solicitor. He opens a can of lemon Fanta. He drinks half of it in one mouthful.

SOLICITOR: Go on/

CASH: Tried tracking him down. He'd disappeared. He'd gone into hiding. Closed down all his social media. Gone. I went via the child support agency. Did things properly. Did things the right way. The legal way. You'd approve. Took them three months to find him. Turns out he'd gone and changed his name by deed poll. Twice. Declared himself bankrupt. Kept moving house. Didn't sign the electoral roll. Refused to take a job. But didn't claim benefits. His parents gave him money. Kept him off grid. *Then* he went to Verbier. Verbier.

SOLICITOR: *Verbier.* It's pronounced Verbier.

CASH: Verbier. That's what I said. Did a ski season. A fucking ski season. He's *lower* middle class. He's aspirational. Skiing. I'm bringing up *his* child on next to nothing and he's in

Switzerland. Working out there. A thirty-five-year-old chalet boy. It's ridiculous. Let me tell you this: He's got tribal tattoos. He buys replica guns on eBay. The only book he's ever read is *The Road* by Cormac McCarthy and he actually *liked* it. He's got a Pomeranian called Nick Clegg. He's got Union Jack wing mirrors on his hire-purchase mini. *That's* the kind of man we're dealing with here.

SOLICITOR: You've made him sound like a *right* prick. Verbier!

My solicitor. He stands up and just walks out the cell. He reappears ten minutes later with a pen. He makes some notes but then it stops working.

SOLICITOR: I'm listening, go on/

CASH: The injustice of it all got to me.

SOLICITOR: Well, the child support agency has very little power.

CASH: I mean, how could he get away with it?

SOLICITOR: Roughly 1.3 million men get away with it each year. Deal with it.

CASH: *But* the CSA tracked him down.

SOLICITOR: After the ski season?

CASH: Post Verbier.

SOLICITOR: He signed on the jobseekers? Couldn't help himself.

CASH: That's how they found him.

SOLICITOR: In which case they'd take five pounds a week direct from his benefits give it straight to you.

CASH: But he denied paternity.

SOLICITOR: How sure are you that he's the dad?

CASH: I've always been sure.

SOLICITOR: 50/50?

CASH: No. 100 per cent.

SOLICITOR: They offer you a DNA?

CASH: I accepted the DNA.

SOLICITOR: You played by the book. I like you, Cash.

My solicitor. He tries to get the pen working. It doesn't work so he starts eating a ham sandwich.

SOLICITOR: Carry on/

CASH: Then he sent me a message via Facebook.

SOLICITOR: He made direct contact?

CASH: Which was in breach of his bail conditions.

SOLICITOR: For the black eye?

CASH: For assaulting me. Yeah. For which they still haven't charged him.

SOLICITOR: Give up on it. He'll never get charged. Your words, his words. Lack of evidence. All that.

CASH: The message was from an anonymous account.

SOLICITOR: But it was clearly him.

CASH: He said — If you want child maintenance you'll need a DNA test.

SOLICITOR: You'd already agreed via the correct and proper channels.

CASH: Then he said — Good luck finding me!

SOLICITOR: Back to Verbier.

CASH: Thirty-five-year-old chalet boy. But he left me a link to a website.

SOLICITOR: What was the website?

CASH: Cash Carraway Gangbang.

SOLICITOR: Cash Carraway Gangbang. I'll check it out.

My solicitor. He spits out his lump of Hubba Bubba. He plays with it in his hands.

SOLICITOR: Gangbang! Go on/

CASH: The website said that my daughter had been conceived in a gangbang.

SOLICITOR: It's up to you what you get up to in your private life.

CASH: I've never had a gangbang.

SOLICITOR: But what about the ten thousand pregnant wanks?

CASH: They were watching me from another room.

SOLICITOR: I see. You were working, they were wanking.

CASH: There was a stud wall between me and the sperm.

SOLICITOR: *Plus* you were already pregnant by then.

CASH: Listen. I'm actually a very traditional person deep down. Despite all *this*.

SOLICITOR: You're saying the website was a fabrication.

CASH: I'm saying the website is a lie.

SOLICITOR: You're saying you've *never* had a gangbang.

CASH: Never. I've never had a gangbang. I'm very romantic really — I want an Aga not AIDS.

SOLICITOR: My wife is desperate for an Aga.

CASH: *You're* married?

SOLICITOR: Twelve years for my sins.

CASH: Fucking hell. Well, I want to go cycling through the Lake District with my soulmate not ride a stranger cowgirl.

SOLICITOR: You always want what you can't have.

My solicitor. He lobs the mass of Hubba Bubba towards the cell toilet. It misses, he doesn't pick it up. He throws another two into his mouth. Orange flavour.

SOLICITOR: Go on/

CASH: Reported it to police.

SOLICITOR: The gangbang website?

CASH: But it destroyed me. Seeing those lies he'd written.

SOLICITOR: It's hurtful to read.

CASH: So. I started drinking again.

SOLICITOR: You're an alcoholic?

CASH: I might be. I suppose. I don't know.

SOLICITOR: You're a 'problem' drinker, as they say.

CASH: Suppose so.

SOLICITOR: It's fair to say you have issues with alcohol.

CASH: It's fair to say that I went to my first AA meeting at nineteen.

SOLICITOR: You still go to AA meetings?

CASH: Only when I lose control.

SOLICITOR: Morning drinker?

CASH: Never. I just binge.

SOLICITOR: Binge until you're out of control.

My solicitor. His laces are undone.

SOLICITOR: Yeah, go on/

CASH: I was sober for twenty months. Didn't drink the entire time I was pregnant, obviously. And when she was born, I was keeping it together, pushing the baby to meetings with me and saying the Serenity Prayer on my knees each morning, even though I'm agnostic. Calling my sponsor. Writing fucking gratitude lists. Didn't touch a drink until I saw that website.

SOLICITOR: Cash Carraway Gangbang.

My solicitor. He walks over to the cell toilet and sneezes down the bowl five times.

SOLICITOR: Go on/

CASH: It drove me to drink.

SOLICITOR: *Don't* mention the drinking in the police interview.

CASH: All because I dared to apply for child support!

SOLICITOR: Makes you look unreliable.

CASH: This is the truth.

SOLICITOR: They don't need the truth.

CASH: But if they know the truth then maybe they'll understand the crime.

SOLICITOR: That's not how the law works.

CASH: I've done nothing wrong.

SOLICITOR: The harassment. You did that.

CASH: It was a mistake.

SOLICITOR: You need to calm down a bit, put on an act.

CASH: You want me to act?

SOLICITOR: You need to appear like a proper mum.

CASH: I *am* a proper mum.

SOLICITOR: Sure, if you don't mention the binge drinking and the twenty thousand wanks.

CASH: Ten thousand wanks.

SOLICITOR: Postnatal depression?

CASH: Just normal depression.

SOLICITOR: You're depressed. Good.

My solicitor. He looks hopeful, like he's found an angle but sweat is trickling fast from his forehead and stinging his eyes.

SOLICITOR: Go on/

CASH: Of course I'm fucking depressed. I'm always depressed. That's why I drink. The doctor has put me on 200mg of Lustral, that's the highest dose, that means I'm really sad. I really am sad. Because — I saw that website. It was set up by Gary and his parents. They set up a website and a Facebook page saying that my daughter was conceived in a gangbang. All because I'd applied for child support. They wrote a website saying that my daughter was conceived in a gangbang, as revenge for asking for money that is legally mine.

SOLICITOR: It's up to you if you have gangbangs.

CASH: I DON'T HAVE GANGBANGS!

SOLICITOR: You sound mad.

CASH: I am justifiably mad.

SOLICITOR: Don't shout in the interview. You need to appear like a victim.

CASH: I sort of am.

SOLICITOR: They'll want a conviction.

CASH: I just want child support for my daughter.

SOLICITOR: Tell me what happened leading up to the arrest.

My solicitor. His white knitted tie falls into the cold coffee. He squeezes it out into the paper cup before taking a gulp and swilling it around his mouth.

SOLICITOR: Go on/

CASH: Gary was the one who requested the test — but he wouldn't take it. He kept delaying it. Changing appointments. Not showing up. Because they don't take the swab from the mother and the child until the man gives *his* DNA. The man has to comply. It's all reliant on the man playing fair. It was dragging out for months. My friend Clover said, and she said it as a joke — She said, Go on *The Jeremy Kyle Show*. I thought about it. I did. I thought it would be funny. I wouldn't actually do it but ... It got my mind thinking. Searching for a solution. Because let's face it — he's not going to turn up on *Jeremy Kyle* if he keeps missing the DNA appointments, is he? Even though they put you up in a lovely Holiday Inn in Manchester for the night, Gary isn't going to sit there on national television and be told to put something on the end of it. Is he?

SOLICITOR: Thirty-five-year-old chalet boy or *Jeremy Kyle Show* guest. What's more degrading?

My solicitor. He's wearing a medallion that reads BEST DAD. *It's not real gold though, because it has left a bruise-like residue on his shaved chest.*

SOLICITOR: Go on/

CASH: I got this crazy idea into my head.

SOLICITOR: I know where this is leading.

CASH: It's obvious, right?

SOLICITOR: No, I've read the notes.

CASH: I thought, I'll bring *The Jeremy Kyle Show* to my flat.

SOLICITOR: The real Jeremy Kyle?

CASH: My own version. I'd be Jeremy. I'm very resourceful.

SOLICITOR: You were so desperate for him to take that test.

CASH: Did a bit of research.

SOLICITOR: Googled DNA tests?

CASH: DNA tests. Lie detector tests. Did you know that you can even book a consultation with the real-life Graham Stanier?

SOLICITOR: The real-life Graham Stanier?

CASH: Graham. Stanier.

SOLICITOR: The *therapist* who Jeremy Kyle credits as 'doing all the aftercare behind the scenes'?

CASH: That's the one. *The* Graham Stanier. Seventy-five quid a session.

SOLICITOR: That's such a good deal. He can turn your life around for that.

CASH: But I didn't involve Graham Stanier. Kept him out of it.

SOLICITOR: Because you couldn't afford it.

CASH: No. But. DNA-testing kits are free.

SOLICITOR: You just pay for the results.

CASH: You get the results within forty-eight hours.

SOLICITOR: You open the envelope. Incontrovertible. He's the dad!

CASH: ... I was really drunk.

SOLICITOR: Because of the gangbang website.

CASH: Because I'd downed a bottle of wine.

SOLICITOR: Because <u>you</u> were angry.

CASH: Because of the anonymous email.

SOLICITOR: Because of the depression.

CASH: Because of the birth certificate situation.

SOLICITOR: Because the dad is a deadbeat! Yeah!

CASH: Filled out his name and address on the DNA website.

SOLICITOR: The last address you have for him.

CASH: His parents' address.

SOLICITOR: They've never met your daughter?

CASH: They've never met their granddaughter.

SOLICITOR: They've never even asked for contact?

CASH: They told me to get an abortion.

SOLICITOR: They *hate* that she exists.

CASH: Found a home DNA-testing company.

SOLICITOR: To disprove the gangbang.

CASH: To make him take responsibility.

SOLICITOR: To make him goddamn pay! Yeah!

CASH: I requested one DNA test.

SOLICITOR: Just the one.

CASH: One DNA.

SOLICITOR: To his parents' address.

CASH: Just the *one* test.

SOLICITOR: You wanted him to take the test.

CASH: But. I did the same again. On another website.

SOLICITOR: You didn't stop.

CASH: I was on a roll.

SOLICITOR: And then another.

CASH: Just to make sure he received *one*.

SOLICITOR: You used ten more websites.

CASH: Was trying to make a point.

SOLICITOR: There are hundreds of DNA-testing companies out there.

CASH: I clicked on every single website.

SOLICITOR: You wanted to make a point.

CASH: It was a clear message.

SOLICITOR: You wanted him to pay up.

CASH: Look here, thirty-five-year-old chalet boy — here's twenty DNA tests in your letterbox! Take — the — fucking — test.

SOLICITOR: Such a succinct point.

CASH: Went to thirty, forty websites.

SOLICITOR: Just to make sure he received one.

CASH: I was making a point.

SOLICITOR: You could almost say it was a political point.

CASH: Too right it's a political point. Yeah. About the ... demonisation of ... single mums.

SOLICITOR: About how men get away with it.

CASH: That they need to take responsibility.

SOLICITOR: And then. The tests arrived at his address. The last address you had for him.

CASH: His parents' address. Next-day delivery.

SOLICITOR: According to their statement — all the tests arrived at once.

CASH: Royal Mail. Nationalisation at its best. All arriving the very next day.

SOLICITOR: You visited one hundred and twenty-seven websites.

CASH: One hundred and twenty-seven websites?

SOLICITOR: One hundred and twenty-seven DNA-testing kits arrived.

CASH: Next-day delivery.

SOLICITOR: Through their letterbox.

CASH: One hundred and twenty-seven DNA kits. Yeah. Well. That's harassment.

SOLICITOR: That's why you're here.

CASH: It ... worked though.

SOLICITOR: He took the test?

CASH: The CSA called us in for our test.

SOLICITOR: He was declared the dad.

CASH: I was never in any doubt.

SOLICITOR: What would Jeremy Kyle say?

CASH: He would say: Next time put something on the end of it.

SOLICITOR: He was ordered to pay.

CASH: Five — pounds — a — week.

SOLICITOR: ... Your daughter is ten months old?

CASH: Eight months when he took the test.

SOLICITOR: And how much child maintenance have you received?

CASH: Not — a — penny.

SOLICITOR: But *you're* the one who's been arrested.

CASH: Well, I'm the one who has committed a crime.

Diary Entry – 13 October 2011

Today it is Biddy's first birthday. I was required to attend bail in Lincolnshire. I thought about skipping, staying at home, attempting to bake a birthday cake and inviting around some of the mums from my mother and baby group but it would have been embarrassing to have the police come and fetch me as we sang 'Wind the Bobbin Up'. So we board a train, Midlands bound. Haven't been back since the day I fled. Didn't use the toilets, because my dad bought me the train ticket. He came up with us. He said it was to support me but he didn't say or do much. I bought a chocolate muffin from the buffet cart and stuck a candle on it. Biddy's first birthday cake. We sang happy birthday in the carriage but the ticket inspector came over to disband our celebration – a passenger had complained about the naked flame. Dad looked disappointed as always.

I was charged with Non-Violent Harassment. I'm due in court in February. If I'm found guilty, I won't go to prison or anything – they'll just stick a restraining order on me. Get social services involved. Give me a fine. If Gary pays the child maintenance, then I can pay the fine with that money but I'm not holding out hope. He's off grid again. Doing another ski season, I suppose. Thirty-five-year-old chalet boy.

My solicitor. He had a huge coughing fit on the phone.

He said we could fight it. That we'd have a good chance of winning.

You've got a good case, he said. Depression, a history of domestic violence, the gangbang website, you're a single mum, driven to despair.

But I'm just going to plead guilty to get it over with.

Then maybe next year we'll be in a position where she can have a normal birthday. Send out John Lewis invitations to all the mothers and toddlers from the local group. Buy a Caterpillar cake from Tesco. Get a pink helium balloon shaped like a 2. Stick birthday bunting round the front door. Ask the guests two months in advance if their kids have allergies. Do an afternoon of soft play. A children's entertainer. Get a pirate fairy, that's normal. Have my dad and his wife over to spoil her with kisses and a Peppa Pig dining set. Buy her a silver locket and insert a picture of us and a lock of her hair. Do a lovely buffet.

I'd like that.

So.

I'm not going to fight him anymore.

Not going to fight anymore.

Well, pick my battles at least.

I'm going to plead guilty. Take the criminal record. Move on.

Then maybe her next birthday will be normal.

Next year our lives will look like everyone else's.

Note: Something went my way for once. Following my arrest I had logged a complaint with the Independent Police Complaints Commission (IPCC) with regard to the treatment of survivors of domestic abuse. Before fleeing Gary early in my pregnancy I had reported the assault that had resulted in my broken cheekbone. Gary had been arrested and whilst on bail had breached his conditions on numerous occasions by goading me via several anonymous Facebook accounts and setting up the website about me. I had reported each of these incidents but they were ignored and after a prolonged period of bail Gary wasn't charged. My complaint was that *my* crime had been treated as an isolated incident of harassment with no regard to the abuse I had endured and reported and how sending the DNA tests had been a response to this prolonged abuse. The IPCC investigation found in my favour and my statements concerning the abuse were submitted to the Crown Prosecution Service (CPS) as evidence. A few days before my trial I received a call from my solicitor with news that the CPS would be dropping the charges against me. I was free.

Speaking up had worked in my favour.

PART TWO:

MOTHERHOOD

6
SCROUNGERESS

I. Subtle Eugenics

IT'S 11AM AND I'M in a kebab shop in Haringey. It's cold and drizzly outside, which only adds to the bleakness of the moment, but things take a turn for the *even* worse when I spot the man I am meeting. We've never met before, but I know it's him because, if I was casting a paedophile in a film, then it would definitely be this guy – *skinny fat, bus shelter tan and holding a dog lead.* He looks just how he sounded on the phone, his voice wet-lipped and high pitched in tone. He is wearing a dirty blue ski jacket and a baseball cap, which he doffs upon seeing me. He is mostly bald and has a lot of moles, which makes me distrust him because my mum's face has literally hundreds of raised brown moles and I tend to take it as a sign of a bad person – and he is definitely the man I'm meeting; after all he is the only person other than myself and the greasy grill boy behind the counter hanging around kebab shops so soberly in the day. He stands to greet me, goes in for a hug but I hold out my hand which he shakes limply. I had anticipated dampness but I think he has eczema or something because I've left the greeting with half of his skin on my sleeve.

'You didn't bring your daughter?'

'She's at school.'

We sit down and he barks at the grill boy for a large doner meat and chips to share.

'Would you like a tin of drink to have all for yourself?'

'Diet Coke. Please.'

He tells me about the room. That's why I'm here. I found the ad in a shop window. It's got a single bed and a small chest of drawers and a faux sheepskin rug – which is machine washable – but the room hasn't got a window. It's a cupboard, really, but it's free, if me and my daughter want it. It's free. He just wants the company, he says. He's telling me he likes to help out single mums in trouble. He knows how tough it is out there for single mums. He was brought up by a single mum himself, he says. He says he is a good guy. To demonstrate just what a gentleman he is he pulls the ring on my diet Coke and pours half of it into the dirty glass, maintaining eye contact like we're sharing some connection, before pushing it my way.

And then: 'If you could stay in my bed for half the week. That's all I'd ask. The room is free. Four nights out of the seven, perhaps. Maybe five. Then your daughter would have her own space. They need their own space, don't they?

At that age. To grow. I'm good with kids, I never had my own, but I love children. Always wanted my own but … I'm away at weekends. Back up to Leicester, my mum she's disabled so I go up and take care of her. Wheel her around Leicester at the weekend. You don't have to do anything with me. The room is free. I'll never ask you to touch me. Although I do love to kiss. It's a simple act really, isn't it? But it means so much. French kiss. That's what I like. Do you like sloppy kisses? You have lovely lips. You don't have to kiss. You don't have to do anything you're uncomfortable with. I promise. Just lay there. In the bed. And sleep. You won't even know I'm there. I won't penetrate you. I just like to touch myself while someone, a woman, is close by. And the last mother who took the room stayed for a whole year – and sometimes she'd let me kiss her, I can't be that bad. I'm a gentle soul really, I'm a generous man, the room is … Have some kebab, I can't eat alone, I got this to share. It's the best kebab in Haringey. This is *all* on me by the way. My treat. My flat is just around the corner from here. I come here a lot. Little bit about me: I work in Maplin in Wood Green. You can use my staff discount if you like. I love my mum. And I'm good at cooking Thai food. Lived out there for a bit. I'll cook us a lovely Massaman on the night you move in. If you and your daughter move in. The room is free.'

I wrap some meat around a chip and dip it into the paper pot of garlic sauce.

It has taken me 80 rejections from estate agents to reach this point.

You walk into the estate agents on the back foot when you're a single mother. They assume low wages and consider self-employment slang for housing benefit (which of course it is these days, if you're part of the underclass) but throw in bad credit and no guarantor and you'll find the door to private renting slammed shut in your face. Even estate agents – considered by *all* enlightened people to be some of the most despicable humans on the planet – are placed higher in society than single mums.

Ranking from bottom to top on the society scum scale:

- Single mums
- Estate agents
- Ian Huntley and whatnot; convicted (male) child-killers get nowhere near the stigma of working-class single mothers. *And* they get a stable home.

These estate agents though, these men in pink ties who think that answering the phone at Foxtons makes them The Wolf of Fucking Wall Street, they won't even try to soften the blow by shaking their heads in a mournful way as they reject you – if anything they get a kick out of ushering me into the gutter with the words 'No unemployed! No DSS!' And despite my protestations that I work full-time, we *all* know that a mother from a single-income household has no chance of passing a credit check on a zero-hours, minimum-wage job.

And I'm one of the lucky ones. My current landlord has agreed to return my *full* deposit, meaning that if I add this month's wages to the moving pot (and forego food and skip on the utilities, which of course I will do – because what's another debt on an already out of control list?) then we'll have £3,000 to our name.

A – whole – three – grand – in – cash.

The things you could do with three grand ... If I could drive then I could buy a cheap car for us to live in – we'd live in a car, that's what we'd do. Families do that all the time these days. *Or* I could blow it on flights to some hick town in America, grab a motel for a few weeks whilst we search for a cult to join – if we pretend to follow the Lord and I become a Mormon's seventh wife then we'll be sorted. We'd be living a lie, but I'd live a lie for the rest of my life for a stab at stability. I now understand why so many people remain in loveless, abusive marriages. I get it. You think they're hanging onto it all for the kitchen island and two Mark Warner holidays each year but it's deeper than that. *The room is free.* When faced with a life of precarity and refused autonomy over housing, jobs and food, give me a black eye in Grantham over this government any day.

But not even a Mormon with a whole bunch of wives would take on the 'burden' of another man's child and the shameful woman who birthed it, no matter how much I fake prayed. So, I have no choice but to keep searching for seemingly outlandish alternatives because £3,000 for rent and deposit won't get you much in London – in fact I'll still have to find some stuff to sell in order to afford the deposit and moving costs. And each move forces us farther out into the suburbs; this next move will probably mean Biddy won't have her own bedroom, we'll have to share a mattress – but we'll find a place. Even if we end up living in a pervert's cupboard above a Halal butchers just off Turnpike Lane. We will find something. *Eventually.*

We tread the underworld of Gumtree, OpenRent and the depravity of handwritten adverts in newsagent windows – masseurs, naked cleaners and slumlords – but most of them insist on credit checks too. Credit checks: The modern equivalent of the discriminatory NO DOGS, NO BLACKS, NO IRISH posters placed in landlords' windows during the 1950s. It's just that these days they're not allowed to be so openly racist, so they have shifted their focus onto classism, which of course (not so secretly) incorporates racism with a dash of misogyny too.

One shop-window landlord refused to rent us a squalid studio on a rough Camden estate with the following words:

Single mothers like you, you seem nice at first, you and your daughter seem lovely and you're charming and you're working, YOU'RE WORKING – good for you! But my experience of women like you is that something always goes

wrong, it always goes WRONG ... and then you stop pay-
ing rent and then I must evict you and then YOU trash
the place, smash holes in the walls and shit in my sink, and
pull up the toilet with your own bare hands and drag it out
onto the balcony ... THAT kind of thing.

I laughed, because she was funny. And she does have a valid point. We will be hit by a sanction or an unavoidable expense and something will go wrong, that's just what happens when life is lived in the gig economy without the safety net of family support. But – I – won't – shit – in – your – sink (I tell her) But. My bank statements, hard cash and landlord reference make no difference when I fail the credit check. That's a 'no', then?

That's – a – no.

If *I'm* rejected for over 80 properties in the space of three weeks, then what hope does someone with absolutely *nothing* have?

The answer is up to 12 years in temporary accommodation and a life that no longer belongs to you. Moved between Travelodges and rat-infested flats on the council's whim, and most *definitely* removed from London. Places like Peterborough prepare to accommodate our temporary 12 years: 12 whole temporary years. That's my daughter's entire childhood wiped out. I'd serve less time for assassinating the Housing Minister. And that's *if* you can get on the housing list. Believe me, I've tried to get on the housing list. I'm obsessed with the housing register. Whilst all my childless friends have reached a point in their lives where they are searching for 'the one' to settle down with, obsessively on sperm search, all I can think about is finding 'the one home' that we can settle into and finally begin living. I've reached a point of realisation where I know I won't be able to have a relationship or plan a family despite desperately wanting more children because all I can think about is where we are going to live in six months time and how we are going to afford to move. It's subtle eugenics. I'm perpetually preoccupied with having a stable home that I can afford in the city I have always lived in. In the city that my daughter has always lived in.

But the government want us out. It's our punishment for our 'reckless lifestyle choices', for not marrying or living with a man. Those women and children who do not fit into the right wing's antiquated ideologies must be impoverished and punished as an example to all.

... If only the myth were true about vile scroungeresses like me breeding aimlessly for a council tenancy, if that were the case, then, according to the *Daily Mail*, I'd have a secure tenancy in a Mayfair mansion block living next door to some Muslims who faked an illegal war in order to seek asylum from it. But there are no council houses for us sponging single mums, nor for the Muslims fleeing horrific atrocities; there are no affordable homes left, and housing benefit is the only thing keeping the working class in their hometowns, but most landlords are refusing to accept it.

The demonisation from the right-wing press has penetrated society to the point where we are deemed untrustworthy. But the fact is we are probably the most trustworthy of all – we would do anything to give our children the stability of a long-term home. The right-wing press say that if we didn't want to be in this position then we shouldn't have 'behaved badly', OPENED OUR LEGS and had kids.

We move every six months. You spend the first three months setting up your new life getting the bills in order, enrolling into a new school and settling in, and the last three months packing up and searching for the next place. I'm a slum-property connoisseur, I'm basically the Kirstie Allsopp of the underclass – in a sweatshop dress and better looking – only I'd never vote Tory because I care about people. But it's getting harder out there. It is getting harder to find a place to stay. The reason for our latest split? Our landlord wants to up the rent by £150 a week to 'market value', despite unresolved damp and a mice infestation. He knows what he can get, and he knows that since the benefits cap came into play that housing benefit won't stretch that far. It's professionals only. No single mums. No kids. No working poor. No benefits.

So, I've been searching tirelessly since he gave us our notice a month ago.

Still no takers.

Still. No. Home.

I stand crying in front of estate agent number 81. I always dress up for the estate agents. Make a real effort. Try to look middle class; a floral dress, soften the accent. It's a hard balance to strike but I can pull it off – you just need to find a sweet spot somewhere between the working-class women stereotypes of hard-faced matriarch in leopard print and the benefits-street chic of tracksuits and exposed steak-bake arms. You're never allowed to be yourself. Sometimes I'll tell them I have a husband who works away. In Dubai. They're much nicer if they think a man is on the scene.

'Surely you must have somewhere disgusting?' I beg. 'A shed? A garage? Our last place had a family of mice. We'll willingly share with rats this time. (The standards drop with each move.) I'm not even on full housing benefit. I work. FULL TIME! Housing benefit is just a top-up because min-imum wage doesn't cover it.'

Even a small amount of benefits makes you untrustworthy, the teenager in the salmon tie informs me.

I've never met a single mother who is proud to be on ben-efits. When we talk about our jobs, we stage whisper about having our rents topped up with housing benefit and how if it wasn't for working tax credits then there is no way we'd be able to afford the childcare to enable us to work the minimum-wage, often zero-hour, jobs that allow us any kind of survival. Fifty-seven per cent of us work, and the reason the majority of those that don't is because they have children under the age of three. Most working-class single mothers are grafters. I know that my daughter thinks all I ever *do* is work.

I take her with me to work and hide her in the corner watching YouTube on my phone to keep her occupied.

Of course I am embarrassed to be working and on benefits.

II. Benefits Slut

Tim said he was entitled to the money. Tim is the only person I've ever met who shamelessly collected benefits with a sense of pride. He was a trainee barrister. From an upper-middle-class family. He was always eager to point out that he was upper middle class; he once sneered about Kingsley, who had attended private school but not the *right* kind of private school, saying that he was the middle of the middle class and being the middle of the middle class is cruder than being poor in the eyes of men like him. Tim had gone to the same private school as some minor royals and Nick Clegg and therefore was a better version of middle class.

I don't know why I was hanging around with him. Bored as always. Searching for something. We met in an AA meeting. In AA there's a loose rule mentioned by 'the elders' when you first go into recovery that men and women should be kept apart because it'll lead to sex and in turn an inevitable relapse. It's true. We had sex. We drank. Can't remember in which order. But we were drinking together and having sex. I was 19. It was my second gap year (the confused working-class kind of gap year where you don't really know how to apply for university because you weren't academically gifted enough for the teachers to have noticed you, that kind of gap year – not the au pair summer followed by the nine months in Thailand kind of gap year). He was typical of his type. He'd been to boarding school, then on to Bristol, then just about made it onto a law conversion course – the normal route for an averagely intelligent directionless man of privilege. If he'd grown up like me there is no doubt his highest professional achievement in life would be making the shortlist for supervisor in the men's section at Debenhams. But he didn't grow up like me. And guys like Tim love a rough girl like me for the summer. Just for the summer. Makes them feel part of the world – or at least lets them live out their romantic perception of what life is like in the 'real world' before they marry their third cousin.

He was about ten years older than me. He was awaiting his call to the Bar (a different kind to the ones we got lost in) and he had a couple of months to kill. One afternoon, we were downing mojitos at the Sanderson Hotel when he blurted out – 'I'm going to *sign on* for the summer. Get myself on the JSA, Bet you've been on the JSA haven't you?! Dirty bitch. My parents have paid into the system for long enough. It's the least I deserve. It's not called National Insurance for nothing, you know. You pay into it and, when you crash the car of life, you get a payout. Consider my car dented. Time for my payout. I'm going to be like all the other benefit sluts.'

Tim was of course referring to his minor royal friends who lived off the state as opposed to future single mums like me. Unfortunately we don't get slogans that sound like bad album titles. Just sneery tabloid headlines. Women like me are simply sluts on benefits.

After Tim downed his mojito he tried to grope a few glamour models before we hailed a taxi to the Archway jobcentre so he could sign up to his new 'lifestyle choice'.

Choice. Not something that people in need of benefits usually get to experience. Food bank – not a choice. Desperation – not a choice. Sanctions – not a fucking choice. Governmental vilification – not a choice.

Lifestyle choice. The birth of Princess Charlotte. The birth of Prince George. The birth of the third one where the benefits still get issued without having to prove it was the result of rape. Lifestyle choice. Birthing in the Lindo Wing. A refurbished Norfolk Manor. A television wedding. A no-expenses-spared christening. Holidays to Kenya. All those pretty dresses from Whistles. That's a lifestyle I'd choose. The royals definitely make me want to go on benefits too, I can see why Tim wanted in. Choice.

If you work full time but don't earn enough to cover your rent and you require some help via Housing Benefit, then you don't get to choose a home. Your home and location choose you. You register with as many landlords as possible and hope one will put you up for at least six months. That's not a lifestyle choice.

The trainee barrister, he *loved* his fortnightly trips to the jobcentre and in the short time we were acquainted he signed on four times. He signed on every other Tuesday at 12.37pm and he'd even dress down for the occasion. He took great pleasure in writing in his job search book to pass on to his work coach. He'd list fast-food chains, H. Samuel, Laser Quest, the bowling alley, the army, the post office, Frankie & Benny's, Burtons. He said the jobcentre reminded him of a day trip he took on an elephant to the slums of India during a spiritual six months back in 1996 when the hedonism of Britpop had become too much for him. He said that the jobcentre had a definable scent; a very specific kind of damp. Like when you dry your washing in a bathroom that doesn't have a window.

Poverty always has a smell.

He said he was entitled to the money. That 70-odd quid each week. Just like his royal friends from school were entitled to their benefits. He'd earned it. His parents had worked bloody hard and paid into the highest tax band for, like, forever, so he deserved a reward. Their hard work had paid for his education, the gap year abusing sex workers in the Far East, the three-bed apartment in Highgate they bought him and the allowance that he was still receiving and probably would continue to receive forever whilst he awaited the rewards of his parents' deaths sometime in the future. They worked hard so he was entitled to it all.

When I gently reminded him that Harry and Wills' parents hadn't ever paid tax, he looked pained. Almost teary. He'd never be a royal no matter how many benefits he claimed over that summer. But when the JSA hit his account every other Thursday he'd hit up the Spearmint Rhino on Tottenham Court Road and in an act of charity would tip it to the girl on day shift he found least attractive. His Lady Di moment.

III. Social Housing Fetishist

It's just gone midday and I've eaten half a doner kebab, so it feels about the right time to check out this cupboard in Haringey. I'm out of options, void of choice. I'm led up four flights of fire escape before being introduced to a studio flat storage cupboard by the front door. There is a single mattress, an IKEA tallboy and above it is an old boiler. On the door there are some hooks where lonely wire hangers await my daughter's school uniform. There is no window. There are no power points. No lights, no way to live a life.

'The last mum left a torch. You can have it if you take the room.' He flashes it on and off to tempt me.

'And she had some beautiful battery-powered fairy lights, with flashing blue hearts, they were lovely, I think she got them from Poundstretcher but she took them when she left. I'm sorry. All that's left of her is that blood stain on the mattress ...'

We look at the dried blood for a while until he confirms – 'It's period blood. I didn't kill her.'

'I know.'

The place smells of dogs and our cupboard home leads onto his bedroom-cum-living room-cum-kitchenette and there is a dirty wok on the camping stove. The walls are woodchip but painted orange and a picture of his disabled mum in Leicester hangs by the door.

'That's my mum.' He points to the picture and I quickly come up with some words because he clearly wants a response – 'You look just like her' is what I give him. And he does. He does look like her.

'She brought me up all alone. I know how hard it is for you.'

I have nothing else for him from my mouth, so I nod.

'The room is free,' he says quietly.

Then I leave.

I think I'm going to take it.

Time is running out. We'll be evicted in a week.

My friend Clover is dating an anarchist who lives in a squat and she takes me along to meet him in the hope we can stay there for a while but he says they're getting moved on every few weeks these days and having a child tagging along would make things even more difficult.

I scout flats in the cheapest boroughs of London. I look at towns on the outskirts with bad transport links that would make it impossible for me to get to work. I view properties that make my skin crawl. I even contact estate agents in Fred

West towns far away where you can rent a mansion for £500! But. Same rules apply. The credit check will fail – this time because by relocating you would be making yourself unemployed and therefore would be 100 per cent reliant on housing benefit. The answer is NO. The answer is *always* NO.

Then some luck comes our way. A high-street estate agent (estate agent number 82) says a landlord is willing to take a risk on us for a horrible two-bed in Holloway for £1,300pcm. I jump at the 'opportunity'. 'Thank you for the opportunity,' I say, bowing my head.

We pay a £300 holding deposit (deductible from total) and £300 in non-refundable fees, of course. And we'll pay the remaining £3,600 of the deposit when we move in at the end of the week.

Then they have a change of heart.

At the final hour, the landlord decides I am a liability.

Self-employed. Single mother. Formerly bankrupt. No guarantor.

A new offer on the table: two months' deposit and SIX MONTHS' RENT IN ADVANCE.

'But I don't have a spare ten grand knocking about …'

Then you're not a suitable tenant.

And no, they won't be refunding the £600.

Things cost more when you're poor.

I call kebab shop man to accept the free cupboard. I lay down my terms: I won't kiss you, I tell him. And I'll cook for myself.

And you don't ever speak to my daughter. OK? He tells me to forget it – he's found another cupboard mum who will share his bed every night *and* kiss him.

Then.

Estate agent number 83. I walk in off the street. I haven't even bothered to dress up. I start crying, tell my sorry tale – you know the moment when you've lost all hope, and pride is something you no longer possess, and you just let it rip? You anticipate defeat, yet you give it a shot anyway.

'Even the kebab shop paedophile who was advertising a mattress in a cupboard in exchange for sex rejected me.'

Then. A glimmer of hope, from estate agent number 83: 'I know a landlord who is a decent bloke. I'll call him.'

I almost hug him. But he is a despicable estate agent, so I *don't*.

I meet with the landlord. Not your typical landlord; a pop-star from the 80s, and the 90s, and he's one now, too.

'What?!' I laugh. '*You* own this flat?!'

He laughs too – 'You don't like it?'

It's a small one-bed, but it's perfect for Biddy and me.

'I love it. I love it. No, I LOVE it. It's just … you are YOU and you own a flat on a … council estate!'

He tells me he grew up here. In this flat. Just him and his mum. The happy memories. It's where he formed the band. His childhood home. The estate even features in some of their most well-known music videos. And when he got rich and famous, he just couldn't let the flat go. 'I don't even agree with

Right to Buy but ...' He doesn't finish his sentence, I think he feels ashamed.

I tell him my story. I'm brutally honest. About the last few years. Everything. My daughter. The bankruptcy. Self-employment. No guarantor. The shit-smeared toilet on the train from Grantham. The refuge. Being homeless. The 82 estate agents leading up to this moment. And of course, the toilet on balcony story ...

'And even if I do fuck up, and you have to evict me ... I just don't have the physical strength to uproot toilets,' I say.

He considers the situation. He accepts my offer of two months' rent. I wince at the amount I'll have to find each month. I take out four payday loans that afternoon to add to my three grand. We sign the contract. We get the keys.

I give our flat, our home, more love than it deserves. I love the neighbourhood, our high ceilings and feel so grateful that we have somewhere to live. I try to overlook the imperfections, the damp and the mould, and the fact my daughter doesn't have her own bedroom.

And of course, we get *all* the negatives of social housing but none of the positives; sharing a communal heating system with 80 other flats, which *doesn't work* – we go for weeks at a time without hot water because the council refuse to fix it; we fall asleep to the soundtrack of moped gangs distributing their wares directly outside our bedroom window ...

We pay *three times* what our neighbours pay for four-bed flats on the same estate because they were lucky enough to be housed by the council 30 years ago.

People say with shock – What?! You pay £1,500 for a one-bed flat on a council estate?! – like I'm some kind of social-housing fetishist, willing to forego a bedroom for my daughter for a taste of the underclass ...

Yes, when times are tough you can swap Sainsbury's for Lidl. Luxury for basic. The gym for a jog. Do a 'no spend' year. A 'no spend' life. Change your energy provider. You can cut back in almost every way. Yet the same cannot be said for housing, not if you're a single mum. Not if you're a scroungeress.

When work doesn't pay and you need to claim benefits to afford a private rental you don't get to experience choice. We live a life where you take what you can get, and get what you are given.

7

OUTSIDERS

Aktion T4

Charlotte Bradley had it in for me. It was summer, and the reason I remember that time so well is because Ireland had made it to the quarter-finals of Italia 90 and that was a big deal in my family.

I also remember it because, up until this point, a lot of my childhood had been spent in the wards of the dilapidated Sydenham Children's Hospital where I would be admitted for weeks at a time for bed rest or yet another painful operation. At the age of two I'd been diagnosed with juvenile arthritis which affected my knees and resulted in me being pushed around in a cheap red buggy until I was about nine.

Like – a – freak.

There was this girl on the same ward as me who had cystic fibrosis.

Her name was Kelly. I liked her a lot. I liked her because she had a My Little Pony nightdress, I liked her because she had a Garbage Pail Kids sticker book and I liked her because her bed was easy for my weak knees to crawl to – she was conveniently located in the bed next to mine. These things are important when you're little and hospital-bound. Sometimes I would climb into her bed and we'd do colouring-in together and, when my dad visited in the evening, he'd read us a book. She loved it because he would do funny voices for all the different characters.

The thing is, though, she couldn't laugh properly because she was really sick; the laugh would get stuck in her throat and sometimes she would cough up so much mucus that her nightdress would be soaked in seconds, and if she found my dad exceptionally hilarious then she would vomit into her paper bowl next to the grapes.

(I was disgusted by her sick but it made me proud that he was humorous enough to make a terminally ill child puke.)

But. I mean, she was really sick. Far sicker than me. At night the nurse would come around and drain the fluid from her lungs. It was annoyingly noisy, and I'd just about got used to the grim 3am wake-up calls when she died.

Anyway, I was discharged a few days later because the doctors said I was in remission and that was that. Kelly was dead, and I was free. It was a miracle: my Nana and my aunty Philomena had brought in a signed Daniel O'Donnell postcard to put by my bed with a note from him saying that he'd pray for me, and the next morning I woke up and my knee wasn't swollen, I wasn't in pain and I could walk without a limp. I don't know if it was thanks to Daniel O'Donnell's powerful prayers or advances in medicine or maybe I'd just outgrown the illness, but the cheap buggy was thrown in the bin.

No – longer – a – freak.

This all happened in 1990 – just in time for the World Cup. That's why I remember it so well. I wore knock-off Ireland shirts from East Street Market and did penalty shoot-outs in the garden.

It was true freedom, running around without swelling or splints.

Of course, there were side effects to the illness; my eyesight would be severely affected and would get worse with time – I'm practically blind these days – and my jaw would be under-developed meaning that everything inside my mouth would be wonky and nothing would fit. Eating would always be awkward, sometimes painful. I'd have a bit of a lisp and terrible diction. But turns out it's actually *perfect* for blow jobs, so that's good; the tight space and rigid jawline creating the ideal environment for cock suction. And my hands wouldn't grow much bigger than a 12-year old's, but I didn't care, I could play football and learn guitar and do Irish dancing. Life was alright. At least I wasn't dead like Kelly.

But Charlotte Bradley. She had it in for me. I was running around the playground as opposed to 'resting' on the bench like I'd been forced to in the past when she turned up on the first day back at school wearing the same coat as me. It was dusty pink and in neon letters on the back read NAFF Co 54.

117

I fucking loved it. It was from Fashion House next door to the Bejam in Penge and I was excited to see that someone else had the same amazing taste in budget coats as me. So I ran over to her.

But Charlotte Bradley was not happy. 'The coat looks better on me. You make the coat look ugly,' she observed.

1990 was also the year that I realised the importance of looks.

The boys ranked all the girls in order of attractiveness (Me? Always mid-table, where I have remained to this day.) and the girls who had started to develop boobs were always the most popular in kiss-chase.

1990 was also the year my adult teeth grew in. My deformed jaw sprouted these mottled speckled goofy tombstones with brown dots (Dental Fluorosis was a side effect of the medication I'd been prescribed for the previous five years) and, whilst no one else bothered to comment (because WHO really cares about that kind of thing?), my new teeth were an endless source of interest for Charlotte Bradley.

Dirty mouth. Bugs Bunny (bit obvious). Tongue prison.

We've all been called horrible names. We've all been hurt. We've all quietly sobbed at night into our pillows at the feelings of injustice from being singled out in cruel ways that tear us apart. Everyone has been attacked at some point.

But.

Some things I've learned about bullies: They are unhappy. They are lacking. They are lost. They are angry. Something somewhere is wrong. Something is missing. They – are – taking – out – their – pain – on – you.

But I didn't know this back then, so by the time I was ten I was sitting in the dentist's chair crying and begging him to rip out every tooth from my useless jaw and give me dentures. RIP THEM OUT. He refused because other than looking disgusting they were perfectly healthy and he told me I'd have to learn to live with them.

Learn to live with the source of attack.

I went home and stared at them for hours. These horrible things in my mouth ruining my face. Then as the years passed and I fell in love with records by Shane MacGowan, Joe Strummer, Freddie Mercury, Mark E. Smith, Justine Frischmann and Paul Westerberg – these unbelievably cool people with demented rock 'n' roll teeth – I realised that I'd fallen into good company.

And I tried to fall in love with myself.

I stopped placing any value on physical appearance. Purely due to being out of all other options. I mean – I would never be perfect, I had to get used to it. Never be a model in a Colgate ad, but then nor would Jarvis Cocker. I learned from a young age that looking nice is subjective and without meaning. Attractiveness (in the view of my very bad eyesight) is the whole spirit of a person; the stories they share and the jokes they tell. The books they've read and the music they love. The beliefs they hold and the kindness they show. I feel so lucky that I found that perspective just as I slipped into my teens – it meant that, although my hands didn't grow to adult size, I had the privilege of becoming a complete person with the confidence to be a little bit odd.

It was almost as if I could make a virtue out of being an outsider. It was who I was, there was nothing I could do about it. I could try to make being an outsider ... cool. It was a trait that stood me well in my twenties as a stripper – I could never compete physically with the Jenna Jameson-esque beauties but could always pull in more cash than them because I knew how to chat to the more cerebral clientele.

We all look shit eventually.

Even the beautiful strippers.

Hair thins and skin sags.

Teeth rot.

We get sick.

The lines dig deep.

We have tumours dug from us.

Limbs lost.

We lose control.

We shit ourselves.

We have the fluid drained from our lungs in the middle of the night.

No one is beautiful enough to fight all that.

So, I decided to try to like myself. It was a wonderful feeling, like that summer of Italia 90 when I could walk properly for the first time. That freedom. I'd laugh a lot and feel good about myself, except in rare moments of vulnerability – like, if I was talking face to face with a guy I really fancied then I might find myself instinctively shielding my mouth with my hand as I cracked a lame joke. It's the one remaining insecurity from that time. *Please don't think I'm disgusting*. Then I quickly remember that if someone is unable to fall in love with me because of a few twisted bones in my mouth then they are probably not the person I'd hoped they'd be.

Take me or leave me.

When I was 14 my mum stood in the middle of our kitchen and pulled down her thick, flesh-coloured tights to flash her freshly shaved vagina at me and my friend Teresa Connally. This kind of occurrence was embarrassing, but not unusual. Last time Teresa Connally was round my mum beat me with a vacuum cleaner, the time before that she sprayed Mr Sheen in my eyes because she didn't want us to watch *Top of the Pops* and Teresa Connally didn't know where the hell to look. So, if anything, the vagina flash was a step up, although I was aware that this was probably the last time Teresa Connally would accept an invitation to my house. This was definitely the breaking point – a 'three strikes and you're out'-type situation.

'I'm having an affair with a military nurse called Micky,' Mum bragged. 'He likes me clean-shaven. I like me shaven. Do you *girls* like me all shaven?' she enquired. The worst thing is that she did this completely sober. She never *ever* drank alcohol so I couldn't roll my eyes and claim she was talking through the booze or that she was some sad junkie – she was devoid of anything that could have altered her mind. Her mind was just naturally screwed and she was just standing there, vagina out for my friend.

Teresa and I agreed that it was very fashionable and that it suited her. It was 1996 and, although neither of us was having sex, we'd stolen enough copies of *Readers' Wives* from WHSmith to know that shaved pussies were 'having a moment' and we'd even prepped ours just in case we *ever* pulled a boy – which was never going to happen because we were goths, obviously.

Anyway, these kinds of things have a way of getting around and next thing you know, as you walk through the school gates the following morning, you're being called FANNY FLASHER.

How do you respond to that? You can't just turn around and say – 'No, I'm not a fanny flasher actually, the fanny flasher is my mum.' Because that's even worse, so you just take it. FANNY FLASHER.

Or there was the time my mum grabbed a cricket stump from under the stairs and chased my ex-friend Nina around our house calling her a paki.

That's when everyone started calling me a racist.

I just accepted it.

Or the time Mum keyed my ex-friend Elaine's Ford KA because Elaine had asked how my dad was. My mum was convinced that Elaine was having an affair with my dad due to her friendly enquiry.

Everyone called me a vandal and my diminishing circle of friends sent me to Coventry until I personally paid for it to be repaired.

Because that kind of stuff gets around the playground.

You just take it.

You accept it.

You're not like the other kids.

You're different.

You're separate.

You have no choice but to embrace it.

You're an outsider.

Take me or leave me.

But then ... motherhood happened. And all that confidence that had helped me survive for so long without the stability of a family went out the window.

Because when you bring a child into the world, all – by – yourself, you're a clear outsider, and that is that. Outsider mums are bad. You're just not up to the job. You're just not like the others. Without the set-up of the nuclear family you are a source of shame, a suspicious character, most definitely immoral and up to no good. The mums on the inside are the nice girls taking weekend burlesque classes in the name of saucy, fun feminism and we're the dirty slut strippers grinding against their husbands to satisfy our *own* carnal immorality. You're even further on the outskirts if you're poor. Because you know what poor people are? They're weak. And you know who's even weaker? Poor women. Poor mothers. Easy targets, a cheap shot. Like a nine-year-old with spazz legs being pushed around in a cheap buggy. Next thing you know you're back in the playground, this time as a single mum, and it's like 1990 again and you're the only one wearing Gola whilst everyone else is wearing Reebok Pumps.

And guess who's back?

It's Charlotte Bradley. Only now she's wearing an £80 Mama jumper and is standing smug next to her impotent Tory-voting husband.

And she's got an Instagram account.

As I take my daughter to school each morning I feel that familiar fear as we approach the gates. The kids were in a pack and now the mothers stand in intimidating packs too. Everyone is still the same really, regardless of how much we try to change or grow. Humans look for the weakness in the weakest and they'll exploit it, no matter how old you are. I used to see old ladies get bullied down the bingo hall when Nana would drag me along, a group of women in their seventies eating chips from the bingo buffet would kiss their teeth at this glamorous woman called Sally-Ann every time she claimed a prize for a line. They did it to her until she picked up her big pens and found another bingo hall three miles away. They chased her out of town. Seven or seventy it never stops. Society always needs to stigmatise someone. The government take from the weakest and the stigma takes hold via the media and it's trickle-down bullying that makes its appearance at the bingo hall or at the school gates.

Bringing a child into the world alone without support puts you in the same vulnerable position as having a vagina-flashing mum does. Single mums are an instant source of suspicion to the mums involved in traditional family structures – I just wish they would see that I don't want to steal their balding, boring husbands who work in advertising.

I find it so hard to fit in in the playground yet I'm desperate to find mother friends. For the first time in my life I want nothing more than want to fit in and I'll do whatever it takes.

So, like the other mums, I join Instagram.

The Fall of Penge

When Biddy was a baby, we lived in Maida Vale by mistake. It's an expensive part of town but this was before the benefits cap and attempts to remove low-income private renters from the inner city. At that time, Westminster Council would cover housing benefit at market value, and because the rents in the borough were so expensive it suited landlords to keep the expensive but badly maintained and rodent-infested properties occupied with the guaranteed income of benefit claimants as opposed to leaving them empty and running at a loss. So for a while we ended up living on the same street as rock 'n' roll stars and Hollywood actors.

With little money and a newborn baby I found myself spending hours of the summer sitting in the Rose Garden at Paddington Rec trying to make conversation with anyone else with a buggy. These women were all incredibly wealthy; the wives of rock stars, household-name actors, or the partners of men who'd sold their souls to the world of advertising. These women. They were so confident. They carried Mulberry bags. They had honey-blonde highlights. Freshly painted nails. Delicate engagement rings. They always smelled so delicious. I was simultaneously in awe of them and their decadent lifestyles yet had a massive chip on my shoulder about the ease and vacuous nature of their existence. They all had nice parents to run away to and stay with in Hertfordshire when things got tough – like if their nanny had filled the dishwasher in a way they didn't like, or their husband had put the recycling in the wrong bin. That type of thing. Because they'd always lose their shit over that *type* of thing and spend hours crying about it in the Rose Garden.

One of these women stopped to chat to me one afternoon and asked me if my dress was Isabel Marant. Had I snapped it up in Paris or was it purchased from Net-A-Porter during a blurry-eyed night feed?! I looked around through the haze of glamorous women to ensure she was talking to me – I was wearing a cheap black jersey dress from my local charity shop – but she was, she was talking to me. She thought I was just like her. Sure, Isabel Marant. Yes, Net-A-Porter, I said. And …

I'm so disgusted at myself, at what I did next, but I

affected

my accent

into this middle-class tone I'd taught myself to do back when
I was at university and dated an Old Harrovian called Giles.

Yeah. You're probably thinking what's a girl like her doing
getting off with a guy called Giles, and you'd be right to think
that, but I guess he found me exotic enough to spend some
time with and ended up taking me home to Somerset for the
weekend to meet his parents. You can tell from his name and
where he'd gone to school that the home he took me back to
was one of those big manor houses with paintings of princes he
was related to above each fireplace. All the fireplaces. So many
fireplaces in one house.

Things were going well with the meeting of the parents; I
knew my place, took the playing piece of the boot when we
played Monopoly and I let his mum win every game. Giles
took the racing car, his dad took the top hat and his mum the
Scottie dog. Everything was in its right place. I'd even managed to use the cutlery correctly and avoided any awkward
'pass the port' situations by being in one of my sober periods.
It went well and I was even allowed to sleep in Giles' bedroom
with the proper linen. The meeting of parents had felt like a
great success, they seemed to like me – until the following

morning when I walked into the kitchen and his dad greeted me with the words 'Here she is: The Wench!'.

He had given me the nickname of 'The Wench' owing to the growls of my strong Penge accent. He even did an impression of it! 'I'm the wench and I'm from Penge!' he said in a mock common voice. And when me and Giles inevitably broke up a few weeks later (because it was never going to work) *all* of his friends started to refer to me as The Wench too. So, I changed my accent whenever I was around people like that, because this terrible accent that my class and location had bestowed upon me was like a glass ceiling. The class ceiling. It's not an acceptable voice to have when dating men with names like Giles and it's not an accent conducive to success in life. So, I have a special voice that I use at job interviews, on the telephone and when registering the birth of my child alone. But on this occasion, in the Rose Garden on Paddington Rec, I took it a step further and not only used my special voice but I also introduced myself to the woman as … Camilla.

'Hi, I'm Camilla.' Not Cash. Cash doesn't sound posh.
Cash – is – not – posh.

Not that Cash is even my real name. 'Cash' is the nickname Kingsley gave me because, whenever I'd return to his flat after my shift at the strip club, I'd throw hundreds of £20 notes onto the kitchen table and count out all my money like some sultry Scrooge. Kingsley would take a cut of my earnings calling me 'his cash' and it stuck. So *you* can call me Cash. I'm talking to you. Yes, *you*. Reader. You don't *need* to know my birth name, you just need to know that it sounds common, a non-descript 1980s working-class name of Irish descent, *you* don't need to know it – because it doesn't mean a *thing* to me. My name is as interchangeable as my accent, my hair, the colour of my nails, my brand of anti-depressants, the style of clothes I choose to wear. I – am – interchangeable. I have no family, which means I have little identity. And. And a woman named something like Jade or Tiffany or Kerry-Marie is *never* going to be allowed to become Prime Minister. Not in this country. Or be a rock star, which was my main plan back in 2007, so I changed it by deed poll to Cash. I hate the name bestowed upon me by FANNY FLASHER because – sharing DNA with her is bad enough. Imagine being named by *that* woman. Imagine living *inside* that woman. I have no attachment to any name, I had no attachment to *anything* until Biddy arrived. Anyway, it's *just* a name. Just a name. Here's my new one: Camilla. *Hi, I'm Camilla*. I can pull it off. In the strip clubs I was Betty, Brandy, Alexandra, Kitty, Roselita, Dolly – living the life of a Bruce Springsteen song. And when you get into trouble, you change your name again by deed poll, get a new passport, bank account and you start again. I do it all the time. That's just what women like me do. Right now, my name is Camilla. New name, new start. And I'll tell you one thing – Giles' dad would never call a woman

I have a horrid little memory from that time, where a group of us were swaying into the early evening, staying upright with the aid of our Bugaboos as we passed by the Little Venice Estate. A group of young mums were enjoying the remnants of summer and having what looked like an impromptu picnic with bags of Monster Munch, Maltesers and a few cans of beer whilst their babies slept in their prams. It looked far more civilised than our afternoon had been despite the backdrop of an inner-city estate and working-class accents.

'Look at them,' uttered one of the mums in my group.

Another one piped up – 'Disgusting.'

We *all* tutted, despite being far more wasted than the women on the estate.

'Alcoholics!'

'Addicts!'

'They should be sterilised!'

'Don't have a baby if you want to act like such a fucking savage!' I sneered like the class traitor I'd always secretly longed to be, because no one grows up proudly working class.

'We're the disgusting ones,' I wanted to say. But instead I just nodded along because I didn't want to blow my cover. I liked that the rich women accepted me, that the acceptable version of motherhood accepted me, and I didn't want to be at the receiving end of their disapproval. And when a rumour circulated around the group that Biddy was the child of a married, successful musician and he was paying our living expenses and for what they assumed were my Isabel

Marant dresses, I didn't quash it, even though the truth was that I was just another working-class single mum nervously awaiting the arrival and implications of the benefits cap. Why would I risk alerting them to the real situation? Privileged mothers have wine o'clock remember – the rest of us have alcoholism.

Then the benefits cap did happen, which turned out to be a blessing and a curse. A curse because it was created to attack working-class single mothers but a small blessing in my case because it meant we had to move away so I could stop pretending to be something I was not. We pack our lives into four wheelie suitcases and hail a taxi to the next place.

Hate & War

Cut to 1992 and it's a Friday and

we'd been studying World War II and

there's that song. The one written by Noel Gay.

About the Luftwaffe.

'Run Rabbit Run.'

Charlotte Bradley stares smirking at me as we watch footage of Hitler as the song accompanies his … antics.

And

this is unfortunate, because around that same time, a Weetabix advert hit the screens featuring Bugs Bunny being chased to – 'Run Rabbit Run'.

So

she would follow me around the playground singing it and she would call me flat face and fat and you're-still-a-freak; sometimes she would pinch me, and she would always trip me up when we played netball. She deliberately poured paint on my submission to the local art competition and, when I brought in my Irish dancing trophy to show off at assembly, she said I was lying and that I hadn't really got second place – that I'd bought the trophy myself, from Tesco (where – she – said – I – got – my – best – clothes). And that I'd never even entered a competition.

And she said it so many times that everyone believed her.

Everyone in the class believed her.

Now they were joining in with her. She had a little gang and they all hated me.

On the Year Six residential trip she threw water into my bed every night so that the teachers assumed I was constantly wetting myself. The worst thing was that everyone in the dorm was in on it. They saw her pouring the water but instead of telling her to stop they said things like: 'It's disgusting that an eleven-year-old still wets the bed, you stink of piss.'

By night three I actually started to believe that I was wetting the bed.

My own reality distorted.

I mean, this girl – Charlotte Bradley, she was horrific.

I hated her. She made my life absolute hell.

So.

... I *planned* the attack on Charlotte Bradley.

By the time we'd returned from the school trip I couldn't take another moment of her unrelenting tirades.

Try as much as you like to exercise self-love, self-preservation, to feel secure in your own true self – but when you are the constant source of negative attention it drains your soul. Their words consume your every moment. You're forever on the edge anticipating their next move. And just when you think they've forgotten about you ...

they strike again.

You will snap eventually. After all, isn't that their point? Isn't their mission to make you lose it? To see you heaped on the floor crying. To see you shouting like you're nuts. To drive you to a place so utterly dismal that they can lift your pain like a trophy for everyone to see. Isn't that the reason they continue to pursue you and harm you as you attempt to live your authentic, weird little life?

I needed to make her stop. My teachers, I'd spoken to them – they couldn't make her stop. My parents, they'd spoken to the teachers – they couldn't make her stop.

I left the school gate, walking just slightly ahead of her. To make it look like she was following me. I wasn't going to be accused of hunting her down. I walked slowly so she could catch up. Because ...

I knew she would bite. Eventually. I knew she wouldn't be able to control herself.

Ignore her. Keep ignoring her. Ignore her. Because eventually all bullies get carried away. They can't help themselves. They push things as far as they can in their quest to inflict pain.

That's when you can get them.

She will say the words that push the button, that hurt more than anything, eventually.

And that's when you get them.

Dirty mouth. Bugs Bunny (still, so obvious). Tongue prison. Deformed jaw. Rotten teeth.

Then. She led her friends in a group rendition of 'Run Rabbit Run'.

I swung around.

Now I can get her.

'Why don't you say all THAT right into my teeth, Charlotte Bradley?'

And she did.

And I threw my school bag into a pub garden.

And – I – lost – it.

I didn't realise that level of violence lived within me. But my mother had taught me well.

Grabbed her knotting, stinking hair hard and pulled her close. She was bigger than me, but she was in shock. Two punches and she was down and that should have made my point, but instead I just carried on. I carried on. It was pissing down with rain; heavy, late-summer rain, and I'm slamming her head deep into a puddle. I'm scratching out her eyes. I'm dragging her face along the kerb. I'm screaming and I'm kicking, tearing chunks of skin out of her plump cheeks with my teeth (that she is so obsessed with) and I'm covered in blood. Charlotte Bradley's bullying blood. Her eyes are closed, and she starts having an asthma attack and, just before her seizure begins, she gently begs me to stop as she falls unconscious.

PLEASE STOP? PLEASE STOP?! FOR TWO YEARS I HAVE BEEN ASKING FOR YOU TO STOP BUT EVERY DAY YOU HAVE MADE MY LIFE HELL. PLEASE STOP? PLEASE STOP? WILL YOU PLEASE STOP? I think I say (but it might have all just remained in my head).

And she is lying on the floor. I am still chewing on her cheek. She is dead? I think she might be dead, but I still don't stop punching. Everything is in slow motion, like really bad sex. Each movement clumsy and pronounced and without satisfaction for either party. But you carry on, until it . . . ends, I guess.

In the retelling of the horrific story years on – 'If her mum hadn't arrived then you would never have stopped.'

I – wouldn't – have – stopped.

She was taken to hospital and the police paid me a visit that weekend, although no charges were brought. Because there were witnesses. For the first time the other kids spoke out. The backing singers from 'Run Rabbit Run'. No 11-year-old wants to lie to the police. They admitted that it had been going on for years and the teachers said they knew too and how long can someone take that much shit before they break?

How long until you start eating a nasty child's cheek in a backstreet in Penge?

. . . I love being a mum. I love my daughter so much.

Despite what I did to Charlotte Bradley, I'm nothing like my mum. I promise you.

I mean, I'm a mess and I can't bake or craft but I'm good at love. That's what my daughter always says anyway.

She says – You're rubbish at doing hair and you burn all the food and you never iron anything so we both look crumpled but you're good at love and you make me feel safe.

And I *know* that I'd never hurt her intentionally or embarrass her in front of her friends. Never. But I do find it hard to connect with other mums. I find it hard to connect with anyone other than Biddy.

It's like I'm expected to dive into a sea of mediocrity and be happy with that. It's like everyone has given up and decided that happiness is never missing an episode of *Britain's Got Talent* or that coffee mornings are something you should naturally want to attend. I can't understand what I'm supposed to have in common with these people except for the fact that some guy did a sperm at exactly the right time and against all odds we created life.

And I don't feel the natural urge to post pictures of gin, or even talk about gin or pose against urban walls. And I find No. 26 'Down Pipe' by Farrow & Ball such a gloomy shade. But everyone else seems really into it. Why aren't I?

I don't want to wear a jumper declaring me 'Mama'. I don't want to join the PTA or make mortgage repayments forever with a man who is emotionally unavailable and exudes toxic masculinity and wears reindeer jumpers and tinsel around his head at the school Christmas Fete. I just can't. But they all seem so content. Why don't I feel this way? Have they forgotten who they were, or were they always like this? Were they just the girls and boys at school who got behind Charlotte Bradley and sang 'Run Rabbit Run' because it was better to be horrible than to be on the outside?

So, I decide I'm going to search online for women like me, for mothers like me on blogs and on Instagram, and in my journey I find lots of mothers sharing about their life. They like Boden dresses and they love teaching their children joyously about capitalism at KidZania and they very much enjoy National Trust properties.

But I want to find women like me, mothers like me, and they are nowhere to be seen, so I decide I'll share my life in the hope of attracting like-minded people. I talk about being working class and our rented flat and being single and struggling under a Tory government, the benefits cap and how I fear we will be pushed out of London. I'm searching for the messed-up mothers like me, the ones with horrible homes, common names and damp and mice and a free-standing gas cooker in our greasy, inadequate kitchens. I'm searching for the alcoholics and problem drinkers like myself who are trying to get a grip on things. The mothers too depressed to put a hashtag next to their mental health issues. Grown-up versions of the kids I was friends with at school – Teresa Connally, Nina and Elaine, before my mum scared them away. And I meet a few outsiders like myself. We become friends.

They are difficult to find though – it's like working-class mothers have been silenced and sidelined, buried beneath Boden and the beautifully curated lives fit for a hashtag ad. Or are we just too scared to share our stories? Because my mind cuts back to the Bullingdon Club of mother and baby groups and I'm quickly reminded that if you don't fit into the stereotype of the middle-class mum then you are a ... bad mum.

'Don't have a baby if you want to behave like a savage,' I once sneered, and now it's being thrown back at me.

Because people didn't like me being my 'authentic self' online.

And some of the mothers from the online playground were rounded up by a grown-up anonymous version of Charlotte Bradley. And once they'd finished tearing apart my mothering skills and lifestyle choices and mocking me for being poor, they moved on to my teeth.

They started attacking my teeth.

And at the age of 37 I was having my physical appearance attacked. Daily.

Because I didn't fit into the stereotype of the typical mum.

Because I'm an outsider.

And they searched for a route of attack.

'Your teeth are so big and disgusting.' The messages came direct to my inbox every day. Not from troubled nine-year-old girls in 1990 but from middle-aged women with their own battles and imperfections and *children* and jobs and husbands.

How do you fight the under-representation of working-class mothers online and the stigmatisation at the school gates when you are oppressed and attacked for merely sharing your own lived experiences? When you merely make a comment that the most commercially successful Insta-mums and bloggers are firmly middle class and conform to the traditional nuclear family structure, you are effectively chased out of town by a mob.

You either learn to live with the source of attack or you do what I did and just delete your account. GO AWAY.

True Instagram story.

... When Charlotte Bradley finally returned to school two weeks after the attack, she was slightly broken. She was pale and withdrawn. Her cheeks hollowed and scabbed. She shook when people spoke to her. A shell of a child. But after a while she reverted back to her old self, because those people always do and she started picking on a girl called Clare Cole who had a lazy eye. She would stand in the playground singing 'Hello, is it me you're looking for?' whenever Clare would shuffle past.

When I returned to school on the Monday after the attack no one could look me in the eye – not the other kids nor their parents nor the teachers – then I was escorted to a special unit for the 'problem kids' on the other side of the school.

I was more of an outsider than ever: when you attack or fight against popular opinion then you are attacking the very system that keeps people in line. And for that you will be made an example of.

Because no one likes outsiders.

8

AGITATION OF THE HEART

MY MEAL FOR ONE is Braised Beef and Mash.

Each morning begins with me making plans for my death, but through no fault of my own I keep making it to dinnertime alive.

My dream ending right now would be falling down the concrete stairs in my flat but failing that I'd take an electric shock as I change a light bulb. Most accidental deaths occur in the home and it's better for my daughter to grow up believing it was 'an accident'.

No one wants to believe their mother left them on purpose.

Tonight, my meal for one is Chicken and Dumplings.

I clean the outside windows by climbing unstable ladders and, as I have no partner to catch me, I assume I'll fall. But I haven't yet.

I'm careless with every appliance and tempt the bath water with my radio.

But I always end up eating dinner.

My meal for one is Linda McCartney's Vegetarian Lasagne.

It is not my last supper.

One day I make a new friend.

Her name is Sarah. We both have children who sit on our knees during Rhyme Time at the library. We walk around Regents Park for a while; she seems nice and almost as sad as I do. I think that's what attracted us to each other. Two depressed mothers just passing time.

On the way home, I spot a Megabus speeding past Swiss Cottage and I hold eyes with the driver hoping he'll lose control and crash into us and our buggies. We don't speak as the coach approaches, she's got her eyes taped to the driver too, maybe she feels the same? Willing our bodies to be crushed underneath the fumes of other lifeless bloodied bodies thrown through the windows – bodies who failed to leave London for the weekend on a budget. At least we wouldn't die alone.

But everyone arrives safely at their destination and Sarah goes home to cook her husband something organic for dinner.

My meal for one tonight is Tesco's Chicken Tikka Masala with Garlic Naan.

The father of Sarah's baby is some big-time rock star. She used to be his lawyer now she is his wife. She doesn't need to work anymore, and I just *can't* work right now, I've been signed off because my mind isn't right, so we spend most days together. She is lonely too, despite having everything you could ever need. Single or coupled motherhood is confusing and hard, but I can't help but be consumed by jealousy that she has someone to share everything with.

After we part ways one evening and she walks through the electronic gates into her town house, I silently urge the man walking too close behind me in the early autumn dark to push me into an alleyway and rape me before dismembering my body, leaving me to be identified by nothing but my shameful Camus-inspired tattoo that steals my upper left arm.

But I make it home for dinner.

My meal for one tonight is Tesco Finest Chilli Con Carne. *Treat myself.*

I watch every single episode of *EastEnders*. Never miss *Question Time*. The sign of a particularly bad day, is an entire episode of *The One Show* – I view it on mute. I watch *The Sopranos* on boxset while pumping my milk supply into bottles, even though I've already watched it at least eight times. I'm obsessed with the episode where Steven Van Zandt's character leads Adriana into the woods to shoot her. I fantasise about having a gangster boyfriend who I can deceive by wearing a wire so a fictional New Jersey strip-club owner can make me disappear. That would be *great*.

I check that my baby is breathing. I obsessively watch her to make sure she is breathing; I'm determined to die but I'm desperate for her to stay alive. I watch *London Tonight* and ask the sky why wasn't I the one attacked with a hammer in the park today? I see a headline about a local woman getting knocked off her bicycle and no one stopping to help. She gets knocked over by a van and then a lorry goes over her head and then a car splits her in half. People stop to take pictures but they forget to call an ambulance. It's too late anyway. They can see she is already dead, and if she's so far beyond help then why not get some decent footage for social media? I buy a secondhand bike the next day. I want people to film my lifeless body on their Samsungs in the hope of a viral tweet.

I try baby-led weaning. I do soft play. I end up in ... places. I'm out and about. I ride the Circle Line in its entirety three times in a row before remembering to get off. Not even someone as useless as me can ride in circles forever. I hop the Victoria Line to Brixton and then all the way to Walthamstow, but when I get off I do not know *where* to go to die in East London. One day I allow myself to be sent along the Northern Line to Morden and I sob along with Biddy for the 15 whole minutes the train is terminated. We wipe away the tears when we're back on the move – only when you are motionless can you see how damaged and difficult everything is. I'm always at least 30 minutes early to health visitor appointments, even though I know they are always running an hour late. I wait and flick through magazines that I have no interest in. *Grazia* from two years ago. *Hello. Vogue.* I do not care for anything contained in their vacuous insides, their words as empty as my heart, but I sit pretending to read, staring through the photographs. I smile at randoms in the street and say sorry to people who bump into *me* just so I can have some kind of human interaction.

My meal for one tonight is Quorn Cottage Pie, it only takes five minutes from frozen.

Sarah tells me she is on 100mg of Lustral. Snap! I say. PND? She asks. No, this is just my life. This is who I am. I've never been happy. I'm – never – happy. We stop meeting up. I do not know whose choice it was.

My doctor confirms that I'm lonely and depressed. I'd already told him that. He asks *why* I'm depressed but I was hoping *he'd* tell *me*, although I already have the answers: I don't have any family, I tell him. It's just me and my daughter. She is all I have. We are each other's only blood. He asks if I am getting out, getting fresh air, walking, eating vegetables, talking to people. Yes, I am. I'm getting out and about. He says I look well. I'm wearing make-up, that's a good sign apparently. My hair is 'done'. Depressed people don't usually *try*, he says. He tells me I look pretty. He is inappropriate but I can see he is trying to make me feel good in the only way that men like him can, but neither his compliments nor prescriptions work. I don't tell him that I only put myself together when I'm in the company of doctors or health visitors because single mothers living below the poverty line aren't allowed to get *too* depressed – it's important that I keep my pain at an acceptable level; hold it together and they'll fob you off with pills, tell them the absolute truth and they'll take your child away.

'Each day I make plans for my death, but ... I hope it'll be in public so that someone can keep my daughter safe' is a sentence I edit from all conversations with health professionals.

Today I went to King's Cross because they've regenerated the whole area and the prostitutes have gone so I thought I'd take the baby out for a walk. The new King's Cross was clinical and corporate, and it made me even sadder, so I drifted into the station and sat upstairs watching people coming off the trains from the north, from places like Retford and Hull, and they're all excited to be here and I ate a tofu curry from Wasabi. The doctor seemed pleased with that.

'The medication seems to be working,' he said.

It isn't. He doesn't realise that I'm hanging out in Central London terminals because they are locations ripe for a terrorist attack.

I stop attending train stations when the threat returns to moderate.

The Lustral isn't working. The Prozac didn't work. The citalopram didn't work. CBT doesn't work for treating serious trauma. If anything, they all make me worse. When I go to heat up my latest meal for one – a spaghetti carbonara – I get excited thinking about what would kill me first: the high sodium and radiation from my microwavable diet or drinking two bottles of wine a night until my liver gives in? Whilst this thought is still happening, I insert my head into the microwave like a Channel 5 version of Sylvia Plath and attempt to cook my face dead.

The plate won't turn with my big head on it. Still alive.

I search the mirror for rare tumours that may have emerged for a quick kill, but my cheeks just look a bit flushed.

It's time to kill myself in the way that makes me feel good, I decide.

It's time to numb myself until I drift into the death that was *destined* for me.

It's time to start drinking again.

… I'm drinking again. And I couldn't be *vaguely* happier.

Back before my only blood relative was my daughter, back when I had a family with parents and grandparents and cousins, we had a ritual that we indulged in every Christmas. All families have them, I suppose. Rituals that mask dark secrets and pain, that make terrible events easier to deal with. One of my friends takes a trip back home with her mother to Seville every birthday and releases balloons from the top of the Giralda, covered with variations of the word 'strength' written in glitter pen because her dad first raped her on her tenth birthday. She releases seven balloons, one for each birthday he ruined. It's a ritual that reclaims her control. Her mother does the same, releasing a balloon for every year she wished her daughter had been able to tell her the truth. And that's how they deal with their pain. Other friends have more conventional traditions: a Boxing Day hike, Easter Egg hunts at National Trust properties sponsored by Cadburys. Those types of family rituals. Rituals that look normal to the outside world but might mask something horrible even if they'll never acknowledge it.

Ours was this: every Christmas Day, after Mass my nana would stay behind at the flat cooking dinner while the rest of the family would form a search party and look for my grandad.

When I say search party, it's not like he was *officially* missing or anything. We're not searching through fields by torchlight like an opening scenes of a McGovern drama. We knew he'd be knocking about somewhere; he'd been spotted back in October shouting at the pigeons on Camberwell Green; we'd heard a rumour he was living in a doss house by the Elephant and Castle; by April he'd been barred from all the pubs on the Old Kent Road. And with these bits of information we created a guide for our Christmas Day hunt. Somewhere a family is playing a cosy game of Cluedo followed by Trivial Pursuit and gammon sandwiches, but my family are searching the streets and alleyways of South East London for my drunk grandad.

My grandad was estranged the way I am now, but for different reasons. He was a chronic alcoholic who had savagely beaten my Nana and my dad. The story goes that he'd been a great man, funny and clever, but when he was 33 he was involved in an accident on the construction site where he worked. A crane had fallen on him and crushed him, he was resuscitated eight times, but finally emerged from the hospital a year later with his legs missing and his job gone. And he hadn't been a day sober since.

The whole family would come together at Christmas to track him down, check up on him, buy him a drink. We'd always find him. We'd find out the name of the last pub he was barred from and we would take it from there. We'd split into groups and cover a small patch of South East London, where he'd been since he'd emigrated to London when he was 21.

We'd start at the Elephant and Castle and make our way down the Walworth Road and into Camberwell before returning for a feast and to update Nana on what he'd been up to. She never wanted to see him, she was terrified of him. I once saw her throw up into a Safeway bag after he barged into her flat one summer, shaking his walking stick at her, but being a strict Catholic she refused to divorce him because *obviously* the fake hell underneath the ground is far worse than the real hell she endured during their time living together. Some of us would take the pubs on the high street and the rest would search the bars and parks hidden between the estates and terraces.

That's when all the stories would come out; the time he threw a glass bottle of ketchup at my dad, his numerous arrests from their flat on the Aylesbury Estate, the time he couldn't be bothered to leave the bar to go to the toilet and just stood their shitting against his wooden legs. My dad always spoke about his dad in the past tense, and he never called him dad, and in turn I never called him grandad. He was only ever referred to as 'the old man'. My dad said he'd already mourned 'the old man' back when he was a child. 'He would have been better off if he'd died at 33,' everyone said.

But despite these horror stories, everyone said I was just like him. They'd all been telling me this since I was about five. 'You're just like the old man.' Whenever I would do something perceived as cheeky or punishable. 'You're just like the old man.' I couldn't understand it, I followed the rules, was high achieving at school and was always trying my best to 'be good' but …

Apparently, I was *just* like the mad, drunk old man from the Christmas Day search party.

By the time I was 12 I'd accepted that I was probably an alcoholic despite never having touched a drop of booze; by the time it touched my lips at 14, numbing my mind for a while, I knew I was in trouble. That beautiful foul-tasting, soul-changing alcohol could drown all the misery in my heart. My glazed eyes acting as gate keepers to my mind. That first sip, taking me away. I really *was* just like the old man.

Eventually we'd find him. We always found him. Covered in his own vomit and shit, shouting in a park at the demons only he could see, slumped in a bar kissing a beautifully ravaged woman. It was the only time of the year we'd ever see him. One Christmas we came into contact with his tuberculosis – the only thing he'd ever threatened to give me. The family trips to the hospital to cure our lungs made me feel close to him for the first time.

I'd *never* done anything as bad as what he'd done, never been violent or abused anyone but it's been 20 years since I've spent Christmas Day with any blood relatives other than my baby.

And as I take another drink alone, I wonder – *Do they think of me at this time of year?* My parents. And I realise that they probably *don't*, so I have no other solution to sadness than to drink until the thoughts no longer exist.

It's normal to have a family, isn't it? Not the one you created yourself but the family who created *you*. It's quite normal. I know that it's normal because Christmas is the time of year when my friends leave London; the ones with northern accents go to places far away and the rest scatter around the Home Counties. It's always been this way.

They leave after the 20 and they return before New Year. They go.

You never forget your first Christmas alone, do you?

I remember mine: my new friends and I had an amazing night out at the Uni Winter Ball, so amazing that we didn't bother going to bed. We got back to halls and drank tea and ate toast. We chatted all night. We'd all got through the first term and we were all going to be friends – for – life! We made plans to go to a party on New Year's Eve – it was going to be even better than the Winter Ball.

The next morning everyone dispersed; to Nottingham, to Edinburgh, to a little village in Kent. Wherever their families were, they went.

I pretend to laugh about it now, but … I packed a *rucksack* to make it look like I was going home too. I walked with a few of them down to Euston Station. Said I'd see them on their way then hop on the 68 bus down to my family in South London where I would be spending Christmas. Instead, after we'd said goodbye, I walked the ten-minute journey back to halls in Camden.

There was no family to go home to.

Leading up to Christmas I kept myself busy. It was just me in halls and every now and again a security guard would patrol the grounds. I'd sleep off my hangover during the day and work as a lap dancer by night. The lonely men in the club somewhat alleviated my own abandonment and, whilst they paid me to get naked, it was me enjoying their company.

Christmas Day I was alone. I hadn't prepared anything other than ensuring I had enough alcohol to help me 'celebrate'. I don't remember much about it, yet vague memories remain – my phone flashed at 11am as my dad called (out of a sense of duty) as he celebrated with his new family.

I – let – it – go – to – voicemail.

I think I watched *The Royle Family* and I watched *Top of the Pops*. Saville presented.

I didn't eat, finally able to enjoy my anorexia in peace.

I read Milton's *Paradise Lost* and wrote an essay six weeks before it was due. And I slept until the 27th when *normality* resumed. When the strip club reopened.

As arranged, my friends and I all met up for the New Year's Eve party, which was as disappointing as you would expect.

The next time my dad called it was in late February to wish me happy birthday for early January.

I let it go to voicemail.

And that's the Christmas melancholy that hits me briefly every year.

I wish someone would search for me.

I drink wine most nights.

But I've got rules.

The bottle doesn't open until the baby is down for the night.

And there is *never* a drink poured in the morning.

But I'm still an alcoholic. I think. That first anaesthetising sip is everything to me.

Most mornings I retrace the night before, follow the trails of embarrassing texts, leftover food on a plate and the call to Kirsty, which lasted 36 seconds and which I do not recall.

These blackouts fill me with so much shame, but without them I'd be plotting my death. Alcoholism is saving my life.

And I'm *not* the only parent who drinks.

Sometimes I meet with the other mums from the toddler group.

'It's wine o'clock,' they say. Most will have the one to 'relax', but I always stop at the supermarket to pick up another bottle on the way home.

The doctor tells me that I'm still lonely and depressed. I *know*.

'Why do you drink?' he asks.

I was hoping that you'd tell me. Is it to anesthetise myself into a slow death? To give myself the courage for suicide? I don't know.

'What kind of suicidal thoughts are you having?'

All the classics, I tell him.

Throwing myself onto the tracks at Penge East as the Eurostar speeds though at 07.29. Jumping from the multi-storey car park in Lewisham. An ex-boyfriend once *showed* me how to inflict an agitation of the heart and I can easily lose an evening searching for the perfect weapon. *All* the classics. Sleeping pills. Slit wrists. Drowning myself in the pointless fountains erected opposite the old Heygate Estate to make the area palatable for the rich people they've moved in. Au-to-erotic asphyxiation is appealing but the Lustral (that you *insist* I take) has depleted my sex drive. All the classics. Marry-ing a member of ISIS so at least I won't be a lonely single mum committing suicide. *All* the classics really.

Sticking my head in the oven.

The doctor looks at me.

Oh.

'You have an Aga?'

No. It's a microwave oven.

'Oh. That won't work,' the doctor confirms.

He attempts to fob me off with some more pills and a promise of CBT and I'm about to accept it like usual, but this time I break down crying.

I can't do it anymore.

Look at my face, I'm not wearing any make-up today. Look at me. My hair hasn't been washed or brushed for weeks. Listen (I mock whisper), I'm not even wearing a bra right now and I have the kind of body shape that always requires a bra. Listen, I haven't cleaned my teeth in four whole days.

I make sure that Biddy is OK and then I just *try* to find ways not to feel.

But I'm in so much pain right now.

I call the Samaritans every evening and even they're bored of me. I can hear them trying to get off the phone. My depression is so dull that even these kind-hearted volunteers make excuses not to talk to me.

I want to stop drinking every day but if I don't drink then all I do is plot to die.

I once jumped on the Metropolitan Line all the way out to Amersham to scout it out as a potential death location – how desperate does a mother have to get in order to be helped? I need to be well for my daughter. I didn't want to tell you all this because it's just me and her and I cannot have her taken away, but I'm running out of ways to survive.

He refers me to the crisis team.

Thank you so much, thank you – I just need some help, I cannot do this on my own anymore.

I don't buy a bottle of wine that night and instead I wheel the buggy to a local AA meeting.

I'm not drinking right now.

NOTE: I'm always a certain amount of days sober, until I'm not sober anymore.

Sometimes I make it through years, sometimes a month or two, but these days the time in between drinks gets smaller. It is said that alcoholism is a progressive illness and I can vouch for that I suppose. Or maybe it just gets worse around certain times of the year. Christmas Day. Mother's Day. Father's Day. Their birthdays. My birthday. Those days you normally spend with your family. Around those times my GP prescribes me a nice high dose of Diazepam and I throw at least four litres of Diet Pepsi down my throat every day – I find it keeps me off the wine.

Loneliness will always hold me I think, it's never far away.

Because I'm rootless. When there is nowhere to go at Christmas, when everyone else disappears for two weeks, you can never feel fully grounded. Whilst there is estrangement and poverty in my life, I will always be asking the bottle for a temporary solution. But I have to hold it together for Biddy. Because I know where I'd be without her:

Under the Eurostar a mile up the tracks from Penge East toward Bromley. Splattered across a spit-covered Lewisham pavement. Up to no good with a belt tied around my neck, an orange in my mouth and my knickers around my ankles in a cheap hotel in Amersham. Alone. Or in 20 years' time awaiting Biddy to form a search party to find me, if I'm lucky.

That's why I go to these AA meetings. Got myself a sponsor who makes me write lists. In AA we make a lot of lists. Lists of things we are grateful for, lists of our defects, lists of people who've fucked us over, lists of people you've actually fucked, kissed, misled, lists of people who have fucked with you, lists of harm and lists of shame. I'm not sure if it's for me or if it's forever but I'll do whatever I need to when I'm desperate.

Because this pain will lift, and it will return, and it will lift again. It's up, down, it changes. This is not always.

I wouldn't have made it this far without her, but I think I will always have an agitation of the heart; there is part of me that will never be fully fused together.

I hope that by breaking the cycle of abuse between parent and child it will slowly heal. Lots of working-class people celebrate the first person in their family who goes to university but I'm celebrating being the first person in my family who hasn't been violent to their child. I am wrong in so many ways but that's the one thing I'm definitely doing right.

So, I need to do whatever I can to make sure that my daughter never feels alone, and I think that means trying to find ways to stay well and living in the world, so I can protect her for as long as I can.

... I keep making it to dinnertime and it's not so bad.

My meal for one is vegetarian paella.

9

HOW TO FIGHT LONELINESS

ROMAN-À-CLEF

THEN ONE DAY HE turned up in a suit. This guy I'd been seeing. An actual suit. It was our seventh date. He wasn't the kind of man to normally wear a suit. I liked that about him. I've always made a point of not getting involved in *any* kind of romantic situation with a man in a suit. It *disgusts* me. Usually it means they have to leave the house by 6am each day. Not – for – me. Don't even want to see a suit on a man on my own wedding day. But he'd shown up in a suit. A fucking suit. It threw me. Me? I looked a mess. The usual. Was too busy with the depression to wash my hair that day so backcombed it up. I can pull it off. We were meeting for an early dinner. The restaurant? It was cosy. The kind of place you take someone you like. But I arrived late and flustered and normally this mess of a look of mine would have complemented his scruffy bohemian attire but he was standing there awkwardly in his suit. Like it was his First Holy Communion or something. His only saving grace was that he wasn't holding flowers. I would have turned and left right there and then if there had been any sign of flowers. But still, I couldn't really look at him to be honest. The *suit*. Didn't want to make a fuss about his image change so I casually asked if he'd been somewhere nice today. Or somewhere terrible? He said he'd come straight from work – the little independent gift shop he owned in Forest Hill. It was a nice shop. The kind of useless place you get with regentrification. Stocked things like paperweights and framed slogan posters and artisan draft excluders. Homemade earrings. Vinyl records. The shop seemingly theme-less. Candles. Witty postcards. Funny tote bags. Nice things. For people into those nice kinds of pointless things. I didn't mention the suit. Or the fact he'd combed and styled his hair. He'd pasted his fringe down with *gel*. He ordered drinks. Made a big deal of remembering my usual. Malbec! Argentine! He was really proud of *that*. Said he'd booked us a quiet table in the corner. As we waited to be seated he asked the waitress to light a candle. It was like his great-aunt had given him a lesson in how to woo a woman. He even pulled out my fucking chair. I'm usually good with the chat. Can crack a few jokes. Settle the atmosphere before the sip of the second drink finally eases all interactional discomfort. But I seized up. Wasn't expecting him to have gone to all this effort. I stared at his shirt. Fresh out of the packet that day. Crisp. Like a teenage boy on his first day of work experience. The suit jacket – an attempt at dapper. Cross between early noughties Essex wideboy his hand as he reeled off his list. I've finally bought bedroom furniture, he told me. A wardrobe. Chest of drawers. Bedside tables. A bed. A sofa. He'd never bought a sofa or a bed before. The futon he'd been sleeping on until recently had been stolen from the set of the television drama he had a minor role in some ten years ago. But I'm growing up now – he said. I never want to own a futon again. What kind of person even owns futons these days? I asked. He stopped talking for a short while to swallow his cheese. I looked around the restaurant during the silence. Smart heels. Blow dries. Office types. I puffed up my greasy hair. Tried to hide my chipped nails. Drank my Malbec through black teeth. He disclosed the cost of his new furniture. The dining table. The breakfast bar stools. The living room rug. Five figures. Not even from a catalogue. Business going well. He started talking about marriage. He planned to get married one day. Did I have those plans too? He asked me what it was like being pregnant. Did I want more children? He asked some questions about my daughter. Not in an intrusive way. In a really caring way. Not in an Ian Watkins way. It was in a non-paedo way. Said he was making plans to move out of his house share. Saving for a mortgage. Expanding his business. He was thinking of opening a second shop in Bromley. There are currently no shops in Bromley selling funny tote bags. Sarcastic fridge magnets. Ironic religious door beads. Theme-less things. He'd seen a gap in the market. He was eating vegetables. Taking driving lessons. Jogging. Weekend drilling. Buying flowers from the market get a husband, will you? Of course I won't. Is my dad a nice man? Of course he is. Do you like sitting on the swing with me for hours and hours and hours until the park closes? Of course I do. Would you ever lie to me, Mummy? Of – course – I – would – I – love – you.

STAIN ON SOCIETY

On Twitter: The reason I joined the Labour Party? It was *all* because of the Tory councillor. He must have been bloated from all the M&S Meal Deals he consumed that day and a little bit angry that the woman he was having an affair with was even more troublesome than his wife. It triggered him into writing bigoted sentences on Twitter. Typical spiel about single mothers and champagne lifestyles. It triggered *me* – I'm a single mum and I don't live a champagne lifestyle, I replied. He said SHUT IT. Get a job. I – do – have – a – job. Stop complaining then – he *at-ed* at me. We live in a society of scroungers. You're either one of them or you're against them, he said. I typed back to him – You're paid to represent me not judge me. *And* you're trying to shut down our local library. My daughter loves that library. He got personal – YOU ARE A STAIN ON SOCIETY he tweeted with two people's worth of gratin potato side dish in his gob – I *imagine*. And I was enraged. First David Cameron on the refuge telly and now *this* greedy prick on my Twitter. I didn't really understand where

I fell on the political spectrum but I knew enough about myself to know I'm not cold and nasty like men like him. So I Googled – Labour Party. I don't know why. But. I did. And joined right there and then. It was 2013.

FAUX FEMINISM

Clover exhales: Listen, Cash. *This* is the truth. The woke men? They are the *worst* of all the men. With their slogan T-shirts and hashtag-friendly dialogue. These pseudo-woke men who declare themselves feminists whilst simultaneously trawling Instagram leaving supportive comments underneath wank-inducing photographs of world-class sex workers in the hope she'll view him as an ally and suck him off for free. Using faux feminism as *currency* to get laid. Given a pass to objectify women because he once went on an anti-austerity march and uses words like boundaries and respect and consent to hypnotise a woman he is mentally undressing before adding her to his ever-growing rotation. Duping sex workers into free fucking, afterwards doing all the 'right things' like making eye contact and holding her close for half an hour before instigating a discussion about Palestine (because he appreciates sex workers can be intellectual too), and dramatically tutting about all those terrible misogynistic men she *normally* has to sleep with to fund her PhD. Because *he's* not like those other men. He's not disgusting like them. He respects her. Even though he can't help but internally high five himself with every spare thought because she usually charges £250 an hour and he got full service for free. The man is a fucking magician. His trick? Woke privilege.

GUTTER BRAVADO

They were ringing my bell: Two of the gypsy women had gotten into my block. One of them said I'd ordered a stripper. *I hadn't ordered a stripper.* Not tonight. But the other one insisted – YOU MADE A BOOKING. Listen, I've just put my daughter to bed, I said. You've got the wrong address. Why you wasting our time? the tall one asked. You don't order a stripper and turn her away. I deserve to be let in. Deserve to do the dance. They pushed into my flat laughing. Be quiet – my daughter is asleep. And I don't have any money. They said it didn't matter. Do you want to see my body? the tall one asked. I'm not really in the mood for a stripper tonight. Is it because you think I'm ugly? the tall one asked. No. You're beautiful. You just have the wrong flat. She said she hadn't. And she was going to lap dance for me. The other one said she needed to use my bathroom. She was in there for ages. About 20 minutes. Rummaging through my stuff. The tall one searched my living room then removed her clothes in one go. She needed to work on her tease technique but I kep my critique to myself. She danced in the silence. After a few minutes I asked: Are you nearly finished? I've got stuff I need to do. Don't you like my body? she asked. Oh, I do. It's very lovely. I didn't want to offend her. Or make her angry. I find gypsy women can be so scary. You can be terrified but you can't call the police on them. That only makes matters worse. She pecked me all over my face and hair and her breath was rotten. Cheap tinned tuna. The other girl finally came out of the toilet. Nothing *much* in here, she told the naked one. She was holding a candelabra from Matalan and a recently opened bar of Dove soap. Can I have these? she asked. Sure. The naked one climbed off me and picked up a jar of coppers. £2 at most. Is this my tip? Yeah sure. Can we have the mop too? Sure. I want your Sports Direct mug, she said aggressively tipping the undiluted squash onto my rug. You can have the Sports Direct mug. We'll be seeing you around, they said as they left.

THE TENDER INDIFFERENCE OF THE WORLD

Clover is still exhaling: Listen to me, Cash. She got conned. We all got conned. Wasn't the first, she won't be the last, and although she feels used she'll remain on good terms with him; retweeting his generic words on class war because he seems so gentle and he once went to a protest at Yarl's Wood so he *must* be on the right side of man. But really he's just another one devoid of humanity. Listen, Cash. There's no love out there. So you need to castrate their balls. Cut off their dicks. That's what I do. Listen to me, Cash. It's getting worse out there. Sex gets cold under a right-wing government. Listen, imagine how the Tories fuck. Zero foreplay. Dive straight in with unlubricated masochism. That's life now. Look around you. Everyone out for what they can get. Coldly rubbing up against each other before moving on to the next. Hoarding. Selling. Disposing of sentiment. Sending out dick pics en masse in the hope that someone somewhere will reply. Someone always does. Another pair of anonymous tits to wank over. Listen, Cash, you need to play the game. Get what you can. Don't give to others. It's survival of the fittest under this regime. It's just the tender indifference of the world.

PLUMMETING STOCK

In a chatroom: This typical pervert suggests meeting in the reception area of the hotel. It's a three-star. In the Watford Gap. I can't drive. He says he'll send me a taxi. His profile doesn't even have a photograph. And his username is Auto_erotic666. That's the kind of shit we're dealing with here. I say, Send me a taxi because I haven't been fucked for six years. He asks why. Are you really that disgusting to look at? he asks. Yes I am. And I make some shit up about how I've been in a mental asylum for my entire thirties. Locked away. Lonely. Losing my best years. He likes that. So much so that he responds with an aubergine emoticon. Classic. He's telling me what he's going to do to me when I get there. Heard it all before. These men have no imagination. So predictable, same old lines but ... for me it's just *knowing* that someone real is behind that horrific username and that alone will keep me wet for a little while. He asks for my address. WHAT DO YOU WANT MY ADDRESS FOR, WEIRDO? For the taxi, he types. And if you stay with me the entire night there's a great little breakfast buffet we can have in the morning. I think about his offer – I do love a buffet. But. No. Can't afford a babysitter. And I'm not *really* going to fuck a stranger called Auto_erotic666 in a service stop hotel. I rub myself off and delete my profile.

THE CANDIDATE

Meeting people: Went to all the local meetings. The Labour Party meetings. It was a sad affair. The group consisting of three middle-aged couples. And me. And Biddy, she sat in the corner. The middle-aged couples gave off the vibe of a village swingers party. But not in a liberated way. In a really sad way where at least one of the group couldn't bear to watch the person they love fuck their friend. But they do it anyway. Because it's better than being alone. The meetings were on the first Tuesday of every month. And on the first Tuesday of every month Biddy and I would go along. Had no choice but to take her, so she'd sit in the corner and draw. Nothing much got done in the meetings but it was something to do. It was nice to sit in a room with people who shared the same beliefs. We set up a stall every Saturday at the local market. Handed out flyers. Spoke about a fair society. But apart from us, people weren't really into it. No one cared. But believing in something filled a hole. Then one day they asked me to stand as a local councillor because no one else wanted to do it. So I did. But we lost. It was 2015.

WOMAN WITHOUT TIES

Getting help: First time I met Clover was on my twenty-third birthday. At an AA meeting in Bloomsbury. She's managed to sneak bottle of red wine into her bag and was drinking it from a foam coffee cup. I was shooting her looks of disapproval. Taking my sobriety seriously. Two years sober. We were the only women in the room. There were about 25 men. Whenever one of the men shared Clover would interrupt with 'all of you should just stop obsessing about your cocks!' then she would laugh manically. The men would blush. One of them asked her to leave. She said no. Told him to put his dick away. Or she'd castrate him. Stop being intimidated by strong women, she shouted. She made me snigger. I'd never seen anyone like her. Like a drunk and angry Mia Farrow. Beautiful and insane. The church hall was full of actors. Mainly faces from theatre but a spattering had made it onto the telly. Some were recognisable from their secondary roles but there were no leading men in the room. One of them going on about how his washing machine had broken that morning. He said he had wanted to drink after the stress of it all. Because of the washing machine. It had been such a terrible day. But thanks to the power of the fellowship he had remained sober. Clover looked at me and smirked. I rolled my eyes. Kindred spirits. We both knew it. She quietly refilled her mug with wine and passed it over to me. We were pissed by the time we got to the Serenity Prayer. Afterwards we went to the indie club at LSE where she was doing her PhD. Took some pills to celebrate my new age. Hung out at her place in Stoke Newington for a few days. I told her the truth about my family. I never usually do that with people I've just met. Usually say they're dead to shut down the conversation. Or end the friendship before it begins. But I told her everything. She didn't have any family either. So we sort of became family. Biddy calls her Aunty. But I wouldn't trust her to be her guardian if I died. She's got her own issues. Her own life. My daughter wouldn't have anywhere safe to go if I died. She'd be alone. Like me.

COURTING CAPITALISM

Swiped right: We're in a bar in King's Cross and he's telling me he hates cats. He's telling me that he works at Google or something and that he has an electric bike and that he finds cats repulsive. Sees one in the street? Kicks it. Threw a rock at one today. Hit it right in the eye. Last weekend in the garden with his nephew he told the kid to kick a cat in the face. Kick the neighbour's cat in the face. The kid did it. Kids always do what adults say. Gave his nephew a high five and a strawberry

Starburst. Do it harder next time and I'll give you a whole box of Heroes. He's telling me that he *loved* cats until his ex ruined his life. Bitch ruined his life *and* his love for cats. Since she left all he can think about is setting their tails on fire. Cutting off their ears. Hey, wouldn't it be funny to see a cat without ears? Laughs so much he spits out his beer. She's a total psycho. The ex. Slut. Flirting with his friends. Checking up on him. Wanting more from him. I tell him I have to leave. Don't even give him an excuse. I'm standing up to leave and he doesn't want me to go and he changes the subject to his electric bike. And his side hustle as an influencer. (Google me, he says.) I'm leaving. I'm walking out but he's following me. These types of guys always follow you. The dickhead is walking behind me. Talking about his ex. She stalks me on social media. She turned up at my work. She asked a police officer to come around to my flat to pick up her stuff because apparently she was 'scared'. I tell him I'm leaving. I know men like you. He grabs my arm. I'll walk you to the bus stop. No thank you. I start to run away. Shouts after me: You're a fucking stuck-up bitch. I wouldn't want to date a single mum anyway. Little slag. He reminded me so much of my mum. But I walked away. Maybe I've broken the cycle?

LOVE FATIGUE

I'm thinking: We've been together since we ran from Grantham. Just me and her. Always talking. Always in love. Quietly living.

Always smiling. Never shouting. Never falling out. Never disappointed. Never had to tell her off. My mum had beaten me at least seven times by the time I'd turned five. But I could never do such a thing. What kind of mother could do such a thing? I'm not like my mum. I'm nothing like her. I'm not like her. I'm not cold. I feel love. Me and my baby hold hands all the time. We spend every minute together. We like the same things. We're poor but it's perfect. Talking all the time. I could never hit someone I love. This cycle of abuse is now broken. It has to be. I was born to be her mum.

That's why I feel so guilty for the all-consuming loneliness that suffocates my every second. But. It's been six years. The last time I had sex was the night I feel pregnant. In *Grantham*. Sex in Grantham sounds like some kind of punishment. Such a long time ago.

EVERYTHING IS FOR SALE

I'm talking: Could sell it on eBay. My six-year virginity. How should I market it? It's an unusual product. An unclassified situation. Wouldn't want to mis-sell. Not worth ruining my 100 per cent feedback for. And it's a nightmare when someone opens a case on PayPal, isn't it? And anyway, would the item description be – BORN AGAIN VIRGIN VAGINA (SIX YEARS OLD) – NEW (OTHER) or would I promote it as a piece of fetishism? Symphorophilia. SCRAP VAGINA – PARTS ONLY . Because I haven't used it for six years. I don't know whether it's healed. Just like new. Or whether it's an accident waiting to happen. How much would I get for it? The freakshow vag would sell for more. But the doctor said the operation had been a success. That the thick scarring that travels all the way from my vagina to my arse actually makes the vagina tighter. Scarring makes the hole smaller. The physio said everything was OK. And I haven't pissed or shat myself in public since Biddy was a year old. Every other mother I know had sex with their partner within the first six months. Six years. What if the wounds are re-established with penetration. What if I'm losing my six-year virginity and then it just prolapses everywhere? Bits of old cunt dropping out all over the place. And – what if it hurts? What if it hurts more than the feeling of being alone?

CYCLE OF ABUSE

A 2am text:

> Cutting you out of my life once and for all. You failed at being a dad to me but you had a chance to be a grandad. Why don't you ever make an effort to see us? We are blood. But like every man I've ever met you are disappointing. I wish you no harm Dad but I hope one day you can reflect on the pain you have caused. Have you ever wondered why I'm a constant source of attack? It's

because you've never had my back. People sense that I'm an easy target. Why have you never stuck up for me? Don't bother replying to that. I wish you all the best Dad but please never make one of your half-arsed attempts to contact me again.

Then I block him. It's the same message I send him every three months. Copy and paste. And in a few weeks I'll unblock him again and the cycle will continue ...

HOW TO TALK TO CAPITALISTS

A phone call: Why don't you just go and get your dick clamped in a dungeon like all the other men in their suits do? Yeah? You make me sick. What you hoping to find inside all of those holes you use? I don't understand you. You pulled out my fucking chair. You wore a *suit*. You think I'm damaged, don't you? And therefore unable to feel connections. Is this why you date single mums? You think we're easy to dispose of? That we don't want to be loved? That we're grateful to be just one of your many women? *Thank you, thank you for the opportunity.* That we'll take anything? That because I already have a child that I'm not deserving of a traditional relationship? Deprived of that one special person? That we just want our fannies serviced around the back of Wetherspoons once a month? That we can't love? Is that what you think? Is that what you really think of women like me? I can't believe I fell for it. I thought you were different. You *wore* a slogan T-shirt. Made placards for Yarl's Wood. And now you've stopped eating cheese and you're a vegan. You say and do all the right things, but you're just greedy. Buying sex, stealing sex – non-monogamy is a capitalist construct. Grabbing as much as you can. In your ill-fitting suit. Getting what you deserve. Claiming to be anti-capitalist whilst indulging in greed and opportunism. Sarcastic fridge magnets. Handmade shoe horns. Your shop doesn't even have a *theme*. Good luck with your second shop in Bromley. And ALL your other shops. Don't – *ever* – call – me – again.

SKINT ESTATE

A crowd has gathered: One of the gypsy women asks me what's wrong. I'm crying in broad daylight. I tell her it's because he'd put gel in his hair. He'd looked stupid. I tell her that it's because he'd called me to talk about it. He'd said he was addicted to sex, he was into all these disgusting things that people usually just keep inside their heads and he is addicted to having all that sex, he just wants to be with everyone and experience everything and *have* everything but then he also said that I was the only woman he'd want to take home to his parents. Don't we all have issues to deal with? he'd asked. This is mine, he'd said. That was my opportunity to tell him about my issues with intimacy. Six years. Six years – I should have said. But I just called him a capitalist. It was the worst thing I could say to him. He'd requested a rep from Hillarys blinds go around to the flat he'd just bought to measure up his window for real wooden venetians. He'd picked the blinds with me in mind. He thought they'd be to my taste. He'd passed his theory test. He's thinking of getting a Land Rover. I'm crying again. A passing old woman hands me a whole pack of tissues. You look like you're going to be crying for hours, she says. Some of the other gypsy girls gather around in their pyjamas and dressing gowns. Some others jump off their horse and cart. They're eating Monster Munch and smoking Sovereigns. The tall one walks towards me. She's going to mug me. She'll take my phone. She invites me to sit in the cart with them. Helps me up. Opens a Diet Pepsi from their multipack and hands it to me. Lights me a smoke. Why you crying, beautiful? She's wearing a Minnie Mouse dressing gown. They all gather around as I tell them about the suit and everything. The night in the restaurant. The price sticker I'd caught a glimpse of on the soles of the brogues. £52.99. From Bally. He must have got them in the January sales. He *opened* the door for me. He's – just – so – gross. They keep taking it in turns to hug me. They'll mug me soon enough. Fuck him, they all say. He's disgusting. He said he wanted to meet my daughter, he wanted to have us both in his life. Start a family. But if he's having sex with everyone else, how does that even work? He buys all that sex, uses all those women, why is he so obsessed with sex? Who needs that much sex? I've been celibate for six years and I'm alright, aren't I? Normal. I'm normal. I'm crying again. The woman in the curlers whips the horse. We'll give you a ride for free around the estate, she says. Thank you. We ride around four times. Are you going to mug me? I ask. Not today, she says. You're too sad.

CONSUMER CASTRATION

Clover is still exhaling: You need to get it done. It's been six years. Get it done tonight. Biddy is at a sleepover. This is your one chance. You're wasting the best years of your life. You're never going to look as good as you did yesterday. She takes my phone. She's swiping on Tinder. Matches me with someone 0.2 miles away. Sends him a message. With a fuck offer. Just get it done. The stranger replies straight away. Of course he does. He'll be there in 30 minutes. What's his name? Clover tells me it doesn't matter, don't even ask his name and best of all, promise me this, Cash – metaphorically castrate him before he leaves.

HOW TO FIGHT LONELINESS

Six years: Giving my pussy a quick wash. Giving it a shave. It's out of control down there. It's been so long. Not normal. My bathroom is at the front of the flat and I can see someone pacing outside. Some stranger. Some man. A message: Have you changed your mind? No I haven't changed my mind, I shout through the window. Then I unlock the chains on the door until I'm face to face with him through my new metal security gate. I start to unlock the gate. He's alright for 3am. Scruffy in the way I like. He hasn't been drinking so he must be as lonely as me to be coming to a stranger's place at this hour. Open up the gate. Lock it behind him. That's it – you can't escape now! I say it as a joke but he looks scared. We kiss in the hallway for a bit. Then lead him to the sofa. He's looking at my book collection. We like the same authors, he says. He's trying to find some sort of *connection*. I don't respond. He starts listing the authors. These are my favourite authors too, he says. I ignore all conversation. Kiss him. I don't feel a thing. He keeps trying to make conversation. Let's not talk, I say. A stranger who turns up at my flat at 3am isn't good enough to be a stepdad to my daughter. He isn't going to be the father of my future children. So I take off my clothes to make my intentions clear. Use it. He's trying to be gentle and caring and he seems like the kind of guy I'd probably like if we'd met outside a gallery or at a political demonstration or something – but we *didn't*. He's collateral damage of my loneliness. He *finally* takes his clothes off. I hand him an extra-thick condom. I put up every barrier possible. We're fucking. Your pussy is so tight. *What?* Your pussy is so tight. That's what he says. Yeah? Say it again. YOUR. PUSSY. IS. SO. FUCKING. TIGHT. It's not falling out? It's all in there, yeah? It feels good? It feels normal? I'm normal? It doesn't feel weird? This isn't some line you use on all women? You don't say this every time you fuck a woman? I'm looking at his face and his expression fact-checks his words. Say it again. He does. He says it again. That's when I cum. Just a small one. But I've lost my six-year virginity. He's still going on with it. Pumping away. Still fucking. You can stop now. I say. Stop please. I put on my dressing gown. This night is over. Thank you very much, it's time for you to go now. I unlock the gate. He is holding the empty extra strong in his hand. Shall I take this with me? he asks. Yeah you can *keep* the condom. He asks me if I want to go for dinner some-time. No. Not with you. You seem like a really nice person and everything but no. I shake his hand, I SHAKE his hand, before he leaves and I lock the gate behind him. Then I just lie on the rug and cry myself to sleep. What an ordeal. But these are the things you do to fight loneliness.

10

IT'S A WONDERFUL LIE

NOT LONG AFTER THE 2015 General Election I became a wife tourist. Biddy and I were evicted from yet another private rental (one that finally threatened to throw us out past Zone 6 and into racist Kent) when I received a text with an offer that no mother needing to feed and home her child in austerity Britain could refuse.

It read: I NEED A FAKE WIFE. DO IT?

Sure, I replied. What's the terms?

I was to pretend to be Kingsley's *wife* in exchange for living rent free in his beautiful cottage on the River Thames. My wifely duties were to include 'the usual': cooking, cleaning, chatting to neighbours over the fence about my wonderful 'husband' as I hung his underwear out to dry, attending family funerals in a stoic yet supportive capacity whenever the deaths occurred, putting up with his bad taste in music and snuggling on the sofa watching episodes of *Mid Morning Matters*.

And because Kingsley is a fully fledged queer these days there'd be no sex involved. It was the perfect solution. We needed a home and Kingsley required a beard to ensure he'd not be cut from the inheritance – his father had recently been diagnosed with cirrhosis of the liver and had made it clear that his vast stash of self-made construction company cash wouldn't be left to any *poofs*. I was happy to help Kingsley blindside his homophobic dad – *plus* he'd offered me a lump sum of £25,000 to be deferred until after the death of his father, once the estate had been settled.

It was a casual job. Like an au pair. Like modern slavery. Like Camp America. Like a gap-year job in an Australian bar. Like a ... marriage on zero hours. Wife tourism is uncontracted work, you don't get a marriage certificate or any kind of contract, you're very much at the heart of the gig economy, but it meant that mine and Biddy's life would change significantly. We'd live in a nice home and have the trappings of a seemingly traditional family albeit within an unorthodox set-up. It was an unusual situation to find myself in, yet not totally out of character for me and I couldn't have entered into a fake marriage with a better person. Kingsley and I share an unusual history, but we are friends I suppose, we've known each other our entire adult lives. He was the man who watched my daughter enter the world, he was the person who babysat when I was in police custody, he is the closest thing my daughter has to a dad. Sure, he's generally of a disagreeable nature, incredibly controlling and has served time for assaulting me, but people can change, can't they? He's practically owned me for the past 16 years so I can live with this man that I do not love for a shot at stability. Millions of women live with men they do not love. Who am I to turn my nose up at this *opportunity*?

All three of us will be living such a wonderful life.

It's a wonderful lie.

Rangemasters and Agas are the same thing. They are owned by the same company. I'm only telling you this because we have a Rangemaster in our new house, which means we *technically* have an Aga. We *have* an Aga. I'm a terrible cook and it's wasted on me and I have no interest in baking biscuits with Biddy but that lump of a cooker perfectly slotted between the pristine marble surface and the shelf of Alessi gadgets is a thing of beauty.

I could stare at it all day. I often do.

I invite friends over just to ogle it. Even Kirsty forces herself to leave Camden for the afternoon, taking the Overground all the way out to see it in action. Clover takes a taxi across the Westway to view it in its sturdy, hot glory and there was even talk of my friend Hannah jetting down from Glasgow to spend the weekend with it, but her mother died suddenly, and she had to cancel. She was absolutely devastated. It was insane. Friends were coming from far and wide to visit the Aga, leaving us without a free weekend for over six months. I hadn't achieved this level of popularity since I appeared on *Mallet's Mallet* back in 1992. It's fair to say I was back in the game. I even took the liberty of purchasing a new Le Creuset kettle to store on the stove, which I would boil right in the faces of the guests as they arrived. Then we'd keep boiling the kettle so we'd have a valid reason to direct our eyes towards the Aga – otherwise it would just be *sordid* – staring at an Aga doing nothing, that would be absurd. To get the full experience of the Aga I've found it's best to put that cooker to use. Boil a kettle, roast a chicken, heat the damn room. Maybe it's the working class in me, I don't know, but I like to make good use of it. That's how you show off an Aga in its best light.

Kirsty and Clover are concerned about my most recent 'lifestyle choice'. They know what Kingsley is like and how quickly things can turn. Kirsty was the one who gave the statement to the police that landed him in jail back in 2009 after he'd picked me up and thrown me across the room – and we thought he'd broken my back, but Kirsty and Clover are trying to be supportive so they help me move the dining table so it's adjacent to the Aga, ensuring we have the kitchen equivalent of top-priced theatre tickets at the front of the stalls. And sometimes, an annoying acquaintance of an audience member would be sat on one of my multicoloured chairs, sipping a fresh Matcha tea, at my new Habitat extendable table whilst taking a long hard look at my *cooker* and they'd turn around and fake apologetically tell me that it wasn't an Aga but a Rangemaster but I'd quickly shut that conversation down with an utter of 'semantics'. It's an Aga. We cook *things* on the *Aga*, I'd say.

Then I'd explain –

Rangemaster is *owned* by Aga.

It's like MDMA and Ecstasy.

It's like crack and cocaine.

They are technically the same thing.

They'll all get you high, they'll fuck you up – they're just packaged and marketed in different ways to suit different audiences.

The fact is: I have an Aga, and that is that.

Deal with it.

My life is different now.

We have an Aga and a shot at stability.

And nothing, nothing is going to ruin this.

Between Biddy's birth and the age of five we've moved eight times. That's the life of the low-earning private renter, always on the run, searching Rightmove, plotting your next six months of space, a place to dump your small stash of belongings – then six months later, another suburb, another Nisa, another shop manager you're begging to save up all their cardboard boxes for you. Private renters: society's acceptable version of the travelling community; only instead of riding ponies around council estates and having flamboyant weddings, we are a community of nomads lining the pockets of 78 per cent of the parliamentary front bench. Having privately rented my entire adult life, I've learned not to become too attached to possessions because those moving costs stack up when you're back on the road every half a year. I have a rule: If I can't fit my entire life into a getaway Uber, then I don't need it. With this nomadic lifestyle I am void of a thirst for *things*. Up until NOW I have been free from the slavery of consumerism.

But this move is a different kind of move.

It's a fake marriage of convenience but there is no expiry date. It could be years until Kingsley's homophobic dad dies. Being a wife tourist is in fact no different to being someone's actual real-life partner and the idea of this new, settled way of life has unleashed the capitalist within. I have been met with a compulsive desire to collect and consume furniture and *things* until we have to find a bigger house to store all of our things. Or at the very least apply for planning permission for an extension. I've really missed *things*. As a child I would spend hours in the company of the Argos and Littlewoods catalogues dreaming of all the things I would own when I got away from my mum. Now, I've only gone and upgraded: From Argos to Habitat. 'Isn't Habitat the same company as Argos?' asks Kirsty. 'Semantics,' I reply. My table, my chairs, my pseudo-retro lampshades – they ain't Argos. My life is different now, deal with it.

'This is my wife,' Kingsley says as he introduces me to my new neighbours. And I smile and I nod my head in what I consider a wifely fashion. I'm trying to act dignified. I am now a woman of integrity. I'm not really sure how to behave. I don't really have integrity, do I? I've never been the marrying kind that's for sure, and when I say the marrying kind, I mean that I'm not the type of woman that men who seek wives want. I've found that even what appear to be the most interesting, cerebral and artistic of men always seek traditional, normative women. If you want to marry a man you need to be mass market. Think Coldplay: conventional, dull, yet ultimately proficient at your instrument. Think of yourself as the Chris Martin of future wives and you're well on your way to getting a certificate. In fact, whilst we're at it, it's my one tip for life: don't have miscarriages in police cells, don't work in a peep show whilst heavily pregnant, don't be a single mum. Play it safe by having a supportive mum and dad, let them give you a deposit to ensure your rung onto the property ladder. Be born middle class – that's THE best plan.

This new wife tourist arrangement has given me the opportunity to leave my old sordid life behind. I'm finally going to be able to live a life like all the other mums out there. One minute I'm trawling dating apps and lying in the foetal position crying onto my fake La Redoute rug after the shame of using a stranger's cock to reassure me that my vagina still works, and the next thing I know I'm a wife tourist in the Royal Borough of Kingston Upon Thames.

This – is – my – fucking – dream.

Let me remind you of my husband: Stereotypically handsome – for such a short man. Wealthy. He wears Casual Connoisseur sweatshirts and limited-edition Clarks desert boots. He cleanses with Dermalogica and moisturises with REN. He once flew out to America for six months to follow Bon Jovi on tour. The only alcohol he drinks is a rare Japanese whiskey that he gets imported on the seventh of every month. He has what he calls 'fuck you' money. He takes menial jobs to fill the pointlessness of his time. Then makes his boss's life a living hell. He took a job as a waiter at Prezzo. When he got caught stealing *toilet roll* he pulled out his banking app to show the manager his seven figure balance. 'I don't need this job. I've got Fuck – You – Money.' He's an avid collector of modern art, our walls are covered with Pure Evil, Mr Bingo and above the fireplace hangs a David Shrigley original. He has a vast vintage vinyl collection, which he never plays. Over 300 pairs of trainers – the majority of which remain unworn and boxed up. He talks about setting up an escort agency, an artisan coffee company, buying a food van and taking it around festivals – but nothing in his life ever makes it past an initial idea. He lights a brand-new Diptyque candle with every fresh bath, which he always fills with Tom Ford Neroli Portofino Oil. He only ever smokes half an American Spirit before sparking up the next. And he doesn't get supermarket deliveries – he receives *food subscription*s: Hello Fresh, Graze, DeGusta, Nutri-Bombz, Abel & Cole, Pasta Evangelists, Carnivore Club. He lives for farmers markets. He has a *driving licence.* He offers stability. He hugs me when I feel unsafe. He accepts my daughter as his own. This is everything I've ever wanted: protection, polished wooden floors and … every single Le Creuset pan in volcanic orange.

We are a proper family.

He hoards *things* and has money.

And now so do I.

That's how marriages work, even fake ones.

That's what happens when you get a husband like Kingsley.

Even if it's only on zero hours.

You get things.

We have *things*.

I suddenly really care about things. And having even more things.

Five years into this motherhood game and I've realised that the only thing making me a bad mother is that I've been unable to own and collect things.

But *this* is normal living.

This is the family situation of everyone I know.

On social media.

This is how I measure my place in the world.

With followers and likes and comments.

If you're drinking Hendrick's Gin, then you're doing alright.

So, I order Hendrick's Gin.

If you're wearing Boden, you're looking the part.

So, I order dresses from their website despite the clothes not suiting me.

If you lose your once carefully curated taste in music and literature, then you're on the right path.

If you used to love Chris Morris but now find yourself whooping at women in Lycra making morning sausage jokes, then you're doing motherhood just right.

I – want – to – be – in – that – club.

Desperately.

So . . .

I'll go along with all that.

I'll sell my soul if I have one.

I'll lose myself if I'm still there.

I'm sick of being a disgusting working-class outsider. Where has being an outsider ever got me? Where has been *proudly* working class ever got me?

You only get to be *proudly* working class when you've left that world behind.

I want *things*. I want things like everyone else has things.

I – want – to – have – a – normal – family.

And now we're in the club.

It's such a wonderful lie.

I get really into it. Embrace the life, like you do. Like you do when you're on a working holiday; got to explore classic suburbia through the eyes of its native middle class – a truly authentic cultural experience. I download Deliciously Ella recipes and cook them on the Aga. I can have two whole bottles of Sav Blanc in one sitting if I fancy it – so long as I post a picture of my drink on Instagram. Then it's alright. Then it's *not* alcoholism.

We both get into it. My 'husband' and me. He looks at me in such a disappointed way – like a *real* husband would; scolding me for running off my political mouth at dinner parties or for snogging all the guests. 'You're an embarrassment!' he proudly slurs as he gives my bum a sleazy slap to push me into the Uber at the end of the night.

I – had – that – middle – class – wife – act – down.

I get *so* into it that I buy a website domain. With the word 'mum' in the title. And then, I go about creating and writing what became a multi-award-nominated blog about my perfect husband and perfect child and perfect home and perfect life and make money doing adverts for brands who exploit the stereotypical aspirational lie of the perfect nuclear family. This – is – such – a – wonderful – life. To live with my actions, with my *embellishments*, I convince myself I'm exploiting *them*; we're both dealing in the currency of lies, therefore our exploitation of each other is … *pure*. In my mind I'm mocking them and *everyone* who buys into the lie of my life. Yet I consider my gains more than just financial; I have been elevated from vilified single mum to an almost respectable woman living the middle-class suburban dream. I mean, I had a kitchen island and *everything*. All I'd had to do was forego *all* my morals – because, after all, what is a working-class woman with morals but a poor one?

Everything is an act. My marriage, my happiness, my *life*.

I document every fake second of it on my new Canon EOS 750D. I put it on self-timer to ensure I am included in every important moment of my new lifestyle; at a Regatta wearing a dress from the Diane von Furstenberg H&M Collection, stuffing Sunday roast into my mouth covered in Ruby Woo MAC lipstick, buying towels from John Lewis, trying out the new Vitalumière Satin Chanel foundation, standing by my Aga spooning organic biscuit mix onto my Joseph Joseph trays. Indoctrinating Biddy into the evils of capitalism via weekly gifted trips to KidZania. A self-timed moment ice skating at Somerset House sponsored by Fortnum & Mason, a self-timed moment on the Ferris wheel sponsored by Samsung at Winter Wonderland. Self-timing doctors injecting Botox into the lines around my lying eyes. Self-timed in Sweaty Betty holding up my David Lloyd peak-time membership. A self-timed moment drinking Matcha tea against the backdrop of teak furniture before filming videos of unboxing Gousto cooking kits, jewellery sets, and all the things I got from this shop, and that shop and all the other shops. My multi-award-nominated lie life.

All these things that I'm *allowed* to own now I have a husband and a house.

And would you look at me now. I'm a real mother. The more stuff you have, the better mother you are. And I *share* every precious moment of my nuclear dream with the world via a hashtag ad. Because the more things you acquire the more pointless things brands will want to *send* you to add to your perfect life; mattresses to replace the perfectly functioning mattress you've already got, a phone to replace the phone that already adequately connects you to the world, a dress that is not to your taste, I mean it's utterly disgusting and shapeless – but you'll wear it for a fee and to ensure you get sent more things not to your taste. My foray into conventionalism is rewarded on every level. And I am documenting every single second of it.

This is the perfect portrayal of motherhood I've craved since pissing on that stick in the shit-smeared toilet. This is everything I have ever wanted. We are the family in the poster advertising car insurance. We are the family around the dinner table in the AO electronics advert on the telly. We are the Instagram post about our trip to Seaworld in Brighton and it has over 3,000 likes. Who – the – hell – is – liking – all – this – shit? This is the life that has 'Mama' emblazoned across an £80 sweatshirt. This is the life of hashtag winging it, whatever the fuck that means. Branded, acceptable, sellable motherhood. And of course, this is also the life of mundanity that creates the breakdowns of middle-aged commuters and this is also the life that fills the swingers' clubs of suburbia. Financial abuse. Family structures in collusion with the patriarchy. A breeding ground for internalised misogyny and the unhappy decades that some women waste just trying to make it all work.

But you'd be fucking mad to leave it.

Do you *know* what it's actually like out there, outside of this bubble? I do. And you don't divorce from this. We have a Loaf sofa and a Sky package. We have original parquet flooring in the kitchen and a restored Victorian bathroom basin. We have exposed beams. According to the conversations I'm having these days at the school gate we also have a thing called 'state till eight' which apparently is Latin for *rape the state education system for as long as possible so we can save ALL OUR MONEY before ensuring our beautiful precious future banker boy doesn't go to secondary school with the black kids from the estate.* And I nod and I say 'yah' because, after all, what is a middle-class woman with morals but an ostracised one?

I am conventional. I am bland. I fit the stereotype. I am the Chris Martin of all the wives.

I find this role I am playing stranger than dancing in a peep show at eight months pregnant. But I much prefer the way people treat me these days. I glide into PTA events with ease. I like it. The women at the school gate confide in me about their terrible *legitimate* marriages and my daughter gets invited to Build a Bear parties. *Finally.*

Now I'm a mum, as opposed to a single mum.

Having a man next to me validates my existence. I am less threatening. Because a man has vouched for me, I get to experience some kind of respect alongside the *things* I've acquired. Kingsley accompanies me to parents' evenings and provides me with a safety net – and at the very least having a man in the background ensures that plumbers don't rip me off.

If you don't look too closely, Kingsley and I manage to pull it off as the typical middle-class married couple, the only give-away is the box of Agent Provocateur underwear he presents to me at Christmas in front of his family to keep up the married act – only gay men and horny teenage boys buy underwear for women – but it appears to send the message required as his dad no longer calls him a poof and Kingsley remains in the will as the executor of his father's estate.

My whole life is a lie, but for once I'm *almost* like everyone else.

It's a wonderful lie.

WHORE has been sprayed across my Farrow & Ball No. 26 'Down Pipe' bedroom wall in red spray paint.

Me and Biddy have barricaded ourselves in our bedroom by placing a vintage teak chest of drawers against the door as we count out the money I've been secretly throwing into the pink Agent Provocateur box each week.

I count out £5,000. We have £5,000.

It's our getaway fund.

We just need to get away.

I'd handed in my notice on my zero-hour marriage about a year ago, but Kingsley won't let us leave. Being a wife tourist isn't like being an au pair or a gap-year job in an Australian bar.

Wife tourism is basically modern slavery. And we're trapped.

We can hear Kingsley downstairs.

He just keeps shouting WHORE. He destroys an expensive object and shouts WHORE.

He kicks off the Rangemaster door and he shouts WHORE.

He rips the David Shrigley original from the wall and shouts WHORE.

He smashes bottles of Japanese whiskey and he shouts WHORE.

He tries to break the Le Creuset pans, but they are very durable.

They have a lifetime guarantee.

I call Kirsty. She knew this would happen. She can hear him in the background. She says she's calling the police. Don't phone the police, I beg her. I'll talk him round.

We can hear him making his way up the stairs. With each step he takes a hammer to the stairs and shouts WHORE.

'Just pretend to be asleep, Biddy,' I say as she lies on top of me shaking. I stroke her hair like it will soothe her through all the WHORES, or something.

Earlier he found our £24.99 Argos suitcases that I had packed for our getaway. We can fit everything we need into a suitcase. If you can't fit it into your getaway car, then you don't need it.

Now he's smashing through the door with the hammer.

Kingsley is about three minutes away from breaking into the room.

I hate getting the cops involved but that's when I bite the bullet and call them.

Kingsley owns me. He owns Biddy. He owns us both. His dad died over a year ago and my wife tourist days are over, but he won't let me leave. He's decided not to give me the £25,000 from the sale of the house but I don't care about that. I just want to leave. But he won't let us. And we cannot afford to escape.

Every penny I earn from writing advertisements on my *multi-award-nominated* blog about our perfect life – he takes from me. He keeps lists of all my clients and the money is transferred directly to him. He is the Cynthia Payne of mum bloggers. A social media trafficker. Insta-pimp. I write on my blog: Look at our dinner at Planet Hollywood. It's the best fast food we have ever eaten. I say, look at these hair straighteners from John Lewis, they are the best hair straighteners I've ever used. Look at what they do to my hair. It's so straight. I write: Look at our daughter in her Joules wellies. They are the best wellies she's ever worn. I write: Look at our matching Bobbin Bikes. Look at the three of us riding our matching Bobbin Bikes through beautiful Bushy Park. They are the best bikes we have ever ridden. Look at the £3,000 bed I just got sent. My husband and I, we love sleeping in our £3,000 bed. We sleep in it together. Like a proper couple. Sleeping. In a bed. It's so comfortable. I write it all down on my domain ending in mum, and I photograph it, but all the money goes straight to Kingsley.

I'm in debt to him. We cannot leave until we have repaid the debt. We are living in luxury and without the burden of rent – we have things and we have Farrow & Ball No. 26 'Down Pipe' covering our bathroom walls and on our bedroom walls (which I have photographed and blogged about). I write: This is the best paint I have ever used, it really is the best of all the paints – in exchange for money. But Biddy and I are the poorest we've ever been. Kingsley controls my bank account and all the money goes straight to him; even when his father dies, and he receives even more money and buys more things to hoard via the inheritance, he still wants control of my money too.

At night he spends his time online gambling thousands of pounds on obscure football matches in the Far East. Sometimes he wins, and to celebrate he'll order himself extravagant aftershaves and make-up brushes or limited-edition trainers. But he doesn't want to do it with *his* money, so he takes out credit cards in my name, transfers his debts to me, and puts all the utilities in my name.

He presents me with a list of all the debts I owe him: the Uber to suburbia, his moving fee, the Christmas tree I insisted we have, a pack of nappies he bought for Biddy back in 2010, the sofa he didn't want that I forced him to buy, the watch he bought me for my birthday, the underwear I never wore – the things I no longer deserve. A long list of all the things I do not deserve.

People in debt are filled with fear when the post arrives and hide behind the sofa with every knock at the door. But I'm sitting on the comfortable, big, velvet, Loaf sofa with my own personal bailiff and there is nowhere to hide.

With him taking all of my earnings, all we have to live on is roughly £70 a week from Child Benefit and Child Tax Credits, which is being paid into an account he doesn't know about. The only thing we have on our side is that I'm not legally married nor am I part of a couple, meaning I am still able to claim them, and I see it as the only thing that can save us. So long as he doesn't find out.

I beg Kingsley to let us leave, to let me have some of the money I've earned from the blog so me and Biddy can get our own flat. I want my life back.

'The only way you'll be leaving is by running to a women's refuge where you belong.' That's what he always says whenever I try to leave.

So, I start plotting our getaway. I spend £20 a week on food and essentials for me and Biddy and then I throw the remaining £50 into the pink Agent Provocateur box. We need £5,000 to escape. I make a list: first month's rent and deposit; an extra-large Argos suitcase; money for an Uber out of suburbia. We don't need anything else. We just need to be free.

I refuse to write any more blogs, refuse to participate in the fake life anymore.

I tell the neighbours I'm not really his wife.

Kingsley tells the neighbours I'm having a breakdown.

My poor wife is losing her mind, he tells them. They feel sorry for him.

Everyone is worried about you because they *know* you are mad, he tells me.

All I can think about is leaving. Every time I bring up my £25k wife fee he just calls me a whore. He says he has decided I don't deserve it, my behaviour is too bad, I've humiliated him.

To supplement the £50 Child Tax Credits, I start to sell on the relics of our fake life on eBay: the unworn Agent Provocateur underwear, the dresses that didn't suit me, the hair straighteners, the matching bikes, the Canon EOS 7500

FUCKING CLEVER, DO YOU, SECRETLY HIDING
MONEY, KEEPING MONEY FROM ME? WHAT YOU
GOING TO DO WITH THE MONEY, WHORE WHORE
WHORE? WHAT KIND OF WOMAN AGREES TO PRE-
TEND TO BE MARRIED? A FUCKING WHORE, YOU
THINK YOU'RE BETTER THAN A WHORE BECAUSE
WE DIDN'T FUCK? BECAUSE I DIDN'T MAKE YOU
SUCK ON MY DICK, LITTLE WHORE. WELL YOU CAN
SUCK ON IT NOW, SUCK ON MY COCK NOW, YOU
DIRTY WHORE. I'LL LET YOU KEEP YOUR MONEY IF
YOU SUCK ON MY COCK. HOW MUCH YOU GOT IN
THERE? 3,000. 4,000. 5,000. 5,000 POUNDS. I'LL LET
YOU KEEP THE 5,000 POUNDS IF YOU SUCK ON IT.
NO. I CAN'T EVEN GET HARD FOR YOU, YOU'RE SO
FUCKING DISGUSTING. YOUR UGLY LITTLE FACE
CAN'T EVEN MAKE ME HARD. YOU'RE TOO MUCH
OF A WHORE TO MAKE ME HARD. WELL THE MONEY
IS MINE, ALL THIS IS MINE, YEAH. WHAT WERE YOU
GOING TO DO? GO A NO GET A FLAT? A DIRTY LITTLE
FLAT FOR YOU AND YOUR BASTARD KID? YOU'RE
NOT TAKING HER AWAY FROM ME. I'M THE CLOS-
EST THING SHE HAS TO A DAD. WE'RE NOT BLOOD
BUT I'M HER DAD, AREN'T I? SHE LOVES ME. YOU
LOVE ME, DON'T YOU? YOU LOVE DADDY, DON'T
YOU? I'M HER DAD. SHE LOVES ME LIKE A DAD. YOU
CAN LEAVE, WHORE, BUT I'M KEEPING THE KID.
HERE, HERE'S A THOUSAND POUNDS, TAKE YOUR

FUCKING WHORE CUNT AND LEAVE THE KID.
YOU'D SELL YOUR KID, WOULDN'T YOU? YOU'LL
SELL ANYTHING. HOW MUCH DO YOU WANT FOR
HER? TWO THOUSAND. HOW'S THAT? LEAVE THE
FUCKING KID. I'M LIKE A DAD TO HER. I'M LIKE A
DAD TO THAT LITTLE GIRL. AND YOU'D TAKE HER
AWAY? BOTH OF YOU ARE WHORES. SHE'S JUST LIKE
YOU. SHE'LL HATE YOU ONE DAY LIKE YOU HATE
YOUR MUM. AND THEN SHE'LL WHORE HERSELF
OUT TOO. YOU'RE BOTH FUCKING WHORES.

He pulls me out of the bed by my hair and collects the money
from the pink box. He gives me his look, the one that keeps
me in line, he does it while grabbing my face.

LOOK AT YOUR UGLY FACE. LOOK AT THAT UGLY
FACE. LOOK AT YOUR DISGUSTING CROOKED
TEETH. YOU'RE A WASHED-UP WHORE. YOU USED
TO BE HALF BEAUTIFUL BUT NOW YOU'RE CHAS-
ING FORTY. NO ONE IS EVER GOING TO WANT YOU
NOW. IF YOU WANT TO LEAVE HERE THEN YOU
GO TO A WOMEN'S REFUGE. YOU CAN GO TO A
WOMEN'S REFUGE. I KNOW YOU DON'T WANT TO
GO TO A WOMEN'S REFUGE BUT YOU'RE SUCH A
SHIT MUM YOU'LL END UP TAKING THAT POOR
BASTARD CHILD TO ONE, WON'T YOU? LOOK AT
HER LITTLE FACE. LOOK AT HER FACE. YOU'RE

MAKING HER CRY. LOOK AT HER LITTLE FACE. SHE LOOKS NOTHING LIKE YOU. I KNOW YOU HATE THAT. SHE LOOKS LIKE THAT PRICK IN GRANTHAM YOU LET FUCK YOU. WHORE. BUT INSIDE SHE'S DARK LIKE YOU. A LITTLE WHORE JUST LIKE HER WHORE MUM. YOU'RE NOT HAVING THE MONEY. THIS IS MY MONEY NOW. THIS IS MY MONEY. STOP CRYING, YOU CUNT. BOTH OF YOU STOP FUCKING CRYING, YOU STUPID WHORES. BOTH WHINGING DIRTY WHORES. I'M GOING TO KILL YOU BOTH. I'M GOING TO KILL THE BIG WHORE AND I'M GOING TO KILL THE LITTLE WHORE. YOU'RE BOTH GO-ING TO DIE. YOU LITTLE WHORES ARE GOING TO DIE. AND THEN I'M GOING TO DIE. I'M GOING TO KILL ALL OF US. YEAH?

That's when the police arrive.

That's when he's arrested.

That's when they find us a place in the refuge.

That's when I go back into the house to collect the Argos suitcase containing everything we need.

That's when I turn around to take one final look at the life and all the *things* I thought I'd always wanted.

I stare at the Rangemaster for a few minutes.

It looks nothing like an Aga.

11

NOTES FROM: A FAILED REVOLUTION

WE ARE ATTEMPTING REVOLUTION.

There are 13 of us in total. We are seven women and six children, and we are all living together in one room. It's the only safe room (in a safehouse that is no longer safe) in a condemned building just off Ladbroke Grove.

We have my laptop, our phones and a couple of battery packs. We each have a pocket torch. We have a supply of candles and the women with babies have nappies and wipes. We are all very different. Different backgrounds, different levels of trauma, and on a normal day we would be fighting each other over something petty (like who the hell is it that leaves the pan of fresh vomit in the bath every single morning) but right now all we have is each other. In an event that took less than 30 seconds to occur I have gained something that feels close to having a family. And we are attempting some kind of revolution.

Twenty-four hours ago, the ceiling in the women's refuge we are living in collapsed on us. I say this not as a metaphor for our lives that are buried beneath the rubble of a society designed to silence survivors of abuse – I am talking in fact. The ceiling *actually* collapsed on us in the middle of the night. And now the walls could topple in on us at any moment and, although water is rising through the floors, we have *no* running water. And we have no electricity. And National Grid came out at 3am to shut off the gas supply. We have nothing.

There is a sign on the notice board with a number to call during an emergency. PLEASE ONLY CALL THIS NUMBER IN A GENUINE EMERGENCY it reads.

Then it lists examples of possible emergencies, just to enlighten its reader as to what an emergency could be – because abused women are assumed stupid of course: fire; flood; the death of a woman on the premises; terrorist attack; invasion of male perpetrator; the death of a child on the premises.

Then underneath, in capitals again.

A BLOCKED TOILET IS <u>NOT</u> AN EMERGENCY. The NOT has been underlined in red felt-tip pen a whole four times. Then there are even more words in capitals: EMERGENCIES ARE LISTED ABOVE. READ THEM AGAIN IF YOU ARE UNSURE. I read them again. And again, just to be sure.

I took a picture of the sign on our first day here. The incongruous wording amused me somewhat amongst the pseudo-calm setting of a 'safe' crumbling house that exists to help fragmented women piece their lives back together. I found myself throwing out a smirk whenever I passed the sign.

Lots of things about living in the women's refuge make me laugh. Obviously the situation that leads to someone seeking shelter from violence and oppression is horrific, and that definitely needs to be said in the age of the *idiot disclaimer*, otherwise that above sentence would be purposefully misconstrued by a perpetual offence-seeker to make me sound like I'm laughing at domestic violence. Idiot disclaimer: violence isn't funny. I know that. I experienced it first hand, I didn't laugh for years. But the truth is that once you stick a group of very messed up people together in a house share with panic buttons then you have the makings of a perfect sitcom.

I started writing it on the night Biddy and I arrived.

My women's refuge sitcom.

Working title: *Refuge Woman*.

I'll find a better title.

I'm working on it.

But the emergency sign *is* funny.

The pan of vomit that is placed in the bathroom each morning (which no one will own up to) is disgusting, but it is also funny.

Here's something funny: a working-class woman gathering a group of shaken, vulnerable people together and attempting to start a *revolution* on a whim with her unconfident, mispronounced and jumbled political views in a women's refuge in the middle of the night. It's funny.

It's like laughing at a funeral, you search for the absurd in order to break the tension. At my grandad's funeral, I laughed so much, it was one of the funniest days of my childhood; I took it upon myself to provide entertainment at the wake and wrote and performed an East 17-style rap with the stories I had collected from all those Christmases when we'd searched the streets for the old man. At first the wake audience ignored me, then they fought with me, then they laughed with me and then I won. To mis-quote Gandhi.

And I've found myself in a refuge as part of this ragtag family who have found ourselves on the unlikely path to mutiny. Soldiers against the patriarchy! Unprepared soldiers. It's funny. Even more so when Monique decides to play the Original London Cast recording of *Les Misérables* through her phone to lift our spirits. 'Lovely Ladies' plays as the fire brigade help us bring down mattresses and blankets from the rooms where the ceilings have yet to fall and they give each of us pocket torches. We lay four mattresses across the floor and one of the officers recommends that at least one person is awake at any time to ensure that we can make a quick exit should a fire break out or if the building loses its foundations. Both outcomes likely.

By the time we've settled into the one safe room Monique has moved onto the *Les Miserables Motion Picture Soundtrack*. As the fire officer instructs us on our potential escape routes should tragedy occur, Sacha Baron Cohen is singing 'Master of the House'.

It's funny. But we are revolting!

I say things like: We stick together on this, we don't let any-one separate us.

I say: We have an important political message to share about the effects of austerity.

I say: We are the walking wounded of a class war.

It's dramatic, but revolutions are, aren't they? That is why *Les Misérables* is the second-longest-running West End show ever. Obviously.

We fast-forward to 'Do You Hear the People Sing?'.

We ALL know *all* the words.

I reiterate to the group: Whatever happens, we don't let *them* separate us. We are only strong as a collective. We only talk as a group.

Everyone seems up for it.

And I write a script that I insist we all stick to when talking to journalists, MPs and the housing officers down at the council. The script is pieced together by some partially formed ideas of my own that have been taking root throughout my awkward political journey and crudely gluing them together with facts from newspaper reports that I've Googled: This is social cleansing! The Tories want us out! Sixty per cent of women who approach a refuge are refused a place due to refuge closures. The government have cut funding to women's refuges by 24 per cent, meaning this was destined to happen. Since the Tories got into power hundreds of women's refuges have closed down. Vulnerable women are getting turned away from refuges every day and the refuges that still exist aren't even fit for purpose. Look at this place! The government ran *this* building into the ground so that they could remove women like us from the richest borough in the country. This is a clear message from the Conservatives stating that they don't want people like *us* living amongst the wealthy!

And then I Google 'Noam Chomsky quotes'.

Finishing the script with: 'To misquote Chomsky – *This* is the standard technique of privatisation: defund, make sure things don't work and then privatise.'

It *sort of* fits with what I think we need to say.

I think.

This political situation I've found myself in. It scares me. It sounds weird, all these words that are said with genuine intention that keep tumbling from my mouth. I feel like a fraud but I'm just trying my best.

Biddy teaches the script to the women whose English is still in its infancy.

We repeat it back to each other. We learn the script by heart.

We are all talking the same language.

As a collective of broken humans we want everyone to know what is happening to vulnerable working-class women like us in Britain.

Somehow, I've found myself leading the revolt and everyone is looking to me for our next move, but like all the other women in the room, I've recently fled violence too. I'm totally out of my depth and terrified. I'm raw. But I put on a strong front. I'm good in a crisis, almost sociopathic. My therapist calls it fight or flight. I make my flight and then I come back to fight once we're safe. That's my life technique, anyway.

It's like the only time I function at my very best is in a crisis. Day to day I'm a bit of a mess but, in my daydreams, I stick myself on a plane bound for an emergency landing or on a packed train mid-terrorist attack and I'm *almost* certain that I'll just take a deep breath, pick my daughter up and calmly make our way to safety.

In the aftermath of Grenfell, as Biddy and I would try to fall asleep in our bunkbed beneath the murdered West London skyline, she would ask me to explain to her shot for shot how I would have got her out of the burning building across the street that night.

'What if we were on the twentieth floor, Mummy? How would you save me?' she asks.

And although we both know in our hearts that there would have been no escape, I read her the same bedtime story every night.

We don't hang about, I say. We get straight out. We don't wait for anyone to help us. First, I soak a big bath towel and then I put it around your whole body, even your face. I'm holding you the whole time. That's when I wet a small towel, like a flannel, that's for *my* face. Then we get the hell out of there. We make our way down those stairs. We don't run of course because I don't want to drop you, but we're quick, we're out of there in less than five minutes. You know I walk fast. We always walk fast, me and you, we're from London. We know how to use escalators properly and we always walk with purpose. We don't speak on the way down because our mouths are covered, but you can feel me the entire time, you know I'll make sure that you're alright, I'm holding you so tight, and if we're moving then that means we're breathing, which means we are still alive. We just keep walking until I make sure you're safe. Then as we take the last steps of our escape, there'll be someone there to give us oxygen …

And we'll be safe.

And we're OK. Hugging each other with our black smoky faces and oxygen masks! It's the happy ending all children's books profess.

'I'd be able to have a few days off school, wouldn't I, because my breathing would be bad?' she asks.

You could *definitely* have a few days off school, is the last line in her bedtime story.

When the ceiling collapsed in the room next to ours and the cracks appeared above mine and Biddy's bunkbed, I placed a blanket around my shaking child, grabbed my rucksack, threw in my laptop, phone, chargers and battery packs. Gave Biddy her favourite toy and shouted at everyone in the refuge to get the fuck out of that building. Much like the hero I am in my daydream, I suppose.

But I know I'm not a hero, I'm just someone who is numb to attack. My doctor says he knows war veterans with PTSD who act similarly. You just switch off.

While everyone else is screaming and sobbing and allowing their emotions to show, I'm planning my next move. Thinking how we're going to get away, what we're going to need to get there, where we are going to go. My mind always plans six months in advance. Where is *this* all leading? Since my mum threw me out for the first time when I was a teenager, I've been forever planning my next move. By the end of a successful first date, for example, I'm already planning our anniversary trip to The Lakes. Six months on from an abnormal smear test and I'm having to call the priest to cancel my funeral. It's happened four times now. Maybe it comes from a lifetime of trauma and having to live in survival mode for long periods, or maybe I'm just dead inside. No, I can't be dead inside, not permanently anyway, because I feel love and I care *too* deeply about things, but in those life or death moments I do have the ability to stop my heart beating temporarily.

It stops when the ceiling collapses, and once we are as safe as we can be, in the only safe room in the safehouse that is no longer safe alongside other women whose only link in life is that we were attacked violently by a man – my pulse slowly returns, and I am now ready to fight.

All seven refuge women are ready to fight. But first we need a name that's hashtag-worthy so that people will hear us. To misquote Karl Marx – Without a decent hashtag your revolution will fall flat. So – The Refuge Seven? The Refuge Thirteen? The 'Survivors'? We keep chucking out names. Starting a revolution in a women's refuge is a *bit* like starting a band only without the groupies.

We each have different skills and pull our resources together.

We are the living embodiment of the sisterhood.

Zainab had worked as a childminder before she'd fled her husband, so she creates a crèche to keep the kids entertained. Amy is a photographer and despite her camera getting crushed in the collapse she navigates the building (wearing a yellow hard hat that the gas man had gifted us after seeing the state of the place), taking pictures of the wreckage so that we can post evidence of our living situation on the Twitter account I've just started. I call us @RefugeWomen and get in contact with some of my influential blogger friends I'd made from my time writing about my wonderful lie of a nuclear family (I had since disclosed the truth), asking them to help us get word out to journalists. It is the most beautiful example of women with privilege using their power to uplift those facing oppression. They don't attempt to speak *for* us, and they don't use our experiences as a conduit to share their own stories of past oppression. They just retweet our messages as they unfurl, with nothing but the intention of helping us and instigating change. They want to help us get word out about how government cuts are harming the most vulnerable in society. It is a beautiful and rare act of solidarity that gives us strength to keep on going and a belief that we are doing the right thing.

We have 26 followers. We have 129 followers. We have 304 followers.

I scroll through my phone for the picture I took of the emergency sign from the safehouse notice board. I post it to Twitter along with the caption: Does the ceiling in a women's refuge crashing on 7 women and 6 children count as an emergency? Because WE think it does but no one will answer us.

Exactly 140 characters.

Monique heads to the 24-hour garage to fetch sundries that do not require refrigeration and Lisa repeatedly calls the emergency line, despite it continuously ringing out.

Our support workers, the housing association and the council are nowhere to be found.

We leave 44 messages but no one will return our calls.

I pop my head up every now and again from the laptop to say things like: hashtag Refuge Women. Everything you post on your personal social media, finish with hashtag Refuge Women. *That*'s our hashtag.

Karl Marx would be proud.

And: We've just had a message from someone at the *Guardian*. They want to come and meet with us!

We all cheer. Even the kids cheer.

We are following every left-wing MP and journalist that springs to mind. Anyone who we think might care about the injustice of cuts to women's services. Every leftie commentator and any person who has ever looked out of place on *Question Time* and given a Tory panellist the side eye. These are our comrades.

It's still the middle of the night so we update our status by torchlight:

The reason the Fire Brigade have had to cut off our electricity supply is so that we don't burn like the other poor people did in the tower across the road from us just a few weeks before – water is streaming through the plug sockets.

Monique returns with supplies. Cigarettes, red wine, crisps, dry roasted peanuts, discounted sandwiches, chocolate, Haribo. *Fuel* for revolution.

Michael Ball would definitely approve.

We're still listening to the *Les Misérables* soundtrack. A different version of it. We're now on *Les Misérables Live! Dream the Dream 2010 Concert Cast Album (25th Anniversary)*. Monique tells us in her broken English that she had tickets for the performance that night at the 02 Arena but her husband had locked her underneath the stairs that week.

As we take hourly fag breaks, we sneak glances at the burned-out shell of Grenfell to remind ourselves how much worse things could be. And then we feel ashamed by our glib thoughts. Those people didn't get a chance to fight. We choke on guilt with each drag. As working-class women, we know that our situation could be a lot worse.

Biddy escapes the makeshift crèche and starts crying when she catches me smoking.

'I don't want you to die, Mummy,' she screams.

It's just one cigarette/Mummy is just stressed – I reassure her that I'm not dying/This is a silly mistake/This won't kill me *today*.

I know it's irresponsible of me to be smoking in front of her; the thought of me leaving her all alone in the world is all that has been on her mind since Grenfell. All she talks about is death these days. Every conversation is about death. She's seven now. Her friends are obsessed with Shopkins and the school of capitalism – KidZania, but she's obsessed with Jessica Urbano Ramirez.

There are over a hundred posters of Jessica on our street alone. Biddy counted them. On every wall and lamp post, there's Jessica – and Biddy feels like she knows her.

The poster reads: MISSING FROM GRENFELL. JESSICA URBANO RAMIREZ.

Biddy stops to stare at every poster of her.

Every day. 'Where *is* Jessica Urbano Ramirez?' she asks. There's Jessica on the lamp post, there's Jessica on the wall – but, where *is* she? Every wall within a mile radius of the refuge is covered with posters of people missing from Grenfell but the only one Biddy notices is Jessica Urbano Ramirez.

'Where *is* she, Mummy? She's dead, isn't she, Mummy?'

Jessica *is* dead. She sighs.

'What floor was she on?' Biddy asks. Because if she was lower than the eighth floor, she would have been alright, she wouldn't be missing. But she was high up and no one could get out from up there, that's where you could see the fire the most, wasn't it? That's where they burned alive, she says.

'I hope they at least find the body of Jessica,' she says.

'Tell me how you'd get me out,' she instructs. So, I do, even when it's not bedtime.

This counts as a normal conversation with my seven-year-old these days.

I stub out my ciggy and tell her it's my last as I usher her inside and try to get her and all the other kids to sleep – we have a revolution to organise.

693 followers. 316 retweets.

The Twitter account has only been up for two hours and the day is only just beginning for most people, but the ones who are awake are listening. More people will be getting up soon (we know this because we are able to turn off our torches and blow out the candles) as the summer sun fills the room – and maybe they'll listen to us too?

Lisa finally gets through on the emergency line. They say they'll call straight back.

They don't.

We post one of Amy's videos of the wreckage.

The entire ceiling had collapsed on her bed – she'd been in the communal living room watching *The Handmaid's Tale* when the concrete landed on what would have been her sleeping body. We joke that if she'd have been in bed not only would she have been the first casualty of our revolution (all revolutions need a climactic casualty – end of Act I) but her limp body would have given us no doubts whether to call the emergency line due to 'the death of a woman on the premises'.

The person from the emergency line calls us back. Finally. It's been almost ten hours since she said she'd call us straight back. I know this because the full soundtrack to *Les Misérables* comes in at around 1 hour and 37 minutes. We're five listens in. I decide I prefer the first act. The second act gets too bogged down with the love story and, when Michael Ball's character chooses Cosette over the far more complex Éponine, it confirms all my life theories about how only the normative and dull can achieve conventional happiness.

Monique, who can barely speak English because her husband never let her leave the house in the whole 16 years she lived in Barking, sings a perfect rendition of 'A Little Fall of Rain'.

We cheer. We are in high spirits.

We post a picture of water seeping through the power sockets. We post a picture of a window that has given up hope and now lies scattered in the cot where Lisa's son normally sleeps. Another tweet with someone's crushed and destroyed belongings. Another with a pile of kids' toys quickly decaying in the vastly deteriorating conditions.

None of us had arrived with much but as we had started to piece our lives back together, we had all begun to accumulate possessions again. Due to the location of the refuge we had been given most of the leftovers from the Grenfell donations. We had new clothes and were given vouchers to buy expensive premium-brand make-up and stacks of new books. Now we were back to nothing. Again.

909 followers. 207 retweets. 84 comments.

Someone should employ me to run their social media accounts, I reckon. Whipping up this kind of engagement within the space of a couple of hours is a proper skill. I'll pop it on my CV if we ever get out of this mess, get myself a 'proper' job.

But for now, this is our HQ. This communal living room, which we are sharing with a family of rats who have just moved in (and vastly outnumber us, we are in their world now), is where we will show the world just what this government does to working-class mothers who fall foul of the patriarchy. In the midst of all of this I become aware of my own strength. I think all of us refuge women do, at this point. We have something important to say, we're standing for something important and not only are we speaking out but we're saying it with conviction. We may be awkward and we don't talk like politicians but our message is simple and clear – this is what happens to working-class women under austerity.

We start giving interviews to the mainstream press, but they don't want to talk about the reason the ceiling collapsed, they just keep asking us to describe the horrible things that men did to us.

How many bruises did you have? they ask.

We refuse to answer those questions.

I remind everyone to stick to the script.

We – have – a – political – point – to – make, we say.

And we stick together and we keep to the script.

The Tories want to cleanse London of women like us.

Our point is proven when the housing association offer to move us all to a refuge in Kent.

I take the call and spend a lot of time shouting: HUN-DREDS OF WOMEN ARE BEING TURNED AWAY FROM REFUGES BECAUSE THERE AREN'T ENOUGH BEDS BECAUSE THERESA MAY KEEPS CLOSING THE REF-UGES DOWN – YET **YOU** HAVE AN *EMPTY* REFUGE OUTSIDE OF LONDON READY AND WAITING TO HOUSE US ALL? THIS IS SOCIAL CLEANSING. WE'RE NOT GOING.

The *Les Misérables* soundtrack continues on low volume. It's the Susan Boyle version, which means our spirits are depleted. The kids are awake and noisy as they run around chasing baby rats.

The news reports are up.

Horrible things are being written about us below the line:

They should leave London. If they cared about their kids, then they wouldn't put them through this 'political act'.

(They use quotation marks around the word political act to ridicule us.)

Maybe we *should* go? Maybe we should just shut up and go to Kent, I think. Maybe this isn't our battle to fight?

What are we actually going to achieve locking ourselves in this dangerous house?

We're all tired.

No one is helping us. The journalists want to talk about domestic violence, they don't want to hear our political message.

It's tiring when no one listens, especially when you're living in squalid conditions.

And let's not forget the smell.

The smell of revolution? Well, that doesn't exist.

But poverty. Poverty always has a smell.

It's the smell of West London in 2017 – burned underprivileged flesh and plastic flammable cladding.

It's the smell of vermin piss on the cheap sagging mattresses our children are sleeping on.

It's the smell of the blocked toilet and two buckets of piss that the 13 refuge women and children are having to use.

It's the smell of the pan of vomit in the bath that *no one* will own up to.

But we maintain our stance. We're trying. We want to be rehoused in a refuge close to our support networks and we want to stay together. We need each other. We're all helping each other recover from some very serious abuse. We're like family now.

A *Guardian* journalist takes us to a members' bar just off Portobello Road and we all get very drunk.

'Drink as much as you like – this is on the wallet of the *Guardian*,' she instructs us, half out of kindness and half in order to loosen our lips. The *Guardian* journalist is on our side and she gives Birmingham Yardley MP Jess Phillips my mobile number. Jess calls me at midnight. She's a woman who knows the meaning of sisterhood. Doesn't dismiss me as an idiot who cannot be trusted with my own opinions. She speaks my language. Understands our purpose. Doesn't approach me as if I'm a victim. Because I'm not, I'm not a victim – I'm trying to raise our voices and seek change. I'm leading a goddamn revolution on no sleep inside a rat-infested room with 12 other traumatised people.

We are 48 hours into our attempted revolution and we have Jess Phillips on side.

The next morning groups of journalists arrive to meet us outside Kensington town hall.

They're here to create poverty porn from abused women.

They keep asking us about the kind of violence we had endured. How many times were we raped? How many bruises did we have? How long were you held hostage? How many skipping ropes were wrapped around your neck? How long were you locked under the stairs for? And just *how* scared do you feel?

Will you go on camera? Will you talk about the abuse you have endured to camera? We'll black out your faces ...

I'm fucking angry. I don't want you to hide my face. Because I don't want to *talk* about domestic violence. This *isn't* a story about domestic violence. This is a story much bigger than that. They've cut the funding on this refuge because they don't want women like us in 'the royal borough'. I want to talk to you about what this government has done, what this government is doing. This government has abused me more than any man could. The ceiling has crashed down – in the safehouse – because of government cuts. They let the building rot so they could sell it off. Don't you think it's strange how, despite the fact we have been complaining about the condition of the property for months, they refused to fix it? And how on the night the ceiling crashed in on us they have an empty property available *right now* in Kent to house all of us? Despite hundreds of women being turned away from refuges?

But they *don't* quote me on that.

The papers print a sad little tale of poverty porn. These poor abused women. They don't quote us about government cuts. Not one little quote. Whilst I was in the council building trying to advocate us all a safe bed for the night, the journalists cornered the women who spoke the least English and asked them how scared they were of their ex-husbands.

'We are very scared,' they said. *Obviously.*

They publish articles about scared vulnerable women with black eyes living in terrible conditions, the typical, but many don't attribute it to austerity. They wouldn't let us share our stories on the impact of government cuts. That would mean giving us a voice, that would mean journalists sharing their privilege with an oppressed group of women.

They don't want to lend us their privilege. Not even one quote's worth.

The comments below the line:

How were these 'refuge women' able to set up a Twitter account?

How were these 'refuge women' able to afford mobile phones and laptops?

(They use quotation marks to ridicule us.)

If these women are *so* worried about their safety, why don't they go where the council want to put them?

These women should be grateful they have been offered another refuge, regardless of location. Be *grateful*.

I pay for these women. My taxes are funding these women to live in the most expensive borough in the country!

These women have never worked a day in their lives.

These women pretend to flee violence in order to get a council house.

These women need to get jobs, so they can look after their kids properly.

What kind of woman has a child by an abusive man?

What kind of mother gets into a relationship with a man who tries to kill her?

These women should not expect to live in luxury.

These women, us women, the Refuge Seven, the Refuge Thirteen, the 'Survivors', the Refuge Women – we cannot fight it. Not on our own. Seventy-two hours into our revolution and without any support we are tired. You cannot bring change without support, without backup. It's hard to find the strength to keep speaking up when you have no money, no resources, when you're living in a condemned building. When the one person attempting to lead the revolution has her own shit going on. When journalists refuse a platform and purposefully condescend because their own agenda is more important to their ego than lifting up oppressed women. When society doesn't want to give a voice to working-class women because no one wants an even playing field. Society needs women like us to look down upon.

We turn off the *Les Misérables* soundtrack. It's over. Our children are hungry and none of us got much sleep, so when the council offer Biddy and me a Travelodge in Cricklewood for two nights we take it. We give up. *Just* like the poor people did in the June Rebellion, which inspired Victor Hugo's novel, our revolution is over before it had begun.

I vow to never listen to that soundtrack again.

The council spread the refuge women across the city's Travelodges. No longer a collective. As lone voices we are easier to control.

As lone voices, we lose the little power we had gained.

Abaisse. As they say in Paris.

Oppressed.

Biddy and I, we spend the summer dragging bin bags from B&B to hostel to temporary flat.

The rest of the women do the same and eventually we all become so preoccupied with our own personal survival that we lose contact and purpose.

It's difficult to raise your voice and create change when surviving is hard enough.

The fight culled before it really got going.

But we tried. The strength we collectively felt in those 72 hours showed me that it is possible to *try* to instigate change.

Next time I hope there will be more of us. Each austerity cut, each attack, bonding more of us together.

Soon there will be loads of angry women like me, and next time we'll be prepared.

End of Act I.

PART THREE:

POVERTY

12

THE WAGE DON'T FIT

MY WORTH IS 14 pence per minute. I live in eight-minute segments. And when those eight minutes are up, I start again. Start with the next 14 pence and slowly work my way through the next eight minutes, as slowly or as quickly as time will allow.

If you are swift of mind you've probably already worked out that eight minutes is £1. Or thereabouts. Well, it's actually £1.12, *exactly* – if your worth is 14 pence per minute.

Eight minutes can feel like a very long time if the situation isn't to your liking. Eight minutes is four pages of dry dialogue in a heavy film script.

Or a more than reasonable amount of time to spend on a rowing machine in the gym.

Eight minutes is far too long to wait for the Tube.

Eight minutes was the length of time it took terrorists to kill eight men and women in the 2017 London Bridge attack.

But you *can* do a lot with eight minutes of time. You can fly from Heathrow to Brighton on a light jet. You can read four chapters of a Bukowski novel. Watch a whole episode of a BBC Three sitcom. You can have a lifesaving conversation with a kind voice at the end of a telephone line with a Samaritan's volunteer. You can even run a whole mile in eight minutes if you're feeling up to the job.

But. You can only ever earn £1.12 in eight minutes if your worth is 14 pence – and that won't get you very far.

I am part of the underclass that is the low-paid self-employed. It consists mainly of single mothers, immigrants and miscellaneous others unable to catch a break in austerity-driven Britain. We are educated yet unemployable. Experienced yet disposable. We are the people without support networks or families. Souls without safety nets. No mum to call when you're having a bad day. No sofa to surf when your relationship breaks down. There are no grandparents for our children. No guarantor for your housing rental. And forget ever owning your own home. You'll never make the deposit. There – is – no – inheritance.

There are lots of us, but we are alone.

There is nowhere to go at Christmas, and there hasn't been for over 20 years now.

We are a subculture of society who can barely afford to feed ourselves, yet we will never be deemed 'in need' enough to qualify for social housing. We pay market rents and share beds with our children. We dance the boundaries of benefits yet sometimes drift into a low tax bracket. We are 'gig economy' workers, devoid of rights, devoid of hours. We are zero. We are less than zero. We are forced into self-employment. We are Aldi's target audience and the cause of Philip Hammond's awkward smirk.

'There are no unemployed,' he lies. Thanks to people like me.

We take what we can, whenever we can. We'll work at 4am for less than minimum wage and at 11pm for the same. We'll work in exchange for a product that we might be able to shift on eBay. Anything, for anything. But it usually amounts to nothing.

And because I am so desperate to keep us in London, our beautiful yet poisonous home city of London, I will do *anything*. Tax returns are often dull but mine depicts a sordid tapestry of life for the modern-day working class: web psychic, writer of porn, sex chat-line operator, mystery shopper, eBay seller, virtual assistant, miscellaneous anything – I'd sell my cunt if peak cunt-selling hours weren't in the evening and so require expensive childcare. I'd sell my own *soul* if someone would put a decent value on it. However, you only have to spend a few minutes on Instagram to see that souls are traded for a hashtag ad with a supermarket coupon if you'll share your undying love for Petits Filous with your 5,000-plus followers. And I can't give *that* to my landlord. My landlord is all good for fromage frais, thank you very much – he earns a fortune from my rent. And the other 16 properties he owns.

I will do *anything*. I've even taken to selling my own dumbed-down and palatable tales of poverty porn and abuse to magazines like *Closer* and *Take a Break* for a quick £400.

Job number 1 – Kiss 'n' tell girl of misery porn

Chat to a young 'journalist' for 20 minutes over the phone about your experience of domestic violence, drug addiction, a friend of a friend who had acid thrown in their face, the six months you spent working on *Babestation* – let them use your name and picture, and they'll create a sad little story around you to suit their agenda that week. Just – give – them – what – they – want. I want to stay in my home city of London and I want to be able to feed my daughter, so I will give *anyone* what they want. It is said that you cannot buy morals and who am I to argue with that? I cannot even afford to buy baked beans some weeks.

Job number 2 – Sort of drug dealer

Without the support of family and without the luxury of affordable childcare you are placed in a position where you must make work fit around school hours. It means you are thrown face to face with the filthy undermining jobs that anyone with healthy self-esteem (otherwise known as privilege) would turn their noses up at, and you end up working every waking hour yet never quite managing to make minimum wage, but *still* having to pay market value for your private rental. How can you possibly compete with that when the playing field was so uneven from the start?

Our rent is £1,500 per month. It's a tiny one-bed flat in Kentish Town, a nice neighbourhood, but my daughter doesn't have her own room. It's basically a studio with a sliding partition shoved in the middle to create a small separate bedroom. Which we share. I'll never have sex ever again and she'll never be able to have a sleepover. It's tiny. It would take just under 14 pence's worth of time to do the full tour.

It's on the ground floor of a rough estate where every night between 5pm and 1am the moped gang hang out to distribute their winnings – mainly iPhones and flashy engagement rings mugged from middle-aged women brazenly dressed in £500 gilets walking toy dogs by the Heath. It's horrible that they get scared by the wild boys of this pov life, but at least they can take solace in their ability to replace what they lost, it's only things. Most of these boys will grow into lost men if they don't get stabbed to death before they turn 16. They come and go in little groups for half an hour at a time, like little Artful Dodgers in baseball caps, bringing back shiny things, and then off the next group go. It seems to work well for them.

Clifton (the guy who owns the boys) sits in his Volvo parked outside my flat eating a seemingly never-ending supply of KFC like some hungry Fagin draped in gold. He looks scary but he's always really nice to me, often helping with my shopping bags when I'm struggling up the road and complimenting Biddy on her Arsenal shirt. He occasionally knocks on my door with a freshly rolled joint in exchange for use of my Wi-Fi. I save up the joints and sell them on to my friends who have spare cash lying around for doing fun things like getting stoned. I sell each joint for a tenner a piece. It's a good profit, the margins are unreal. Although I cannot work out what the profit margins are on something you get for free but could potentially impact on your liberty. Although, to be honest, I'm more worried about the weird things KFC Fagin could be searching for on my IP address. I'm constantly anxious that I could be implicated in the thefts, but it's a risk I'm willing to take for a whole ten pounds.

That's the electricity topped up.

'You get the best weed, you're my favourite dealer,' Clover says, and sometimes she'll kindly share the joint with me.

Job number 3: Sell-out

I first met the artist Reg Williams whilst living in Soho in my twenties. I write his name in full like you might have heard of him, but you haven't. He was just another talented, beautiful loser living in obscurity. The night I met him, some years before the economic crash, I'd been on a first date with a man whose name I cannot recall. I'd informed my date that I appreciated the gesture of someone making a date memorable and he really did try his best – he took me as his plus one to his recently deceased father's funeral. It was a bold move and one I appreciated but didn't much enjoy. You don't get to see someone in their best light as they weep over the sausage roll buffet at the wake. And despite it being one of my more memorable first dates I cannot for the life of me remember his name no matter how hard I try. I remember he had crackhead cheekbones and wore mascara like those kinds of guys did back then but …

But I *do* remember Reg Williams. And how it was the night we became friends. I'd not that long ago chucked Kingsley out of our shared flat and got an injunction against him after he'd held a pink Gillette lady razor to my throat, and since then I was living life with a sense of abandon. I always did whenever I got free of him for a few months. During the day I worked as a theatrical agent and by night as a stripper. In between all that I wrote plays and stories and hung out with celebrities at AA meetings. In my head I was part of the secret Soho scene, a hedonistic crew.

But really, I was just a chancer and a fake, searching for a version of myself that could never exist. I've never been hip. But meeting Reg Williams completed the image of myself I was desperate to create. He made me want to dress like one of those sexy hipster women who hang off the arm of Terry Richardson types, in bondage clothes and fedora hats and stylishly smudged lipstick like all those girls who hang around with artists always do. Who speak in a language of innuendo and smut. Who grew up with nice families and strong safety nets but like to pretend to be on the difficult end of life for a few years. Living on tins of chickpeas and sofa surfing in Dalston. Method actors of the middle class. Doing an entertaining impersonation of a woman going off the rails. Starting a blog about their bi-monthly drug addiction. Giving blow jobs to everyone on the tour bus of some crappy band from Berlin. Selling sex for a week as a bit of fun to shock their friends back in Godalming and curating witty self-aware Facebook statuses about how many STDs they caught this week – safe in the knowledge it's easy to live on the edge when you know you can return home at any time. I've always wanted to be like that.

After the wake with the nameless date, I suggested we stop off for a green tea and cheesecake at Bar Italia on Frith Street as an attempt to cheer him up. We sat outside chain-smoking Marlboro Menthols and taking in suburbia's finest on a night out 'up west' searching for sex and bohemia, and because I had no intention of getting off with the man in mourning with mascara down his face, I ended up falling into conversation with a group of musicians who had just performed over the road at Ronnie Scott's and some trumpet player introduced me to 'the Soho legend' Reg Williams.

He was the most wonderful creature I had ever encountered. He looked like Charles Bukowski, all scarred face, scowling and ravaged from some kind of traumatic life I used to consider romantic. But as he took my hand to shake it, he said, 'Pleased to meet you' in a gentle voice like Ben Whishaw as Paddington Bear, before flashing a smile to reveal a tongue in prison to his last remaining teeth. He looked about 75, older, and he smelled like a man who had given up on taking care of himself some decades before. He had long, matted grey hair pulled into a bun at the back of his head that was of course topped with a fedora. He had a walking stick and a constant cough that erupted out of him with every exhale of smoke. He looked like a man who used to be tall and strong, perhaps even handsome, but he was now hunched over with a skin so bleached yellow I could view all his veins and organs slowly failing him. I think I even glimpsed some fragments of his soul which were haemorrhaging from its frail old core. I was capti- vated by him in the most platonic way possible and it appeared that the feeling was mutual. He was smoking weed and passed the joint my way.

We chatted into the night about nothing I can remember but it was a beautiful connection, and it meant I was able to ignore my gormless date who by now was reciting his dead dad's poetry into the lap of a Bulgarian waitress whose English wasn't good enough to tell him to shut up. At 5am they close Bar Italia for an hour to prepare for the 9-to-5ers and that was when I helped Reg walk back to his flat, which I discovered was only a street away from mine.

He lived on the top floor of William Blake House, a high- rise on the edge of Soho's crack triangle. He was one of the few remaining council tenants left in the block, most of the flats had been bought up in the 80s and had since been traded in and sold to buy-to-let landlords for up to £1 million.

'The snakes from the local estate agents are always wait- ing around in the corridors to slither up my trousers. One cornered me in the lift and offered to lend me the money for

Right to Buy – I get a big discount because I've been here for forty years – then in three years' time I sell up and we split the profits. Half a million in his pocket, half a million in mine – minus the £400,000 they loaned me. I'm not falling for it, it'll price me out, they just want the bums and artists like me out of Soho. They place no value on community.'

His small studio was cluttered and smoke stained. Worth a whole £1 million if you're willing to sell your morals. He didn't have a bed, just a mattress on the floor, there were beer cans close to where he lay his head and an ashtray that looked as if it hadn't been emptied in months by normal standards, but probably only two days in Reg Williams' case. Despite the chaos there was a surprising number of potted plants forming a jungle by the balcony which he obviously tended to in lieu of himself, and covering every space of the wall were the most beautiful pieces of art I had ever seen. Crudely painted nudes of the same woman over and over, and a bloody tryptic of war planes crashing.

'Why are you not rich and famous, Reg Williams?' I asked.

He lit another joint and laughed for a short while, which prompted his emphysema to consume his body for a few minutes, and I sat there not knowing what to do as he reached for his oxygen mask. After about ten minutes he was able to answer.

'Because I never sold out,' he growled as he grabbed the oxygen mask once again.

When he was able to breathe almost normally again (in between coughing fits where he would throw up chunks of bright blood into a never-ending series of clean kerchiefs), he told me how as a young man he'd managed to make some kind of living selling his paintings in Covent Garden alongside his sculptress wife (who had since gone away yet remained living on his walls), thanks to being given a council flat and affordable rent. He was happy living a simple life, selling his own work and taking the odd commission whilst having enough to eat and travel. Then one day in the 1980s he was approached with a life-changing offer. He told me that a high-street chemist had wanted to replicate one of his pieces and mass produce it on plates, mugs and teapots. It was a small fortune that would have enabled him and his wife to buy their council flat and eventually sell it on for a profit that would provide for them both forever.

He turned down their offer because he hated the idea of a chemist profiting from art, and they pulled in another artist to rip off his work for a quarter of the cost. He didn't have enough money to pursue a claim in court; his wife was resentful that he had turned down the opportunity for a more affluent life and she left him a year later for his best friend. He hadn't picked up a paint brush since, preferring instead to live a life of self-sabotage like a true artist.

'I couldn't sell out to a corporation. When you take the money, you murder the truth.'

And that was the night I met my great friend, the artist Reg Williams.

He was someone I looked up to, and over the years, as our friendship grew, he treated me like the daughter he'd always wanted (he was estranged from his real one, the child of the woman in the paintings). He came to see all my half-formed plays and sat in dingy bars watching my terrible country punk band – named after a chapter in the Alcoholics Anonymous Big Book, and Reg said it was the worst piece of shit he'd ever heard (and he was right) but he always encouraged me to keep on writing my little stories and plays despite the constant rejection letters. He never once looked at me with disappointment. He was the closest thing I'd had to a father since I left my parents and their abuse behind as a teenager.

He was upset when I fell pregnant though. He felt I had great things to achieve and becoming a single mum would hamper everything. But when Biddy was born, he proudly took on the role of grandad and restored a beautiful old Victorian rocking horse for her that he'd pulled from a skip in Mayfair. He even spoke about how he might start painting again, the energy of a new birth providing him with a short-lived lease of life.

Reg was on the way out, he had been since the night we met. But the day was getting ever closer now so when Biddy was at nursery I'd go around to his studio, cook him some food, which was a pointless gesture because he'd lost the remainder of his teeth, and tidy up the place. When I was washing up that was when he'd wank. He never asked me to get involved and he somehow managed to keep an air of dignity during the act. Maybe it was because I had so much admiration for him that he could get away with it. He'd start off discreetly, staring at the plants on the balcony that looked all the way to Waterloo, but the emphysema breath always gave the game away. When you mix an orgasm with terminal lung disease, you are always one breath away from death. I always hoped I would be able to make it out of there with him still alive. As he finished, I would throw him the tea towel so he could mop the clumps of dying man's cum off his trousers and then he'd help me finish the dishes.

He'd always hand me £20 as I left.

That's the food shop covered.

A few days before he died, he said that one day if I ever got the opportunity to write about all of this that I shouldn't hold back. 'Never be afraid to tell the absolute truth. Let everyone know what it's like out there and the horrible things you have to do. Tell everyone what a dirty old man I was. And how I sold out by following my base instincts and murdered the truth of our friendship.'

I sold out too, I said, as I slipped the twenty into my pocket.

Everyone has their price. It's just not always monetary, I realised. Mine is though. £20.

And I'm not sure how to describe this role on my tax return so I let it slide like some kind of silent and pointless act of defiance against corporate tax havens – but one that is now likely to land me in shit after admitting it *here*. I probably shouldn't share these kinds of things under a government that encourages multinational corporations to avoid tax yet forces the poorest and most vulnerable to starve to death in a choice between heating or eating. But what's the point in all this if you don't read the truth?

When Reg died, I lost another source of income, and the closest thing I'd ever had to a father.

I didn't go to his funeral because I didn't want to say goodbye to the fantasy life I'd created – plus I couldn't find a date. I only go to funerals these days if it's a first date. So instead of heading to the church I stopped by his flat, collected up his cruelly unsold art and ... stole them. I placed them around my tiny overpriced flat because deep down in my heart I knew that I could sell them on eBay for a few quid if I ever needed to. I think it's what Reg Williams would have wanted.

Job number 4 – Sex chat-line operator

Biddy is at school. I'm preparing dinner. I allocate three eight-minute segments to the task. Then, when she gets home, I can just bung it in the oven. You know the drill.

I'm using the best-quality mince I can find from a budget supermarket. I like to mix in a large tablespoon of honey, *indulge* a big dollop of Lazy Garlic from a jar and then I pop in quite a lot of salt, whatever cheap dried herbs are in the cupboard and a little bit of pepper too.

I don't really enjoy mixing up raw meat with my hands because it gets messy and also because I'm trying to be vegan, but Deliciously Ella takes me over budget, and Biddy does need to eat so I've decided that it's worth it.

The phone rings.

Don't stop what you are doing.

Make – sure – you – answer – that – phone.

(I like to multitask during my eight-minute segments.)

The thing is, you can't *not* multitask when 14 pence is at stake, even if that *is* all you are worth.

So, whether it is mixing up cheap cuts of fatty meat, doing the washing up or cleaning your teeth – you answer that phone.

And you make that task goddamn sexual.

'What's that noise?' my callers ask. They like to believe you are engaged in the moment, that you are there with them, hanging out in your bed all day bonking yourself silly with your lesbian flatmate's dildo or fucking all the plumbers that keep arriving at your door whilst awaiting their 14 pence of stereotypical sex chat (because they *all* say exactly the same thing).

So.

The burger mince is my fanny. The – *sound* – of – mince – mixed – with – budget – honey – is – my – fanny.

Doing the washing up translates as having a 'kinky time' in a soapy bath, and cleaning your teeth becomes sucking your vibrator, obvs – because who *doesn't* suck their vibrator for fun?!

It keeps them cumming and it keeps them coming back.

Return callers are your bread and butter.

A loaf of bread? Six times 14p.

Butter? Eleven times 14p.

And if they happen to call you whilst your buttering the toasted bread? Well, it's obvious, isn't it – you're scraping dried shit off your bedsheets.

Some of your callers *will* be into that.

But when the phone stops ringing, or you just don't have the emotional energy to make soul-destroying sex noises in response to sweet nothings about scatting, then you need to tackle one of the other low-ranking jobs on your list.

Job number 5 – Web psychic

Translation: Lying to people desperate to believe that someday *someone* might fall in love with them. Or pretending their dead mum has a message for them. They love a dead mum message on the psychic webchat. Mother said: *You're going to get through all of this – you're going to be OK*. If my mum was dead, that's the message I'd want to receive.

Job number 6 – Selling what's left of your life on eBay

The artwork of Reg Williams. Starting bid – 0.99p. No reserve. Collection only.

Job number 7 – Mystery shopper

'Get a proper job!' reads the comments section in the *Daily Mail*.

How? I ask. Proper jobs just don't exist for people in my position.

And the wage don't fit.

An email hits my inbox: I've just been offered a 'job' that will make me a grand total of £10. I'll take it, I grab it, I'll do it – I say. When you are part of the self-employed underclass every tenner counts. It's a 30-minute job, which actually is a nice little deal in my desperate little world.

It's a simple job. I have to go to a shoe shop, try on a pair of shoes and purchase them. I return the shoes to the mystery shopping company along with the receipt. I fill in a question-naire judging the sales adviser's performance and the mystery shopper company pay me my tenner at the end of their working week. They also refund the purchase and postage. Done deal.

Of course, the whole concept is insane, you're poor yet you're investing £80 on shoes plus £11 on Special Delivery postage before you've even made your £10. All that spend-ing for £10. But that's the kind of thing you do when you're forced into self-employment. Every single penny counts. Like, you'll walk the rapey route home alone at 2am after another low-paid, miscellaneous job instead of spending £1.50 on the bus. £1.50 means so much to you that you'll risk a rape.

Every penny, you need *every* penny. When the cashier at the Co-op hands you change for a twenty instead of a ten – you don't speak up. You're not in a position right now to afford morals. Maybe one day. That's the dream, isn't it? To afford morals. To afford morals and some Converse trainers without holes in. That's actually the dream.

Little wins: Someone forgetting to pick up a £5 note at the self-service till, discovering some change in a coat you haven't worn for a year, a *generous* £2 tip from a caller on the sex chatline.

I winced as I handed over the £80 for the shoes. For the mystery shop. Because, £80, well that's roughly our monthly food and toiletries bill. But I'd done other jobs for this particular company before and I knew they were good for the money. I just kept telling myself – it's only half an hour's work, and you won't have to please a man, and you won't have to feel ashamed and the money will be back in your account by the end of the week.

But they said I hadn't returned the shoes even though I'd emailed them proof of postage and sent them the receipt for the shoes.

A week passed. A couple of weeks passed. Our food supplies dwindling until every meal was a bowl of pasta. Pasta topped with sugar for breakfast and plain for all the other meals apart from the time I found a pound coin outside Gospel Oak train station and I splurged on a tin of tomatoes, an onion, a bulb of garlic and a Freddo bar from the Co-op.

After at least 15 consecutive bowls of pasta I decided it was time to call the mystery shopping company.

We'd been exchanging emails for weeks.

They had received the receipt for the shoes.

And the special delivery receipt with the tracking number.

But the tracking number said the parcel was still in the post office in Kentish Town.

I'd been to the post office in Kentish Town, they said they'd tried to deliver it to the company.

I was advised to put in a claim with Royal Mail.

I put in a claim.

Royal Mail said they'd tried to deliver it, so they cancelled the claim.

That's privatisation for you.

And the company were refusing to pay.

I was as confused as that whole sorry tale sounds. But the point is that my account remained empty and that £80 was gone, and the £11 postage was gone, and I still hadn't been paid my tenner despite filling out the questionnaire. Half an hour's work, and I'd paid £91 for the privilege.

'All I want is my money, I really … *need* it.' I sobbed down the phone. 'Can I speak to your manager?'

'No.'

'Can I email your manager?'

'No.'

'Can I have your manager's name?'

'No.'

'Well … I'll just … *Google* your manager's name!'

'Google him. He won't speak to you. He wouldn't want to speak to *you.*'

'But. My money,' I say.

'You're NOT going to get your money,' she said, with a cruelty reserved for *PMQs*. '*But*. As a gesture of good will, we've agreed to pay for the postage and your £10 fee.'

'A gesture of good will?! That's *my* £80. £80! I'm going to have to go to a food bank this afternoon. My doctor gave me a voucher for the food bank this morning. Your company has put me and my daughter in a really *shitty* situation ...'

'DON'T YOU DARE SWEAR AT ME!'

'I'm not swearing at you. I promise. I just meant that this is a shitty situation.'

'You're swearing at me! Don't you dare swear at me.'

'I'm not, I just mean ...'

I paused.

'I'm not getting my money back, am I?'

'No.'

Then, I searched my mind for the obscenest words I could think of: 'NASTY TORY. YOU VOTED TORY. DIDN'T YOU? I BET YOU DID. YOU LACK COMPASSION AND KINDNESS AND EMPATHY. TORY!'

She didn't deny it. So, I called her stupid.

'Don't swear at me!' she said.

'Oh. COME ON. What world are you in where *stupid* is a swear word?! You really are stupid! And *that's* why YOU vote Tory, because you're STUPID. You work as an office manager, at a mystery shopping company in *Staffordshire*, which means you can't earn more than twenty grand a year.

Twenty grand. If that! At most! And you're a *Tory* voter. On a measly twenty grand. STUPID! You're a nasty Tory who lacks compassion and empathy. You're stupid! You're stupid! STUPID!'

'Don't swear at me! Stop swearing at me! Don't swear at me!'

'I'm not swearing at you.'

Wait.

'Wait. *Sorry*. Please. *Please*.' (I begged.) 'Please just listen to me. I'm desperate. Please. Just pay me what you owe me. Please. I know it's not a lot to you. Not to you. With your twenty-grand job in Staffordshire, because up there you're rich on that. You're a success! But. That £80. It's *my* money. That £80 is *everything* to me. Everything. *Please*. I can't go to the food bank. I can't take my daughter to a food bank. Please. If we can just have our £80, we can eat like normal people.'

She said no.

Then I called her a cunt and that was the end of that.

Nothing is my main source of income, it's a drip here, a drip there. Every silver bit of change that comes my way gets thrown in a jar to save up for Christmas to buy my daughter a gift that she won't be ashamed to tell her friends about but there is always a bill that requires every last bit of cash.

The jar gets filled briefly but it is nearly always emptied again.

It's not an ideal situation but at least we have a home for the time being, until one of the income streams die and the eviction process begins.

It is a constant struggle to make rent. I need an absolute minimum of 12,000 minutes-worth of 14ps and only then will I just about make the rent, then I have to dive into one of my other jobs in order to look for something else to make the council tax too.

There's food and utilities too, but remember, I've got joints and wanks for that. And every Friday is the joy of tax credits, which you can scrape by on for a short while on the weeks when zero hours really does mean zero.

This is why I currently have six jobs. This is the reason I live my life in eight-minute segments.

But that's just life for single mothers (with no family support or savings) on low wages in Tory Britain. The choice between listening to a man pleasure himself or visiting a food bank. The choice between a compromised dignity or none at all. Between zero hours humiliation or homelessness.

So, make a fucking choice. Take every demoralising job that comes your way or kill yourself in the midst of a housing benefits sanction, which will happen eventually when they decide they need to cleanse some more women and children out of the city. Everyone living in underclass precarity is just one housing benefit 'investigation' away from homelessness. However, keep this in your head – if you take 14 sleeping pills with as much alcohol as you can stomach without vomiting (remember not to vomit or it voids your mission), then it will take roughly eight minutes for your body to shut down. For good. Eight minutes, or thereabouts.

Remember: you are only *ever* eight minutes away from a way out.

13
FOOD HAUL

THE COUNTRY IS NOT in an official state of emergency but the Salvation Army Centre in Chalk Farm is filled with the walking wounded of austerity. A team of upbeat volunteers sit inside makeshift booths separated by plastic curtains like the underfunded beds in A&E and the queue leads all the way around the corner to the side street with well-maintained Georgian houses that stand pristine in the shadow of gentrified cladded towers. Biddy and I make it to the front and we hand over our green food-bank voucher to a man who signs us in. He tells us that we'll only be allowed three visits in the year and each visit will grant us with three days' worth of food. He delivers it in the most upbeat way possible, like 'yes, it is laryngeal cancer but it's only stage 2 – there's a lot we can do!' It's like some kind of disaster party in here. A passer-by could easily mistake us for guests at a cheap shotgun-wedding if we didn't have so much desperation sweating off us. If we weren't so zealously collecting tinned foods. He takes the voucher and asks how many people are in my household – it's just me and my daughter – and he takes my name. In exchange for all of this we are given a raffle ticket, which doesn't offer the hope of winning a cheap sweet Hungarian wine like you would at the school summer fayre tombola, but some kindly donated tins and instant mash would be wonderful.

Another volunteer, a woman in a wheelchair, glides us across the hall to the waiting area where we are told to sit with some other families on those brown faux-leather chairs usually found in hospices.

'They'll call your number when they have your food!' She is *so* upbeat, wheeling around the church hall like a TGI Friday's waitress working her arse off for tips – I half expect her to hand me the cocktail menu and point me in the direction of the specials board, but she just smiles before zooming off to fetch the next food-bank family. She is being hospitable for *free*.

Outside the hall, a crowd of mothers with toddlers in buggies hold their food vouchers in their hands nervously, waiting to get into the room with the bags of food that will erase the feelings of emptiness for the next few days. The woman on the chair next to me (who I hadn't noticed until she spoke) is sitting with her teenage daughter and leans over to ask how long this usually takes because she's got to get back to work.

'I don't know, this is my first time.' I talk low and stare ahead as I try not to notice her.

We don't speak again.

It's rowdy in here. It's like Friday night at closing time and we're the last few standing awaiting an invitation to the pub lock-in. The ones who create noise to hide the shame of the early-daylight drink, the part of the night where you have to force the fun otherwise you start to question the point of your existence. The invisible loudmouths. And just like them, us queuing at the food bank don't dare make eye contact in our shame despite the fact we are sharing this unique moment together. We are talking, we are even laughing, but we are numbing our minds to the event. We are all filled with so much shame. Deleting each moment from our minds as it happens. Consciously blurring the faces and muting the voices around me. The woman who has just spoken to me, I couldn't tell you what she looks like, but I know she is carrying a mop and bucket and wearing a pink tabard. I don't smile at or acknowledge the children drinking squash at the table opposite me, but I notice the squash is orange and that the volunteers have placed red and white chequered cloths on the buffet tables.

I don't want to ever have to remember that people had to do this.

Eventually you just get tired, don't you? All humans do at some point. I'm not talking about being a bit run-down or needing a holiday or those early days of motherhood that go by in a blur due to sleep deprivation. I'm talking about being *so* tired from just about surviving on the smallest amounts of cash despite working every hour you can find and finally realising that you're out of options. There is no way out of this. No matter how hard you work you can't afford to fill the cupboards to feed your daughter. You are no longer surviving. You're begging. This is the final humiliation – and where do you go from there? I am so close to giving up. To writing my resignation letter.

One thing I've noticed over the years about friends who've died from terminal diseases is how happy they become in the days leading up to their death. It's like their mind has had a conversation with their body and they've reached a ceasefire. They've signed a treaty and said – wouldn't it just be great if we didn't have to worry about all this? If we didn't have to go into battle each day? Let's have an amicable divorce. Let's just accept that this is over.

And with the burden of battle off their shoulders they are full of life again. Like they haven't spent the last few months chained to drips being pumped full of poison. Their skin becomes luminous, their smiles stretch wide, they crave platters of fruit to nurture them and there is no talk of the past or future. They are so at ease with themselves that they can fully live in the moment.

A few days before my friend Simone died, I went and sat with her for a few hours in her room at the St Christopher's Hospice in Sydenham. I'd been trying to avoid visiting her for a while, not because I'm a terrible human who didn't want to spend time with her but because the Simone who I was visiting was no longer the person I had known. She was only 27 but she looked hard-life late forties. She was already dead as far as I was concerned, her scrawny face was contorted into a perpetual look of terror and she talked morphine gibberish to all who visited. It didn't seem to matter if anyone was with her and I didn't want to remember her like this, so I ignored her, put her away and awaited my funeral invite.

Six months earlier she had been diagnosed with a rare vaginal tumour and in order to save her life the doctors had to cut out her *entire* vagina. The whole thing was dug out of her. The ovaries and the cervix and the lips all gone. The entire area an infected war zone wound. And Simone was a woman who loved her vagina, she used hers more than anyone I had ever met. But she took the removal well, all things considered, and went into remission. She joked that she was a J.G. Ballard creation (*Crash* was her favourite book) and, when the extra-large tampon she was forced to wear to protect her wound fell out of her on a busy Sunday morning at Parliament Hill Lido, she got a kick out of the humiliation it caused other people. The middle-class parents shielding their precious children's eyes from the filth of disease. She even made the lifeguard pick up the jumbo tampon because she wanted to witness the disgust on his face. *Nothing* could embarrass Simone.

The next thing we heard the cancer was back, and now it was *everywhere*. Within weeks her parents wheeled her into the hospice to die. I visited regularly and feigned optimistic chatter but then I stopped going.

However, rumour had come my way that she was on her final few days and I decided that despite not wanting to see her weak life finish I knew that the *right* thing to do would be to head over to the hospice and say one last goodbye, despite the fact I'd said my official farewells when she was still lucid. I did it to appease my own guilt for abandoning her, not to give her comfort. I'm as selfish as everyone else there during visiting hours. When I walked into her room I was surprised to find her sat up in one of those brown chairs, continuously eating satsumas and watching old episodes of our favourite show, *Brass Eye*. She no longer looked scared so I got under the blanket with her and we didn't make a sound except to laugh throughout 'Paedogeddon'. As the credits rolled I turned to her to tell her that she looked like her old self. Maybe she was getting better? The doctors can get these things wrong. I was glad I came. I spouted the usual comments about how she was 'so brave' and that I wish I had the courage to live my life without fear, like she did.

She peeled another satsuma and started talking:

It was only when I knew it was over that I started living.
  She confided.
We spend our lives attempting to save face.
Worrying about what people think of us.
Curating an image to portray to the world.
People pleasing.
Doing things we don't want to do.
Not saying what we mean.
Holding back.
Never taking chances.

We don't tell that guy we like him.

Or that abusive prick that we NEED to leave.

Spending hours second-guessing.

Apologising for things we haven't even done.

Trying not to offend.

Never happy with ourselves.

Dressing to flatter our bodies.

Whatever THAT even means.

Worried we'll be held up as fools.

By who?

Another human fool.

But nothing is as humiliating as death.

As you start to die, everything that is within is desperate
    to crawl out.

Everything that has been trapped within.

It needs to come out.

Here's something that needs to come out:

You were a cunt, a proper cunt for not visiting me.

You're a cunt, Cash.

That's out there now.

And I forgive you.

Everything comes out. Everything within the human.

It has to come out.

The most humiliating thing of all is yet to happen.

For me, for you, for everyone.

The piss, shit, vomit, semen, blood.

All of it.

Escaping because you no longer provide it with purpose.
The ultimate humiliation.
That's the only point when we face real humiliation.
Nothing can truly worry you when you realise that.
The final humiliation will come.
But if it happens we're dead, so we don't even know
about it!

I left thinking that I'd probably see her again, but within days her body exploded all over the hospice walls. Blood, piss, shit and guts everywhere. How embarrassing.

So, I'm here, I'm at the food bank and we're finally being called into one of the curtained-off booths and I remember Simone's words as I attempt to convince myself that visiting a food bank in order to feed my daughter *isn't* the most humiliating thing that will ever happen to me. I remind myself that I am merely a product of a systematic government-sanctioned attack on the most vulnerable in society and, although it brings me to my knees, there are worse things that can happen, right? The worst is yet to come.

Nothing breaks me. Does it? The black eye. The train. The peep show. The DNA paternity test. The arrest. The low-paid dehumanising jobs that do not even allow me to survive. They don't break me. Nothing breaks me. I almost enjoyed those moments in exchange for the stories I will get to tell in the future. I'm always alright. Aren't I? Those times were tough but none of them smacked me hard in the gut.

This might not be the most humiliating thing that can happen to me but this *is* my breaking point. And I'm starting to realise that once you've been broken you will never fully heal. My broken cheekbone from Grantham? Whenever my right cheekbone hurts I know it is about to rain. It's not because I've got 'the gift', it's because damp has an effect on broken bones. I'll always be weakened by the attack. By all the attacks. Always be slightly cracked. I mean, you can use the best superglue on the market to stick the handle back on your favourite Sports Direct mug, but it'll smash to pieces eventually.

And this is it. This is where I break. It's big. This is O.J. Simpson's comeuppance. This is Lance Armstrong's final drug test. This is Charlie Sheen's positive result. Since the day I fled violence, my life has been leading up to this and I think it's only going to get worse; once you're on your knees doesn't that just become your way of life?

In Alcoholics Anonymous they have a saying that only when you hit rock bottom can you rise up. But if you're a working-class woman living in modern Britain then rock bottom is the first day of accepting that you'll never be able to get back on your feet again and just getting on with it. When there is no one to reach out their hand to lift you to your feet, where do you find the energy to rise up?

Breaking point:
   'Have you been eating?' my doctor asks.

I'd gone in to ask for a Valium prescription, something to take the edge of my decline – why is she asking me about my diet?

'I'm really stressed right now, I just need a few nights' sleep,' I tell her.

This much is true. The night-time is relentless, I haven't slept properly in months.

I couldn't even tell you what day it is. My daughter reminds me if it is a school day or not. She could easily get out of school if she wanted, tell me it's a Saturday, I wouldn't know. But she goes to school, probably to escape the misery of me. I've fallen behind on all four of my payday loans because payday hasn't happened in quite some time and I seem to spend a lot of my life hiding behind the sofa and walking around in the dark, so it looks like no one is home when the bailiffs come knocking.

'I'm eating,' I tell the doctor.

The pasta and sugar diet. It bloats your tummy, makes your face rubbery. I have a slim, albeit watery physique at this time and I'll never meet the love of my life looking like this, but I've got other things on my plate (not – food – though) beyond being concerned about my physical appearance. I go three days at a time without washing, I do the school run bra-less, my hair is rarely brushed and I always look like I'm heading off on a park run, but of course I do not have the energy to exercise. Because it does something to your sleep, the food of poverty, it's unsustainable – you are in a constant state of lethargy, yet your eyes never remain closed for long.

'I just need a few nights' sleep,' I say again.

But she's asking all these questions, prying into my life.

Asking what I do for work, who I live with, how often I exercise, just how low my mood has been recently and most crucially – WHAT ARE WE EATING?

'The last few weeks? Just pasta,' I say.

'And your daughter? Is she getting enough fruit and vegetables?'

'My daughter is *fine*. She eats enough, she's alright, I promise. She's really healthy. All the kids get fruit and vegetables at school.'

Free school dinners, they are the only thing keeping her strong right now. The only thing stopping her from slipping into hunger's version of the perpetual bad acid trip that I am currently on *is* the free school dinners. But this week is half-term so the hot meal at lunch is gone and the break-time fruit snack is not available and it's just … pasta. It's *just* pasta. And although she never complains I know she'd do anything for a Chicken Cottage bucket or a bunch of grapes to gorge on, anything that is not plain pasta.

'But we're doing OK!' I have suddenly gained the overly vivacious persona and gurning smile of a YouTuber. You get good at pretending everything is going OK. I do it for Biddy.

I never cry. Not these days. Not even when I'm alone. My mind is always taking me back to the yellow-eyed solicitor at Charing Cross Police Station – don't act mad or they'll refer you to social services. You don't act mad in front of the feds and you don't start sobbing about your lack of food in front of your doctor. I cannot have my daughter taken away, we are hungry but at least we have each other – we are each other's only blood. And one day, if I keep working hard then I will be deserving enough to feed her properly.

The doctor is really young. Straight out of medical school, I reckon, and she seems eager to help. She pulls out a green voucher from her drawer, it's for the food bank. It looks like something from the 1950s, like a relic in a glass case at the Imperial War Museum depicting the demoralising period of rationing. She gently tells me the opening hours and prints off a map, and I collect Biddy from the waiting area and we head on down to the Salvation Army by Chalk Farm.

Half of the room is being used as a soup kitchen and the other half consists of the queue for the food bank. The homeless queue is all men, the food-bank queue is all women and children. It's like the beginning of a school disco, the nervous boys and girls coyly distancing themselves from each other as they prepare to make their moves, only we are all devoid of the anticipation of beautiful possibilities and an awkward kiss at the end of the night. It's just sad. The only thing you'll be leaving here with is tins and a battered ego.

... They are lovely. The volunteers at the food bank.

'I'm sorry about the wait. We're really busy today. We're always busy over school holidays!'

The woman in the wheelchair gives Biddy a Danish pastry and some toys which she stuffs in her pocket, along with a handful of biscuits she has secretly stashed for later.

Biddy pulls out her notepad and pen. She carries a unicorn notepad everywhere with her that she fills with poems and playlets. She always reads them to me. She's incredibly prolific, they just tumble out of her. They are mostly funny. We listen to Radio 4 in the evenings, so she writes that type of thing mainly, the kind of thing a white man from boarding school would come up with. She even does that rising inflection like they do at the end of a sentence to indicate the punchline. Her favourite subjects to write about currently are dogs, Minecraft and Pizza Express. And here she is in the food bank jotting down every moment happening whilst the adults are attempting to block this moment out of our lives. She is drinking in every last bit of this strange experience. She is never going to forget. She is hurriedly swallowing her Danish and scribbling down words with the speed they leave her brain. Studying the faces, taking in the voices and then she asks the name of the wheelchair woman who is about select some food for us.

Her name is Vivian. Biddy scribbles it down.

She – picks – up – on – everything.

Another volunteer runs over and asks if we'd like some hot food and some squash.

'We're fine, thank you.'

'We've got lots left over today. Come and have some food with us.'

'Well ... I don't want it to go to waste,' I say, pretending that I'm the one doing them a favour.

Some of us women and children go and sit with the men and someone brings out plates of sausage and mash for us all. A tear splashes into the gravy but I quickly regain composure because I'm not going to ruin my first proper meal in over a month. I'm very much failing at being vegan, but it feels so good to eat something that isn't stale wheat. It feels like the best meal of my life. For the first time in weeks I am tasting *something*, and I suddenly feel very awake and present, like the way Simone did on the day she died.

I'm on a food high, I'm in great spirits, and I seek out the cook to hug her and tell her just how much her food means to me. Then we get ready to take away a selection of tins and sustainable foodstuffs that kind people donate to places like this with women like me in mind.

Vivian coasts out with heavy bags. 'I've thrown in a few extras for you and the little one,' she whispers. 'And some sanitary towels.'

She's given us so much it's a struggle to carry it all home but Clifton from the estate spots us and runs over to help.

'Red bags,' he notes. 'Food bank?'

I nod.

He carries our bags to the door and he offers Biddy some of his KFC, which she accepts with delight despite having recently eaten. She never refuses food these days even when she's full up, because she never knows when the next proper meal is going to be.

Once we get inside I place our food across the kitchen counter like a YouTuber showing off her haul for the week. If only I had the animated voice and carefree persona to pull it off, then I could add YouTuber to my floundering income streams. I flash Biddy my biggest smile as I rehearse my potential new job into her face, pretending she is my camera:

Hey, guys! Just back from an amazing morning at the food bank and wanted to show you what we begged for today! Let's start with the tins, shall we?! Corned beef – hmmm, corned beef is my fave! Tuna, tomatoes, pineapple, three tins of baked beans, carrots, new potatoes, spaghetti, pasta sauce, seven cans of sweetcorn, spam, tomato soup. What else have we got? There's pasta! Oh, we love pasta here, don't we?! We could live off pasta! And boil-in-the-bag rice. A packet of Rich Tea biscuits. Tea bags! UHT milk. Cornflakes. A multipack of crisps. Sugar sachets from a hotel in ... Durham.

Biddy laughs and mimes giving the camera to me before taking over in a high-pitched YouTuber accent:

Hey, guys! Gonna make a lovely tinned potato and baked bean and Spam stew! Looks like puke in a pan, guys, yum!

Guys, I've popped the recipe in the description box below so you can eat puke for your dinner too and don't forget to subscribe for more food-bank hauls, guys! Bye, guys!

We can live off *all* this for weeks. And of course, we will.

Biddy stands staring at the food in front of us.

'I've written a new play,' she finally says.

'Do you want to read it to me while I put the food away?'

'Yes, Mummy. It's called *The Food Bank*. It's about a mum taking her daughter to a food bank to get some food because they are hungry because Tories are starving poor people and burning them.'

And then she reads it to me. And it is just as I place the tinned corned beef on top of the tinned baked beans when those guttural sobs finally smack me.

I am most definitely broken.

'Are you humiliated, Mummy?'

And I remember Simone again.

The most humiliating thing is yet to come.

'No, darling. Just injured. I'll cook us up a pan of puke and then I'll be ready to go back into battle.'

14

NOTES FROM: THE RED

AS I HURTLE TOWARDS my final decline, I am pounced on by the commissioning editor of a popular financial website. I've been asked to list my weekly spending habits to entertain their readership with the real-life budget of a single mum factotum living below the poverty line. She asks me to do this in exchange for £100 in Love2Shop gift vouchers. I know full well what kind of article this is going to be but I'm in no position to decline; this isn't worthy journalism written to evoke empathy nor is it a dispatch from the underclass rejecting objectivity and providing a soundbite from the under-represented. This is an attack. And I am offering myself up to be publicly slaughtered across social media, a complicit participant in the war against class, not for the good of my kind but for nothing more than a £100 Love2Shop gift voucher.

In exchange for the gift voucher I make a list of my weekly outgoings.

In exchange for the gift voucher I make a list of my debts.

In exchange for the gift voucher I play the part of scapegoat and slave to the genre of poverty porn.

FANTASY FICTION

One of my most favourite things about period poverty is that it allows me to justify my desire to shoplift. Inspired by Ken Loach's fictional dystopian fantasy *I, Daniel Blake*, I set off to Morrisons to steal as many packs of Always Night-Time with wings as I can. Not worried about getting caught – because like in the fictional film which *isn't* based on reality whatsoever, I'll just take a fictional job in a brothel and befriend one of the fictional 120,000 sick and disabled people who fictionally died whilst on a fictional phoneline listening to Vivaldi's *Spring* – a fictional piece of music composed specifically for Loach's satire.

Down the Morrisons I distract the security guard by pretending to be a good human who cares about food poverty and I performatively place a pack of 49p M Savers pasta in the food-bank donations trolley before running out with a whole 17 packs of sanitary towels stuffed down my bum pockets.

In exchange for the Love2Shop voucher I list my spending for the day:

49p (to charity)

Potential loss of liberty (for period-product theft) culminating in a three-week prison stint due to having previous convictions, £1,000 a week (courtesy of the taxpayer).

Total spend: £3,000.49

LITERARY FICTION (ADAPTED FOR THE BIG SCREEN)

One of my favourite things about period poverty (on – the – whole) is that on the days my shifts are cancelled (without notice) I can indulge in a much-needed day of self-care. We all need to practise self-care and the great thing about low-paid flexible work is that I'm getting to do it more and more these days. This week I'm having a rather heavy period and after greedily devouring a whole 17 packs of sanitary towels with my raging fertility I'm now lying on my sofa with nothing to do but bleed onto facial flannels whilst rewatching old Argos adverts and repeats of *Take Me Out: The After-party* on my enormous television from BrightHouse – one of the few places I'm allowed to shop these days (real cost: £2,041.02/repayment cost: £4,056.00). And when the facial flannels become too bloodied, I have no choice but to wash them in my BrightHouse-owned washing machine (real cost: £1,020.51/repayment cost: £2,028.00).

In exchange for the voucher I list my spending for the day:

The doubled debt of the BrightHouse big screen.

The loaned-out washing machine.

Total spend: £6,084

META FICTION

One of my favourite things about period poverty (generally) is using payday loan companies to help me stock up on sanitary products and painkillers. I'm applying for another loan today because ironically I won't be getting much of a payday this month. I apply for £200 at the *very* reasonable APR of 1,333 per cent from a well-known loan shark with the intention of splashing out on a year's supply of tampons. I brazenly lied to the lender. Told them I worked at the *Daily Mail* as a cleaner where I earn 2 million pounds a week and the computer fell for it and immediately deposited £200 into my account! I'll spread the repayments over the next 24 weeks meaning we won't be able to afford food or utilities or anything, but it's worth it for having the extra money that I'll briefly feel like I own.

In exchange for the voucher I list my spending for the day:

1 pay day loan. £200. Plus 1,333 per cent APR.

Total spend: £386.61

CHILDREN'S FICTION

One of my favourite things about period poverty (overall) is that I get to indulge in crafting. It's a great technique for distracting children below the breadline from their empty grumbling guts. My daughter is sick today so she's off school and we wile away the morning playing hide 'n' seek with the curtains closed and the radio off until the bailiffs go away. The game is free *today* but when they finally catch up with us it'll cost us roughly £40,000. We take a stroll to Morrisons to get lunch. I try to lure my daughter to the cheap fruits, but she keeps picking up Medjool dates even though I've always made it clear that these foodstuffs are *not* intended for children like her. We compromise with a punnet of strawberries, which she stuffs greedily into her gob like she hasn't eaten since lunchtime yesterday before we even reach the till.

We spend the afternoon crafting DIY sanitary towels made from her pull-up pants. Due to the trauma of knowing that poor people get burned alive she's started wetting the bed again. But from my POV it's worth it for the crafting opportunities; it's simple really, you cut up the nappy and use a little bit of sticky tape to mould it into the shape of your undercarriage and, before you know it, you're got yourself a homemade sanitary towel. Cheap, and a useful lesson for her about the degradation of poverty, which I believe is one of the most important things you can teach your child, especially as this is her *fictional* future too.

In exchange for the voucher I list my spending for the day:

£2 on Strawberries.

£5.99 on pull-up pants.

Total spend: £7.99

FANTASY FICTION

One of my most favourite things about period poverty is that I sometimes get to bleed on Iain Duncan Smith's face. *Fact.* This week is such a heavy week – it's like all my eggs are hatching out of me at once – I've had to resort to special measures. I grab a copy of my free, local, Tory-supporting rag – the *Evening Standard* – and I scrunch it up into something cervix shaped, shove it in and let it flow all over his ghastly face. Sometimes I use Dominic Raab's face or Jacob Rees Mogg, but I only let them have the brown stringy bits of womb residue that come out on the *very* last day.

The thing with this technique is that you never know who has fingered the paper with their germy hands before it reached you, so dealing with your period poverty in this way means that dying of Toxic Shock Syndrome could potentially become a political act. *Or*, if rolled out correctly as a government initiative, could become a great tool to rid the country of fertile working-class women scrounging from the state.

In exchange for the voucher I list my spending for the day:

For once I live within my means.

Total spend: £0

POV FICTION

It's been a quiet week so on Saturday I decide some entertainment is in order. Just because we're poor doesn't mean we can't have fun. My period is over, yay! Which means I'm able to leave the house without worrying about nappies slipping out of my jeans. I've found myself shoplifting in the Morrisons again – just for the thrill of it! I steal a pack of Bodyform and head to my local food bank, where I seek women roaming around the cold church hall with hot water bottles pressed against their bloated stomachs. I approach one with the overly empathetic eyes of a proper journalist desperate for a book deal and gently ask if I can help in any way. I offer up an unwrapped Bodyform at almost touching distance. As she bows her worn head and cups her M Savers budget washing-up-liquid-cracked hands to shamefully accept the pad, I pull out my lighter and burn the sanny right in front of her face like I'm in some kind of poverty porn Bullingdon Club initiation ritual! I fling the burning Bodyform to the ground.

In exchange for the voucher I list my spending for the day:

Entertainment via the ridiculing of people worse off than you is absolutely FREE!

Total spend: Who the fuck cares, the journalists will make it all up anyway …

For the £100 voucher, they ask me to make a list of my weekly outgoings: Our high rent, the gas, electricity, the Wi-Fi and the phone (that – I – do – not – deserve). Transport and food and all the basic *things* that require real money.

My list is viewed and analysed by the fictional financial guru and former journalist-turned-blogger Mummy_Loves_Bunting.

Here is her detailed crucifixion:

Quite the poor little victim is Cash, isn't she?! Methinks Cash just needs to stop being poor and stop lying about being poor. Poor people don't own £4000 televisions or even *know* what the Bullingdon Club is. How does she know what rich people get up to if she lives in this 'so-called poverty'? She needs to stop blaming others for her bad lifestyle choices, which she clearly made by being born poor. Her life is a car crash of her own making not because she is poor but because she is bitter. And I'm sure that Cash will agree with me that it was wrong of her to feed her daughter such expensive fruits like berries because berries are not for children like hers, sometimes even I don't even give my children berries and I work BLOODY hard. Me and my hubby Mr Mummy_ Loves_Bunting both have good, respectable, well-paid jobs and we keep costs down by only having one car, asking our parents to babysit and making sure that at least one of our holidays each year consists of staying with our friends who emigrated abroad to a very nice Italian villa which they inherited. We budget and make do and mend, why can't Cash do the same? The problem with Cash is that she feels entitled to things. She needs to learn to *budget* and live within her means. And stay away from our berries! And branded sanitary products! Bodyform – what an indulgence! Methinks, if she could just be a bit more grateful for what she *does* have and stopped playing the 'poor me' victim card, then I'm sure that she would have a lot more money. We all know that there is no such thing as modern poverty, but there *is* such a thing as being bitter, which of course is what all working-class people are. But if she takes my expert advice on board and works bloody hard like the rest of us, then, one day, one day – she might get what she deserves; a small shared ownership home that she'll never fully own, in somewhere like Pontefract where I propose all women like her should go and live if they can't afford London. Now there's a solution – methinks you should put all the fictional poor people in Pontefract, keep them out of sight and away from the berries and Bodyform. And if she takes her head out of her arse and follows my expert advice then methinks she'll be a super happy mummy like me!

For the £100 voucher they ask me to make a lists of all my debts: The 12 or so payday loans, the catalogues, the BrightHouse *situation,* the thousands of pounds in credit cards and utility bills from my time as the wife tourist in the financially abusive relationship. I don't earn enough to repay my student loan.

Below the (poverty denial) line:

- NEVER. HAPPENED.
- This kind of poverty just doesn't exist!
- Get a 'proper' job.
- Can't believe she gave her daughter berries and expects us to feel sorry for her.

- Cash sounds like a bitter bully.
- How does she afford a phone to babysit her daughter?
- This is utter drivel, you don't have to steal sanitary towels these days there are plenty of charities giving them away for free.
- There is no such thing as poverty.
- Where's the dad?
- Methinks someone believes Ken Loach's lies! It's a good film but it's all lies!
- Whilst I agree that period poverty *does* exist she could have used this opportunity, this *platform* to share some statistics to give people the real facts about poverty but instead she chose to mock vulnerable women by burning sanitary products that could have been put to good use. Vile!

Here's some stats, etc.

Stat: One in ten teenage girls has, at some point, been unable to afford sanitary products.

Another stat: One in seven teenage girls has had to borrow tampons or sanitary towels from a friend because they couldn't afford to buy their own.

Here's one more stat: The average UK woman will spend more than £18,000 on periods over her lifetime.

But this isn't a book of stats so you either believe me or you don't.

Non-Fiction

I approached one of those housewife rags requesting a quick £250 in real money in exchange for my latest poverty kiss 'n' tell story. I was on my knees. No subject was too humiliating for me to put my face to. Yes, I'm willing to go on the front cover, I said. Yes, I'm willing to expose my steak-bake arms, I said. They requested a photograph of me looking sad and bloated from drinking gallons of undiluted tropical squash from my Sports Direct mug, in my rubbish kitchen, next to my deep fat fryer, just looking really sad, whilst stirring some beans and casually holding a tampon. Biddy snapped the photo. I am a walking talking *Take A Break* magazine article. I am a stain on society. I am a statistic of shame. But this isn't a book about stats. All of this happened. I even gifted the magazine the perfect headline: MY PERIOD MADE ME BANKRUPT! NOW I'M BLEEDIN' BROKE. I wrote the piece, but it never made it to print. After some discussion the editor considered it to be in bad taste, my poverty porn too hardcore for the high street – which is a huge achievement because their other published stories that week included STALKED BY THE GHOST OF A BAILIFF BECAUSE OF GARY BARLOW, CARJACKED THEN FORCE-FED TINNED MEAT PIES. And I SMOKED HEROIN BUT DOT COTTON SAVED ME. Luckily they agreed to pay me. I put the money towards declaring myself bankrupt for the second time in my life, reaching my lowest point yet.

15

CRACKLE & DRAG

TEN DAYS AFTER 'THE incident' we are driven out of the city.

A removals guy called Donald from Sierra Leone loads our entire lives into his transit van and we make our exit stage south. We are leaving but this is not a choice. This is not some aspirational move out to the countryside seeking a better life, we're not searching for quiet, more space or better schools.

This – is – *not* – a – choice.

The thought of better air quality *appals* me. I don't seek life in a quaint village with only one shop that closes for an hour at lunchtime and doesn't even open on a Monday.

That is *disgusting* to me. I don't want scenic bike rides over the weald – I want to dice with death *every day* on my fold-up bicycle between Kennington and Vauxhall where reality abruptly interrupts regentrification on the A202. Forever.

We are being dragged. It's all over bar the shouting, but I don't even have the energy for *that* these days. There is *nothing* left inside. And ... we're officially out – we've just passed a sign that says WELCOME TO KENT, which means we're not that far from being dumped in the kind of town I've lived in fear of for years. The type of place I vowed I'd never live. The kind of town they send women like me to these days. To throw us away, to hide us away.

This was always going to happen.

Maybe my mum was right all along, maybe I *do* have 'the gift' – *I'd call her right now if I had her number* – because I *saw* all this happening back in 2010 when I was pregnant in the refuge. I foresaw all this happening. Eight years ago. Working for nothing, losing everything. I pictured me and my daughter living this half-life before she existed to be held in my arms; packing up, driven out of the city. I'd even witnessed 'the incident' from above my body as I faded out of consciousness and away from this life.

Because I'd been hearing things, we'd all been hearing things. The women I'd bump into down the food bank, on the estate, in the temporary flats, at bus stops heading off to their fourth job of the day – we'd *all* heard stuff. And it ter-rified us. The families moved out to Peterborough, Margate, Wolverhampton. It wasn't an urban legend, we all knew at least one person cleansed from London. Placed into flats on run-down streets hundreds of miles from their friends and support networks. Nowhere towns where you don't know a soul or a street and where your accent doesn't make sense to the locals. Where a woman and her child are hand-delivered outsiders and ordered to restart life from scratch.

That's us now.

As three elections passed, the things we heard got worse, like a game of Chinese Whispers on a bad batch of Angel Dust; first they killed off 120,000 of the disabled, then they took food from the low waged, and then they started cleansing the cities of the women and children.

That's *us* now.

People sat in cinemas crying after watching *I, Daniel Blake*, knowing these things were true, yet they elected the Tories for a third time. 'Are people really that selfish?' I screamed at the telly as the idiots welcomed Theresa May back into Downing Street.

That was when they came for the single mums, the low-waged mums, the families without support networks trying to hold it together in the capital.

They wanted people like us out of the city.

That's us *now*.

But we don't want to move out of London! This is our home. Tough. Get out. You shouldn't be so poor. Or a woman.

Because it's the weakest women and children who are out first. The Conservative governments cleansing of London is like a gentle nudge of a Nazi extermination camp. We're the demonised drains on society offering no contribution. So, we are removed. The government treat us like we are subhuman: *Untermenschen* – the term the Nazis used to describe the weakest of humans they wanted rid of.

I watched David Cameron walk into Downing Street when I was six months pregnant – I knew my days were numbered before my daughter was even born. The only thing I'm surprised about is how we got away with it for so long. Eight years we held on for.

Eight years of trying and lying and convincing myself that there was always something far more humiliating that could happen to me than the humiliating thing that was currently happening. I must be quite strong, I reckon, deep down, despite 'the incident' to keep holding on and plugging away fighting constant battles.

Even though I knew I would have to leave eventually. And that it might be the end of me.

I'd been Googling the same phrase (or variations of the phrase) for over a month from our cramped temporary flat in Gospel Oak.

'How to disappear'

'How do you disappear?'

'Is it possible to disappear and start again?'

'How to erase yourself'

'How to erase yourself completely'

'Is it possible to disappear from the world?'

'How to disappear completely' – but that one just kept leading me to the Radiohead song from *Kid A*, my least favourite of all the Radiohead albums, which kept making me even more depressed.

I scrap that sentence from my search.

Either way, I was going to disappear. I couldn't afford the rent on our tiny one-bed flat, I couldn't afford to feed my daughter, so I decided the only thing to do was to disappear on my own terms.

You probably didn't notice me anyway: I was the woman standing outside the betting shop doing the survey and customer count for a whole £7; I was the woman walking around Asda with a scanner doing a self-employed audit (£10); I was the woman working from the online zero-hour call centre selling Cancer Research lottery tickets (£7.50 per hour); I was the woman on the psychic webcam, or on the sex chat-line. I was the woman who thought about selling her actual real-life cunt (I met with the head of an escort agency who valued it at around £150 per hour – my age and worn out features depreciating my price) but just couldn't find the time – it doesn't really fit in around the school run.

But I would have. I would have sold my cunt. I'd sold everything else by this point. And maybe having regular intimacy would have made me feel like a normal human again.

This life isn't normal, is it? Constantly searching for ways to keep yourself slightly afloat until the next battle. It isn't supposed to be like this, is it? No one deserves this, do they?

Forced self-employment: it means you are always on the back foot. You are always scrabbling around. Bad weeks, less bad weeks. Constantly having to declare your earnings. Reveal your every pathetic attempt at living. Some weeks you can get full housing benefit, some weeks you can't. It's almost a full-time job informing the council what you're up to, printing out forms, seeking evidence, watching that you don't earn too little or too much. Why can't anyone see that if I could just be paid a proper wage then I'd be able to afford my rent?

Then.

Then. Something amazing happened. *Then*. Something life changing happened to me.

And I could smile properly for the first time in years because it looked like I was on the way to finding a legitimate route out of poverty for us.

I received an advance payment to write a play. For an actual theatre. I was being paid to do something I was good at, because I'm really bad at sex chat, I'm far too angry. When a caller asks if he can call me 'mistress', I immediately think he's pathetic and I cannot help but tell him so, but of course he gets off on *that*, which obviously makes me even angrier. He's agreeing with me saying, 'Yes, mistress, I'm pathetic,' and I'm going out of my mind because the last thing I want is for him to be satisfied and I end up slamming the phone down losing yet another 14p. I'm just not a customer service type.

Underneath my common accent, zero-hours 'lifestyle' and jumble-sale bra (because who can actually afford a fucking bra these days) is a woman who writes stuff. I hadn't stopped writing the entire time I was working these less-than-minimum-wage jobs. There was always this tiny bit of hope that I could turn this strange decade of my life into something artistic, or at least create something useful to someone else. So, every morning I'd get up at 4am and for the first three hours of my day I would write continuously, before getting Biddy up and ready for school. I'd write anything that came into my head: plays, sitcom treatments, short stories, gonzo-style confessionals, and every now and again the odd one would get picked up by a website and I'd land a much-needed £200. One morning I got a phone call about a new play I'd written and they offered me £5,000 for it. A whole five grand. And a few days later I got signed to a really big agent. It felt life changing. For a couple of joyous weeks it made me smirk as I took sex calls knowing I had a play about to tour the UK and that, after all these years of trying and failing, I had an agent who considered me a 'proper' writer – but because the money for these things takes so long to come through, in order to feed my daughter, every morning I was listening to a man lining his kitchen floor with bin liners so it would be easier for him to clean up his cum and shit once he'd made a mess of everything.

Unsurprisingly, it becomes easier to live that life when you can see a way out. I could finally see an escape out of this decade lost to poverty. I was so close to leaving poverty behind that I almost convinced myself I was a tourist.

Anyway, eventually I received a lump sum of money to finish up my play script.

It wasn't a life-changing sum; £5,000 isn't a lot of money in the grand scheme of things but it was enough to do proper food shops that actually filled up the fridge and the cupboards for a few months, and I was even able to replace my one pair of shoes. I treated myself to a new pair of Converse. And I settled some debts with friends who'd helped me out.

But because of that *one* payment the council suspended my housing benefit – without notice – on the day my rent was due. The council assumed that this one-off lump sum (an advance payment to cover me for six months' work) was my monthly wage! When you are low-waged, self-employed and in receipt of benefits, you are required to declare all your earnings or any changes as they happen. So, I did, I was honest, I showed them my earnings and after they scrutinised my bank statements and 'did checks' they realised their mistake and said it would take six weeks to reinstate. It was more stress that I didn't need, but I had become accustomed to living in this bureaucratic system that constantly holds those on low wages under suspicion and, when I explained the situation to my landlord, he agreed to hold off taking any action so long as I caught up with all my rent once those six weeks were up. But, once those six weeks were up, the council said they were investigating me for *fraud*.

What makes you think I've committed fraud? I've been totally honest with you.

They couldn't, they wouldn't, tell me the reason. They suspected fraud and that was that. They don't have to explain anything to you.

The way they see it, £5,000 goes into the account of someone attempting to rise up from below the poverty line and they immediately suspect that you're up to no good. That's why it's so hard to rise up. That's why it's easier to just give up. And by this point I was three months behind on the rent which meant eviction was imminent. We were going to be made homeless. Again.

Hard work *doesn't* pay. I was worse off than ever.

This is because the government don't really believe that *hard work* pays. Not for the working class anyway. That is the reason my bookshelves and why theatres are filled with the words of people of privilege. They can *afford* to sit around and be poor whilst they await their publication advance without the worry of needing housing benefit to keep a roof over their heads.

And with housing benefit no longer being a safety net to top up my rent, and no more payday loan companies left to tap, my landlord handed me a section 21. We'd be out within the month.

And I thought: I can't do this anymore. I cannot continue to be this poor. I cannot fight another minute. I cannot see my daughter go hungry for another day. I work hard – any hour I can find, doing degrading things day upon day. And I declare every measly penny of it. Yet I am being investigated for fraud because for the first time in *years* I have made money that equates to more than £3.09 an hour (because in forced self-employment you rarely make minimum wage).

And by the way, £5,000 for a six-month period, working full-time, equates to just over £5 per hour. I was *still* working for less than minimum wage, and *now* I'm being accused of fraud.

I went down the council and said I urgently needed to get on the housing list. We need housing that we can afford. My next-door neighbours live in a three-bed council flat for a quarter of my rent, and we have a tiny one-bed, how is this system fair? If we had social housing, with affordable rent, then maybe we'd have a shot at a normal life. They turned us away.

They said that I didn't have a local connection.

The council said I had no local connection.

What do you mean I have no local connection?

I am 37 years old. I was born in Lambeth, I grew up in Penge and I have contributed to this city my *entire* life. I've paid the high rents to the local economy since I was a teenager. All the money I've earned since I was a 15-year-old girl working in the clip joint, it has all been put back into this city. I buy from the local shop. I send my daughter to the local school, care for my community. My money and soul feeds this city. This place, this *London* – it's the only place I know. I couldn't be *more* locally connected.

But when the Tories came in they changed housing law so that you are not eligible to be put on the housing register unless you have resided in the borough for at least five years.

When you are constantly having to move every six months it becomes almost impossible to remain in the same borough as you are pushed farther and farther out. It is a rare success that someone privately renting whilst living in poverty gets the opportunity of five years' worth of stability.

The system is *created* to cleanse.

I was done with it all.

We would disappear. I'd change my name to something like Catherine West, something Google doesn't give a shit about. I'd be Cathy to my new friends – CATHY! We'd really fit in, in Oldham or somewhere like that. I wouldn't *try* anymore.

I'd stop getting up at 4am to write. I'd know my place. Accept whatever it is I'm supposed to accept. 'Stop trying to be something you're not,' as my dad always said. That was the problem. Always trying to be something I'm not. All those mornings getting up to write – who was I kidding? I needed to accept that working-class women rarely get to own, never mind change, their narrative. I should have married a nice builder who was interested in getting a mortgage and maybe got myself a 9 to 5 back when those jobs were available 'because you're bright, you could be a PA at an advertising agency' – as my dad always said. I always thought he said those things because he didn't think I was good enough to amount to much, but in this moment I realise that he had wanted me to follow a simple path so that I didn't get hurt. That's why he failed in his ambitions too. OK. It's never too late. I'll follow a simple path. And I'll change my daughter's name to Sophie or Charlotte because those are the kinds of names that get you places in this world.

Good plan.

No, it's a *terrible* plan.

I don't look like a *Cathy*. It's too late for me.

This – is – over.

'THE INCIDENT'

So. 'The incident', etc.

That's what we'll call it.

That's how the doctors referred to it whenever Biddy was in the room.

Which was always. Because where else could she go?

Nobody needs to know how I tried to do it, but I did try to do it, and you can reach your own conclusion on how because there are so many ways to end it. There are all the classics. I've never had a driving lesson in my life but in early 2018 you could be sure to find me taking an interest in London's tallest multistorey car parks, and I stockpiled packets of paracetamol, the cheap 25p packs. I stalked my flat for the best spot that would hold the weight of a heavy rope and I found a website giving you step by step instructions on how to remove your own heart.

(I liked the idea of watching my own heart stop beating – only when you've seen it for yourself can you truly believe that all of this is over.)

So, one night I decided to have my last supper – it's lucky I don't have any disciples because I couldn't afford anything more than a meal for two. And I blew the budget because from tomorrow there would be no bills to pay. There would be no rent, no council tax, no utilities, no food, no payday loan repayments. Money wouldn't be important because I would be gone. Poverty wouldn't mean a thing in the morning.

I took us out for a lovely Pizza Express and I didn't even use a voucher code. I said to the only person in the world that I'd want to eat my last meal with – have *whatever* you want. My daughter started with dough balls and I went for the mozzarella and tomato salad. She ordered a Classic Margarita and I went for an American Hot, which I upgraded to Romana. I ordered a large glass of rosé. I let my baby have a Diet Coke. She told me about this online game she plays called Minecraft, which I do not understand but I smiled as she told me everything about how to play it. I just wanted to hear her speak for as long as I could. We ate until every plate was finished. We ordered desserts to share.

I didn't look at the bill, I just paid it – and I frivolously handed the waiter a £20 tip.

We walked home via the Heath and we did cartwheels before going on the zipwire.

I told her she didn't have to do her homework and we hugged on the bed until she fell asleep.

I closed the bedroom door behind me and that was when 'the incident' happened.

The incident. It's on the list of classics but it's the least dramatic of the suicides. It's the one that doesn't leave behind a blood trail and the one that doesn't require a visit to B&Q. It happened over hours and hours and each second seemed to last longer than I'd ever been alive. And as I lay slowly dying, as my body fought angrily not to leave (because your stupid body does that even when you're the one who has instructed your brain to help you die) suddenly my eyes opened wide as it dawned on me that my baby would find the body. I'd been so sad and scared that I hadn't really thought this bit through, the discovery of the body. I was already drenched in sweat, covered in my own vomit, and I slid along the broken vinyl flooring into the bedroom we shared and watched her beautiful snores for a while before heaving all over myself again. I realised that in a few hours from now she was going to find me getting cold on the living-room rug.

I was between a rock and a heartbeat when I called the ambulance.

You can change your name to Cathy West, you can change your daughter's name, change the way you dress, you can cut your hair, dye it, move up to Aberdeen, get a new phone number, deactivate all your social media accounts, delete your shit meaningless blog, run away – but the debts never truly dissolve. Your credit record is always recording, and your mind refuses to erase the pain it cohabits with.

You cannot truly disappear. Not if you're alive.

That's why I tried to die. I had already been cleansed of my dignity, and now we were about to be cleansed from our city, so I decided that I wanted to be removed in every way. The hospital discharged me quickly with the usual list of helplines because physically I was well – ironically, my body had rejected death due to the amount of Pizza Express I'd consumed. Greed had saved me. And anyway you only have to look at Jesus to see that last suppers rarely lead to a successful demise.

… When I saw Biddy's beautiful face the next day, when she came into the kitchen for a cuddle and a demand for Coco

Pops, I felt so grateful that I hadn't watched my heart stop beating on that kitchen floor. Once your broken heart is in your hands there is no going back from that. And later on that evening I laughed with my friend as we shared a bottle of prosecco on Hampstead Heath, as a Jazz band played and our kids ran around together in the adventure playground, about how I couldn't afford a pair of scissors sharp enough for *that* job – cutting out your own heart is such a middle-class suicide!

So. I didn't disappear completely. I didn't die. My daughter isn't an orphan. And we're *here,* somewhere on the motorway. We're being driven out in a transit van by Donald to a homeless hostel in Kent. WELCOME TO KENT – GARDEN OF ENGLAND, the sign reads. This is it now. We're out. The road is starting to wind and where we're going is trying to hide, but it is time to admit defeat.

It's the day of the Royal Wedding. Another one. This one is the Meghan and Harry one. Donald is really digging it, he's listening to the service on the radio. He's joining in with the prayers and he's singing the praises of the royal family. This makes me dislike Donald very much. And I didn't think my day could get any worse but by the time we make it to the hostel all of our furniture is crushed. Turns out that he hadn't packed it correctly – he'd just thrown it in the back of the van. As Donald and his assistant pull my crushed sofa out, he gets cut and bleeds all over the cushions.

Royalist Donald has bled over and destroyed all of our furniture.

I – didn't – think – my – day – could – get – any – worse.

The last of everything we had. Smashed.

'I'm not paying you for this,' I say.

'You owe me £500!'

'No. You owe *me* £500, Donald. At least.'

And I didn't think that my day could get any worse but then Donald starts *speaking in tongues* and declares that he is putting a voodoo spell on me. Right – there– in – the – middle – of – Maidstone. And Biddy is clinging onto me in fear as he dances around us shaking his arms, doing this voodoo spell. This is actually happening, Kent is worse than I had ever imagined, but it doesn't really register because I am still numb from 'the incident'.

'Fuck's sake, Donald. Not a voodoo spell, Donald, please. Things cannot get any worse, Donald,' I sigh.

'My mummy is being sarcastic,' Biddy tells Donald.

'You will NEVER feel contentness, you will NEVER feel peace,' he shouts.

'"Contentness" isn't actually a word so your voodoo is factually incorrect, Donald,' I smirk.

Then. He stops and takes a deep breath before saying – 'You, Cash. You'll never rise up and shine like Meghan Markle.'

He's got me.

I know, Donald. I know.

He throws the rest of my crushed life into the middle of the street, turns the National Anthem up to full blast and drives off screaming 'voodoo' out of the window, right over the Queen's special song. And Biddy and I sit on the blood-covered sofa and cuddle for a bit. For ages, actually.

Then these two young women, in nice coats and glossy weaves, who look like they have been out for the afternoon trying to sell god, stop by the bloody sofa and look at us for a while.

'Are you OK?' one of them asks.

'I'm not sure anymore.'

'It's your lucky day,' one of them tells me.

They are going to help us carry our broken belongings up to our hostel flat on the eighth floor.

And they do. They take hours out of their day. We drag all the remains up to the top floor of the hostel.

They give me a hug and a flyer for their church. I promise I'll pop along, even though I know I won't. But their unexpected kindness had saved me for yet another day.

We're living in a hostel. It's in one of those towns. Those towns they send women like me to these days. It's an art deco building, a former office block, that has been turned into luxury flats and sold off to investors who rent them to the council. It's called Star House. And Biddy is in hysterics because on the welcome mat in the hostel foyer are the words – STAR HOUSE LUXURY LIVING.

'But this is a homeless shelter!' she laughs in disbelief. At everything.

Every London borough is represented. I talk to the women in the lift. It is mainly women and children here. And a couple of old junkie men, but they are too out of it to be noticed. Tower Hamlets. Newham. Islington. Hackney. All the London boroughs.

We're flying the flag for Camden.

How long have you been here? I ask everyone I meet.

Six months. Three years. Nearly 12 months.

A woman a few doors down moved in with a newborn just a few days before us.

Shipped out without family support as she begins motherhood.

She's just like me. I wonder, will she still be doing all this in eight years' time?

Will she be visiting food banks and working zero-hour jobs and stigmatised and broken too. I wonder that about everyone I see in the lift as I eventually join in with the silence of all the other unheard voices who've given up bothering to speak.

The hostel is so quiet.

I've lost my voice too.

I don't think I'll ever fight again.

I am alive.

But.

I'm done.

In terms of hostels we have lucked out. These are nice apartments; underfloor heating, new kitchen, power shower, all the *things* that people like.

Not your typical hostel.

The only clue that it's not luxury apartments is the fact that we all look poor, and none of us wants to be in this terrible town and it makes us depressed and there are signs on the walls showing hypodermic needles and begging the residents not to take drugs – because that's what they think mothers like us in homeless shelters do …

Anyway, we're here for now. I quite like it. Sort of. We like the quiet, for now. I mean, we don't have a choice in the matter so we'll make of it the best we can. I feel anonymous and I'm treating this as time away to recover from everything. Recover from everything that has happened in the last eight years. We don't know how long we'll be here or if they'll ever let us back into London. Our hostel – it's in one of those towns I vowed I'd never live in, in that dismal place between the sea and the city.

It's only temporary, but that's all any of this is. I hope.

16

CLEANSED

This lad on the way down here
this lad, he starts chatting
to me
on the train platform and
he's like
your bag looks heavy and I'm like yeah
and that was the *end* of our conversation but
the train comes in and we're both getting on the train and
I'm struggling to pull it onto the train, my bag, and this
   lad, the same lad, comes up behind, acting the hero,
   acting the gentleman, swoops up my suitcase, chucks
   it over his shoulder and
thanks I say. That's the end of the conversation. I go and
   get a seat.
But he sits right opposite me.

We're in this empty carriage. Just me and him. Which pisses
   me off because I can't just walk away, it's difficult to move

because he's put my heavy suitcase in the overhead compartment but

men pull this shit all the time, dont they? And I don't want to cause a scene, want to keep myself safe, get to where I'm going – and he's just trying his luck – but he's not my type so I grab a newspaper on the seat across the aisle

but it's the *Sun* and I'm like

fuck this and

chuck it in the bin and I pull out my phone and pretend to reply to messages or something but

my battery is dying and

he asks where I'm going. In his head it's clearly not the end of the conversation. So I tell him. Tell him where I'm headed.

That's a lovely place, he tells me.

Is it? Is it a lovely place? Well, that's good I say. Because I'm being forced to move there.

We were in a homeless hostel and now we're

being removed from London permanently and sent to this *place*.

He say's I'm lucky. It's a really lovely place. His gran used to live there.

Then he blurts out, like he can't help himself, he says – you're really lucky, no blacks or Muslims

FOR MILES.

When we were

given the keys to the flat we took a stroll around the
estate.

The first three houses we passed had UKIP posters on
the window.

Biddy laughed when she saw my angry face.

She said, in her posh North London accent: Oh, Mummy.
Oh, Mummy! Where have they put us?! What is this
place?! You're going to have so many FIGHTS with
the neighbours!

She just couldn't stop laughing.

The flat was a right state. No flooring. Dried blood on
the tiles. Holes in the walls.

But we can fix it up.

Went and introduced myself to the neighbour, she said the
woman who had lived in our flat previously had died
in the flat.

Slit her throat.

She was very unhappy.

That explains the blood.

My friend Clover, she was helping us move in – she'd over-
heard us chatting and popped her head out the door
and said she *knew* that from the moment she'd walked
into the flat that it had a bad energy

and she was going to call a priest and get him to come
around and cleanse the place.

I started telling the neighbour I was planning on putting
   Biddy in the local school and
she said the local school is great.
Lovely village school.
Really great school.
Biddy will settle in well.
Really lovely teachers.
Safe.
None of that black or Muslim nonsense that you have to
   deal with in London. You'll like it here. Because they
   don't *come* around here. YOU WON'T SEE ONE
   FOR MILES. They know they're not welcome
because there's no
mosque. There'd be
UPROAR
if there was a mosque or one of those Sikh dens or some-
   thing planned within twenty *miles* of here, there'd be
PROTESTS
RIOTS and
everything.
We'd fight against them.
Until they went away.
But. What *you* need to watch *out* for
around
here
are the *Poles*.
Watch out for the Poles.

They're sneaky ones, they are. They blend in. Fair
   enough, they normally keep themselves to themselves
   – apart from the
pretty ones
who marry the Englishmen
for the money obviously and because they're
deviants in bed they are
dirty girls – sneaky little Poles.
Because
you can't *tell*, can you?
They look just like us, don't they?
Apart from the ones with the harsh faces who work in
   the factory. But most of them keep to themselves. *Very*
   sneaky though. Because they can pass as one of us
but they're …
From a third-world country
Poland
don't you forget that Poland is a
third-world country – third-world country out there.

… It *isn't*, I said.
She said IT IS IT IS it's a third-world country – have *you*
   ever been to Poland?
and I said yeah, *yeah*, I have been to Poland and – and she
   said well you've been taken in by all their sneaky little
   lies then, haven't you?
ALL – THEIR – LIES

and she said that she'd have to watch out for me but
I'd learn the truth soon enough because they fit in but
   when you get to know them, they don't fit in.
Very odd bunch.
If *she*, if your *daughter*, starts playing with someone with
   a funny surname then you'll find out for yourself,
   won't you
that will learn you
unless you're one of them? You one of them? Keep her
   away from them if you love your daughter but yeah the
   school is good it's a very good school my little ones
   went there but they're grown up now ...

It's
horrible out here. There is no way out. There's this one bus.
   One bus a day that leaves the village at 06.07 and returns
   at 15.43. One bus. Everyday. One bus a day. I checked it.
   Goes to fucking Tunbridge Wells. The *one* bus
you sit on a bus for a whole 90 minutes and your final
   destination is Tunbridge Wells
what the hell are you supposed to do when you get to
   Tunbridge Wells?

Have a Pizza Express? Or something. Go to fucking Zizzi's?

and
there *is* this bad energy around here

there is and

we've been told that THIS is home now

they told us that's what they said

take it or leave it

so we took it

the council said take it or leave it – but you *have* to take it

they *pretend* you're making a choice

but

there

is

no

choice so

this is our home

the council said take it or leave it but

you have to take it because when you're

homeless

you get one offer and if you refuse then they say you've
    made yourself

intentionally homeless

and – and we are no longer homeless

and I guess that's a good thing it's a good thing I mean
yeah

we're not in a hostel anymore

we have a stable home so

so

so it's not like I can … it's not like I can *moan*

about it now because *now* people will just say

BE GRATEFUL be grateful be

grateful

that's what they'll say, they'll say just be happy and be
    grateful that you have a home like

don't be so ungrateful because you have a home now

it doesn't matter where it is

you wanted a stable home and now you've got one. And
    that's the end of the story like this – this – is – the –
    end – of – the – fucking – story

that just like

having a roof over your head

is the solution to EVERYTHING

to all of *this*

no matter where they put you

50 miles away

100 miles away

alone in the middle of nowhere

and of course it is a good thing that we are not

homeless anymore we're grateful we're no longer

homeless

I mean, when we *were* homeless back then

when we were homeless

when we were homeless when we were still in the hostel
    – we still had hope

hope that we wouldn't be ... – hope that we wouldn't be
    cleansed

that we'd get back

that we'd get back
that we'd get back
home
you've got people in hostels waiting 6, 7, 8 years
waiting to get housed in their borough near their families and
this one woman I met
this one woman I met in the hospital after
'The Incident'
just before they shipped us out
she told me that she was about to be sent to Mansfield
    any day now
after being in a hostel in Camden for eight years
and she had lived in Camden all her life, nearly all her life
she came over from Somalia with her aunt when she was six
but she went to St Patrick's Primary in Kentish Town and
    then on to Haverstock where Ed Miliband went
he was a few years above her
yeah – he went there and she went there
and she'd lived in a private rental all that time from the
    age of six and she even went to Uni in the borough
    and she'd got a job in the borough working for a char-
    ity and she lived there her entire life but
when she split up with her husband because he was beat-
    ing up their three-year-old son with a belt
every night like
he'd like whip him, her little boy, her son, in his toddler
    bed because

I dunno, maybe he, maybe he hated himself for not being able

to get a proper job because he was on the zero hours and they kept sending him home or maybe he was just outright evil

but he'd whip his son with his belt and of course she didn't know about it but then as soon as she did, as soon as she found out – she left him because that's what you do, isn't it? You don't hang around when your husband is beating your three-year-old son, she did the *right* thing but

she couldn't afford

the private rent on her own and

she moved in with her aunt and then her aunt decided to move up to Liverpool

but she didn't want to go to Liverpool so she went to the council

and they put her in the hostel

you know the hostel on England's Lane near Belsize Park Tube, yeah?

It looks like a nice building, an old tenement block but there are like 200 families living in there

and each family has one small room and

there are just mice everywhere and cockroaches and apparently a couple recently got brutally stabbed on the stairwell.

This is what she was telling me down the hospital; some bloke brought another man back from the pub for sex,

just for sex, and his wife – she catches him DOING IT.
Catches her husband doing it in the stairwell
and she goes back to her room
where their four kids are sleeping and she gets
a bread knife, she's just had enough of all this shit
she's shouting in the stairwell and waving the knife
around and
its just a threat
she's not going to use it but the bloke from the pub, the
sex man he brought back, well HE grabs the knife and
just kills them both
Just like that
stabs the man
right up the arse
and the mother she gets it in the eyes and she gets it in
the head, I mean –
they found the bread knife buried deep in her skull
right after it had been up her husband's arse and
their four kids are sleeping in bed
one of them was a newborn and
no one knows where the queer stabber bloke has disappeared to but
that's another family off the council list I suppose
that's what she *heard* anyway
she doesn't know if it's true, or if it's just a rumour
she never saw the body, she didn't know the family, she
said they *could* have got stabbed in the stairwell or they

could have just killed themselves or more likely they
were just moved

to *Wakefield* or

somewhere

that's the *thing* one minute you're there and the next
you've disappeared. Gone Cleansed.

no one knows but she said it's a dark place, bad energy
in that hostel

she was there for eight years

EIGHT YEARS and then one day they said they were
sending her to

Mansfield.

A private rental in Mansfield.

An eight-year prison sentence in a hostel only to be sent
to Mansfield.

I guess we're lucky we only got sent as far as racist Kent.

My friend Zainab

we lived in the refuge together, when the ceiling collapsed and we kept in touch.

I don't make a habit of staying friends with people in
refuges because

I like to move on, put it all behind me but we

we get on well

she said she wanted to bring her boys down to visit, to
get out of London for the weekend and

she's so lovely

she got so excited when she heard that Biddy finally got
   her own bedroom that
she bought her some My Little Pony curtains from B&M
   Bargains but
I can't let her come down *here*, can I?
She's my friend, she
wears the full burka and
I just worry that something will happen to her around
   here so I suppose
we'll drift apart because you can't expose your friends to
   that and Kirsty has already told me she *won't* be visiting
after I told her about the
conversation I had on the train
with the lad, the lad who carried my suitcase
I told her what he said and she
she
she said
she's not coming down, she's sorry and everything
but she's
worried that the gangs on the estate will make
monkey noises at her and
the thing is I think that they might
they might make monkey noises at my friend they
probably will and I get why she wants to stay away.

This lad though
the lad on the train he just wouldn't stop talking and

he tells me, *informs* me that he's just come from an EDL
   march and I'm

looking out the window and there isn't a stop for about
   30 minutes so it's just me and him in the carriage and
   he's already scaring me

making me uncomfortable and then he asks –

have you ever slept with a black man? I'm like, what –
   business – is – it – of – yours – who – I've – slept – with
   – and ...

and I'm trying not to be too antagonistic because it's just
   me and him

in the train carriage and I don't want him to

rape me or

hit me and he can see I'm shaken so

he starts telling me about his daughter, she's seven, she stays
   with him every other weekend and all that, it's like he's
   trying to *convince* me that he's safe and he's not going to

attack *me* but I am honestly worried about

him raping me because why would he be asking about
   who I have and haven't slept with if he isn't thinking
   about my vagina and he goes quiet for a while and I
   look out of the window but

every now and again he'll ask me if I've ever slept with
   a black man or would I be friends with a Muslim
   and have I ever walked past a mosque when they get
   together to pray because they are like rats going in all
   the RATS – rats in cloaks – why can't they just dress

314

like *us* this is OUR COUNTRY it's yours and mine
and they are like rats.

I said *this* is not my country

I'm Irish

and he says yeah I'm Irish too. Like we're the same.

He's trying to make out that I'm like him. That we're on
the same team.

We're the same me and you, he says. We're not the same,
I want to say.

But I'm keeping my mouth shut. it's just me and him and

and he asks me again if I have any Muslim friends and
I'm just trying to talk to him about his daughter – Are
you close? Does she enjoy school? What's her favourite
subject? Because it's too late to ignore him. I'm trying
not to give him the conversation he wants whilst trying to keep him calm so he doesn't rape me. And he
asks me again if I've ever slept with a black man.

And I

GIGGLE. I fucking giggle.

And I say (and I'm trying to keep it 'light') – it's none of
your business who I've slept with and he says well that
means you HAVE

you *have* – you've slept with a black man

you've slept with a black man I can tell you have and if
you *won't* answer then you probably have slept with a
black man and

YOU'RE UTTER FILTH he says

A CLASS TRAITOR
A RACE TRAITOR
Stay in London if you're into that kind of thing.
GO BACK TO LONDON TAKE YOUR BLACK
   COCK-LOVING PUSSY BACK TO LONDON
   because THAT KIND OF BEHAVIOUR will NOT
   be tolerated around here you
fucking whore
and
he *spits* into his paper coffee cup and then he swigs it
   back – *which is proper weird* – and my stop is next so
   I stand up and he says –
if I saw a black man going into a white woman's flat
if I saw a black or a Pakistani – notice how I don't use
   slurs, he said – because it's NOT racism it's OPINION
   based in fact, he's saying – if I was a racist I'd use the N
   word or the P word but I don't –
but
if I *saw* a black *man* or a Pakistani *man* come out of your
   flat, a white woman's flat then
I'd put dog shit through your letterbox
no questions asked and
so would *hundreds* of others.

What, *hundreds* of others? I ask. *Hundreds* of people
would be putting dog shit through my letterbox. *Hundreds*? Actual hundreds?

I said –

hundreds?

Hundreds

hundreds of others?

hundreds of others would put dog shit through my letterbox?

He said, well I would put dog shit through your letterbox but I can't speak for *anyone* else but I reckon at least a *few* people would put shit through your letterbox because

I would FOR SURE put shit through your letterbox *definitely* so it means that hundreds would I reckon …

He took my suitcase down.

From the overhead compartment.

He helped me off the train with it.

Like he was a normal, nice person. And there is part of me hoping that even despite his opinions he must surely have kindness within

surely he is not as evil as his words

surely he's just another victim of this government

surely he doesn't have that much hatred within him

because

he hated seeing me struggle with the suitcase even though he had scared me and I was worried that he was going to rape me or hit me or put shit through my letterbox

but that's just what happens around here he said
you better get used to it he said and
and
this is where we live now
home ...

Clover called the priest. Father Nolan, he came around
within hours.
He was excited to be at our flat.
After raping altar boys – exorcisms are a priest's favourite
   thing.
He said there was a bad energy. In the flat.
From the woman who'd killed herself.
So. He did a prayer with us and he flung around some
   holy water and
he said he had cleansed it.
He had cleansed our new home.

17

LUXURY AMBULANCE

THERE IS A FIFTY-POUND note at the back of the cutlery drawer. It's been there for about three months now. A fifty-pound note. Been there since the day I received my book advance. Since the day the funds hit my account. I remember the cashier handing me the fifty-pound note. It was at the post office in the village. The only cash machine within a ten-mile radius of our flat charges for withdrawals so you've got to get to the post office before they close. Otherwise you have to pay extra for your own money. So, I got to the post office. It was the *day* my book advance hit the account. It was a Friday and it was sometime in October. The October just gone, the most recent one. A whole three months after I got the call offering me the deal. We were without money for the first three months of writing this. We were living in the hostel at the time. When I got the deal. Picture this: we're living in this homeless hostel in *Maidstone* when I'm offered a book deal. It's with the biggest publisher in the world. It makes me smile now: homeless shelter, book deal. I can smile about it *now*. It's the grubby kind of story I love. We'd been in the shelter for a month when I got the call with the offer. But it took three months to get the first part of my advance. Didn't receive a penny for three months. And so much had changed in that time. I mean it would, it was a whole three months.

We moved into our permanent flat, painted it, got some carpets laid, took my play on tour around the UK – the play that I wrote that got us cleansed from London. Biddy enrolled in yet another new school and I started dating this political journalist guy. Things had changed; a new life, a new start. But at the same time, a lot *hadn't* changed because we were still living below the poverty line. I was still doing precarious work in between it all, playing catch-up from all the moves, applying for Universal Credit and doing naked video chats on a porn app. My side hustle was pretending to get myself off whilst in my underwear on some app but as I waited for men to choose me I'd productively knock out a few hundred words here and there. These words, perhaps. However, when the men didn't choose me we'd have to use the food bank. To those on the outside my life looked like it was turning around; my one-woman show was on tour and people would want selfies with me afterwards and journalists were keen to talk about my 'writing process' and all that but *then* I'd get back to our flat, put Biddy to bed and log onto the porn app for a few hours.

I was doing all that whilst attempting to write this book.

I kept saying to anyone who would listen at that time: this – is – why – women – like – me – don't – get – to – write

– books. Because time had passed, and things *were* different, but precarity was still prevalent. In fact, writing this book only added to the burden of our poverty. It was an extra job that required full-time attention for which I wasn't getting paid. I didn't even have a computer. My old laptop had given up on me back when we were still in London, so I had to write the first half of this book by hand. This – is – the – grubby – kind – of – story – I – LOVE. Would set my alarm every morning for 3.50am and I'd be out of my bed by four. Stumble into the kitchen, fill the kettle, flick on the radio, pull out my notebook and write. Three hours of scribbles. I'd get Biddy up at 7am, into breakfast club at her school for 7.30, finish my six-mile run by nine and slip into the library where I'd type up the pages I'd written earlier that morning before forwarding them on to my agent and editor.

After a few weeks I became of interest to the librarians Lorraine and Steve. They wanted to know what I was up to each day. What were all these scribbled pages I was hurriedly typing into the communal computer between 9am and 1.30pm before the library shut.

Lorraine smirked at me and mocked in that special way only the Kent accent can, 'What are you doing, writing a memoir?' She said it like I couldn't *possibly* be writing a memoir, who the hell would be interested in my inconsequential failure of a life and then Steve rolled his eyes and chuckled at me gently like he just couldn't be bothered to put the effort into laughing at me properly.

And I said, 'Well, yeah, I *am* actually.'

Then they laughed again, which made me really angry.

'Well, actually I'm signed to Penguin.'

Then they laughed some more, and Steve laughed so much that his big belly was silently jiggling by my face and it made me want to puke. They assumed that I was some mad fantasist just like all the others who sat in the library every day chatting to their dead wives in the History section.

And on the *day* my book advance came in, I went and splashed out on a new laptop so I wouldn't have to see Lorraine and Steve ever again, so I could write a book in the same way that all the other writers signed to Penguin Random House did and after I picked up Biddy from school at 3pm we popped in to the village post office. I requested £100. Dave behind the counter called me a big spender – and he wasn't wrong – then he said, 'How do you want it, Miss Moneybags?' and I asked for a fifty-pound note and five tens. The fifty-pound note went straight in my pocket. And with the five tenners I bought:

A fish and chip supper.

A stash of magazines and sweets.

Topped up the gas and electricity.

And I treated myself to the most expensive bottle of wine in the post office to celebrate. It was called Villa Maria Private Bin, a New Zealand Sav Blanc, which cost me £9.99.

When we got home, before we ate, before I poured myself that first dangerous glass that would once again be sure to lead me to oblivion and regret, I slipped the fifty-pound note into a brown envelope on which I wrote LUXURY AMBULANCE, and I stuck it at the back of the cutlery drawer.

I like to be prepared. I always have an escape plan these days. Whether it's from a relationship or a collapsing building. My life on constant risk assessment – is this man I'm dating a threat? Or, how many bones will we break if we jump from the kitchen window because the stairwell is on fire? We live out in the middle of nowhere and the nearest hospital is roughly 30 minutes away, so, if Biddy falls ill in an emergency and I call an ambulance, we're looking at a minimum of an hour before we're anywhere close to a doctor. It's a killer, it's a literal killer. I'm always looking at ways to survive, ways to protect us, ways to make the little we have go further. Freezing the bread, sticking insoles in shoes with holes, cutting up the toothpaste tube to use every last little bit, ordering a taxi instead of waiting to die.

On the morning my advance comes through I even call the local firm – How much am I looking at for a cab to hospital from here?

Between forty and fifty quid.

Fuck, that's a lot.

But we have that fifty-pound note. It's there. If we need it.

We're lucky to have this option.

It's just a precaution but, if we need it, we've got the money right there.

My good friend, who's dead now, the artist Reg Wilson, he once said to me that you shouldn't get in a taxi or have a meal in a restaurant if you can't afford the tip. It's a rule I always stick by. So, if we have an emergency we have enough to get to the hospital and if there's no traffic there'll be a tip for the driver. And I've upped the odds against my daughter dying. Everybody wins. Maybe.

I stuff the money in the envelope.

The fifty pounds for the luxury ambulance.

I forget it's there. For months I forget about it. What an extravagance to *forget* you have money in a drawer. I'd never experienced that before.

But my book advance had come through and my play had sold out every show and things were looking better for us.

We can spare fifty pounds.

It's at the back of the cutlery drawer.

I *honestly* forget that it is there. The fifty-pound note.

Until the day when I am forced to remember.

Is this poverty porn? Does this turn you on? Is your cock twitching? Your pussy wet? Do I make you want to watch every single episode of *Can't Pay? We'll Take It Away!* Are you hard? You like seeing me naked? Have I written the most grotesque, gratuitous piece of poverty porn ever? Do I make you want to pull on your semi-erect dick as you utter – SO BRAVE, YOU'RE SO FUCKING BRAVE? Do you want to cum all over me as you whisper into my ear with heavy breath – THIS MUST BE SO CATHARTIC? IS WRITING THIS CATHARTIC? Are you so woke that you'll even ask me for permission first, you'll get my explicit consent, you'll say – Can I cum on you? Then you'll say: THANK YOU, THANK YOU, THANK YOU FOR SHARING YOUR STORY, THANK YOU, YOU'RE SO BRAVE, YOU'RE SO FUCKING BRAVE, THANK YOU, YOUR STORY IS SO IMPORTANT. PEOPLE – SO – NEED – TO – HEAR – YOUR – STORY. THANK YOU FOR SHARING YOUR TRUTH. That's when you spunk on my cheap dress (in the most respectful way possible, of course).

Is this making you hard? Are you wet for this? Is *this* poverty porn? Have I written the filthiest book of all time? Should this be banned? Is this obscene? Do I disgust you? Do you think I'm vile? You think I'm vile, don't you? 'She's so VILE!' they'll write on Instagram. They'll write it on the forums. Oh yeah! Is … *this* some kind of literary spit roast? Are you getting off on degrading me? Are you getting off on me degrading myself? Am I basically in Huddersfield's only four-star hotel with two premiership reserve players from a lower-half team? Are they double-ending me? Are they tag-teaming me and filming me as they sweat all over me whilst thrusting into me and shouting as they climax – WELL DONE FOR TELL-ING YOUR OWN STORY, WELL DONE FOR SPEAKING YOUR TRUTH? THANK YOU FOR SPEAKING YOUR TRUTH. Thank you for SHARING your story. Are they high fiving each other as they say it? Do I deserve this? Is it rape? Or am I too vile to even bother raping? Did I ask for it? Did I consent? Have I been used? Am I a whore? Am I like some kind of poverty-porn kiss 'n' tell girl but getting paid a porn stars who rose and quickly fell before me? Because that's what happens to working-class women, isn't it? Isn't it? They do something that digs them out of poverty and then they must fall again, that's what happens, isn't it? Because we don't *deserve* things. And will I have to do a Jade Goody and get a terminal illness and die on a cable channel reality show in order to receive redemption?

Is this book basically a manual on how to create Channel 5-esque content or can I actually make a difference with this story? Can I make my voice heard? What if all of this throws me even deeper into precarity and ridicule?

These are the questions I ask myself every day.

And I'm terrified of the answers.

That's why women like me don't speak up.

The nurse pulls me to the side. You did the right thing, she says. Your daughter is going to be OK. Stop crying, it's OK, she's going to be alright. You were right to bring her to the hospital when you did. If you'd left her a couple of hours, then she'd be in Resus. If you'd left it six hours then you'd be looking at a best-case scenario of some amputated limbs and a childhood spent on Carer's Allowance. If you'd left her overnight to sleep it off then next thing you know you'd be setting up a page on JustGiving begging strangers to fund your kid's funeral. You did the right thing. You spotted the signs and you got her straight here. You're a good mum.

Biddy is lying in the hospital bed tied to an IV feeding her antibiotics to stave off the virus. She is going to be OK. She is sleeping now and recovering. The nurse said I'd done the right thing.

I can't stop pacing and making calls to everyone I've ever met repeating over and over how lucky it was that on the day I received the advance I put away that fifty-pound note. I tell them the story: I put it in the envelope and on that I wrote LUXURY AMBULANCE. I didn't think I'd ever have to use it but I'm lucky that I had that £50 to get us to the hospital. I even tipped the driver. The nurse told me that I'm a good mum. Does that mean the mums who don't have £50 are bad? The ones who put their kids to bed with Calpol to see if they're better in the morning, are they bad mums? The ones who wait until the morning to see if they're better and when they're not they call the ambulance, but it takes at least an hour for them to get to a doctor and by then … They're not good mums?

It's just me and her at the hospital. Just Biddy and me. It's always just me and her, and right now I have never been more grateful. I make more calls. I'm telling everyone the story of the fifty-pound note and how it might have saved my daughter's life.

I'm on a Facetime with Kirsty.

I'm on a Facetime with Clover.

I call my dad and, although he is worried, he doesn't come and visit her. It's just too far away, he says. I'm not surprised by his reaction. But if I could see him, I'd reflect back at him his disappointed eyes, the look he's used on me forever to make me feel worthless. I realise it's just too painful to have him in my life. I send him one final text message. The one I send him every three months. But this *is* the last. I promise. It has to be the last. His granddaughter is seriously ill in hospital and that isn't enough to make him care. I'll just have to mourn him through the remainder of his life in the same way he did with 'the old man'. Another cycle complete.

I think about resurrecting my mum again so I can hear her say, 'I've been expecting your call' – but I don't want her. Or need her. I'd only have to kill her off again.

I think about calling this guy I've been sleeping with for the past few months, this political journalist guy who I'm trying my best to fall for but just can't bring myself to open up to because I can't live without being on guard. And in my head, I'm composing the message I'll leave on his phone – because of course I only choose people as avoidant as me, so he'll let me go to voicemail:

... You know all those pseudo-deep conversations about internalised misogyny, brutalism and our mutual distain for ALL Radiohead albums post OK Computer, *that we have in your bedroom after we have that really nice sex? Well ... I, I need you right now. I'd like you to be here with me. Right now. And once you've listened to*

this message I want you to call me straight back so I can give you the address and you can get here right away. And I don't want you to text me back with some annoying hipster quip like you always *do to make out that you are beyond loving another human – because – I need a proper grown-up person with me right now. The person that you are in the morning when you make me endless cups of tea, when you talk about your family and you don't try and be cool, because you can't be cool, because no one in the world is cool when they wake up at 6am mid-nightmare, semi-erect and stumbling around without their glasses. A human at their most fragile.* That *person. Yeah? Because my daughter is really sick right now, she's really fucking sick and . . . it's just me and her, she's in hospital, we're at the hospital in the middle of nowhere, that's where we are and she is filled with all these tubes and I'd like . . . some-one, I'd like YOU, to be standing next to me right now, someone who at least wants to pretend to have a connec-tion with me (because after all, what is a connection but an act of rare rationality shared between two people who can no longer stand to indulge in false interactions) and I want you to tell me that it's all going to be OK. Can you do that? I just want you to stand next to me and put your arm around me and maybe kiss my head like you did that one time in Hastings when the stones from the hailstorm got in my eyes and irritated my contact lenses – because you made me feel protected for a few seconds and – It's*

*just, I don't know how a person lives an entire life alone
without any support, I don't know how, but I have and I
don't want that anymore because it's really fucking hard
and I just wondered if you were up for joining forces in
some small way ... Meet me at the hospital?*

But I don't call. I delete his number. Right there and then.
He's gone. I'm by the vending machine at the hospital buying
Biddy an overpriced bag of Maltesers and I just block him.
Because. It's all too complicated. Because it's a lot to ask of
someone, isn't it? To invite them into your decade of hell. I've
never had anyone really care about me and it's probably too
late to start expecting that now and ... It's better if there are
no more casualties in all this, it's better if it's just ...

If it's just me and her. It's just Biddy and me. It's just the
two of us. Like it always has been.

And she's going to be alright. I don't need anyone else. We
don't need anyone.

She is still here, and she is everything, and she is beautiful,
and she is alive, and she is all I need. And we are all each other
needs for now.

I'm just glad I had the money to get us to the hospital.

That fifty quid, the money I put aside for the luxury ambulance, the minicab that would get us to A&E because we live
in the middle of nowhere and we don't know anyone, and I
can't drive – it might just have saved her life. I'm lucky, and
she's ALL I need. Three months ago, I wouldn't have had

that money to pay for a taxi. And I know what I would have done. I'd have given her Calpol and put her to bed to sleep it off. And the nurse wouldn't have said that I'm a good mum. She wouldn't have said that to me. And instead of writing this chapter I might be mourning my daughter.

But that's just life and death below the poverty line I suppose.

I write this from my kitchen table, in my council flat, far from the city. I'm wearing tracksuit bottoms, a baggy T-shirt and my hair is scraped up into a Croydon facelift because I've just completed my morning run. And I'd love nothing more than to be conforming to the myth of the troubled, drunk writer / champagne-lifestyle single mum courtesy of the taxpayer (delete as applicable), complete with fag butt-filled coffee mug and menthol super king hanging from my glossy lips, but I'm off the ciggies and on a health kick. And I don't wear vest tops (my tattoo embarrasses me far too much) *or* drink Lambrini. I never did, I never drank Lambrini, but regardless of all that the point is I'm sober right now. And I don't know if it's forever because nothing ever is (even – if – it – sometimes – feels – like – it – might – be) but I'm not drinking. Not today.

And.

I don't own an iPhone X and I don't get my fanny serviced round the back of Wetherspoons, but I *will* hold my hands up and admit that, when I celebrate my birthday at the Harvester, I *do* visit the salad bar an unacceptable amount of times,

I fucking love it. And regrettably, my daughter does have bad attendance at school – a result of having to take her to work with me. What choice do I have? If I'm offered a show all the way in somewhere like Carlisle, I can't afford to turn it down, but I also can't afford the childcare. And any support network I had established back home in London is firmly in the past, we're out on our own here, so sometimes I have to take her to work with me. And I just have to resign myself to the fact that the people who condemn me for that are the same ones who would slam me for being unemployed or would say 'get a proper job' and by that they mean something demeaning designed to destroy all hope and keep you in line and on the cusp of struggle, even though there are *no jobs* – 'proper' or otherwise – in the wasteland far from civilisation where we have been forced to live so … I take her to work with me, she sometimes misses school. The only good thing about her having to change schools so often is that I can always kill off Mother again to ensure we have a funeral excuse. I go with heart attack these days, I find murdered prostitute is a too bit harsh for the ears of the admin staff at the primary school office.

But whatever, Biddy is top of her class. And she doesn't live on a diet of Chicken Cottage – she is currently attempting veganism after being inspired by a piece of art she recently saw about climate change. Look at me, trying to prove that we're not the working-class stereotype created by Channel 5. But my daughter is amazing. Not *despite* what she's been through, or *in spite of* her background – she is just amazing. I know that

'Political' – I use quotation marks to ridicule myself before anyone else gets in there.

Because whenever I've attempted to publicly articulate my desire for an equal society, I have been mocked by the middle class of social media for having what they consider an A-level standard of political discourse. And of course, on hearing that critique I feel ashamed and embarrassed, because it's true. I am entry level. An entry-level woman. The reason I sound like someone with an emerging, confused and aggressively hopeful and excitable appetite for politics is because I'm still piecing together the life I have been leading and connecting it to government policy and patriarchal structures that demonise me and my peers. I am not an intellectual, and it's not something I seek to be. I am a mouthy working-class woman who, through struggle and failure, has found something to be passionate about. My daughter has given me a reason to fight for change. Some kind of meaning behind these terrible tales of mine. A reason to keep existing when things get bad. And the idea that you shouldn't be allowed to voice your discontent until your opinions are fully formed, or of 'graduate standard', or until you are able to mimic the voices of those in power, is just another way to silence and ostracise the working class.

When I stood as a Labour Party candidate a few years back, I spoke out about how poverty was harming the mental health of the most vulnerable in my community, citing my own experiences, sharing my own stories of depravation and depression to humanise the effects of cruel policies, exposing my own life and struggles to help people understand – but my attempts at discussion were met with the hashtag MadCash which was started by a Conservative counsellor and used on Twitter to discredit and mock me. A few years later, when I posted pictures of my empty fridge on Instagram alongside my stories of food banks and homelessness, I was called a liar, accused of fabricating my poverty to gain followers and cause drama and told again and again that I wasn't the 'right person' to be discussing working-class issues – deemed too aggressive for not using 'nice language'. Acceptable middle-class language. Tone policing being the first defence for those in a position of privilege, a successful technique used to silence oppressed voices as we start to rise; painting us as vulgar belligerent bullies who cannot be trusted to behave correctly as we fight to make our point heard – our experiences lost as we shout back to defend ourselves, alienating others from our original purpose and being forced into hiding again. Remaining unheard, further demonised and traumatised by incessant gaslighting as the soldiers of the patriarchy rip us apart and leave us for dead.

A vocal group of women even attempted to have my book deal taken away from me.

This book.

This book that might provide me and my daughter with the opportunity to raise our heads above the poverty line.

They tried to stop me from writing this book.

To keep my lived experiences and stories unheard.

To silence my voice.

And it takes so much emotional labour to fight all that, an energy that is already running on empty when you're just about surviving, when you've got bigger things to worry about, like feeding your kid or finding a new home, and that's why it's sometimes easier just to shut up and go away.

You sound thick.

You sound mad.

You're too aggressive.

You're not the 'right' person to be talking about these things.

But who is better to speak up than the women who are experiencing this oppression and deprivation? And one person speaking out does not deprive another – there is space for *all* of us to use our voices.

And.

… I think it's OK to be unsure, it is normal to be afraid. My approach to politics will probably always remain emotion led and visceral, and that's alright. I blame it on the accent of Penge! And on the lack of confidence that results from a lifetime of stigma and oppression, from those headlines created to demonise us by the people of privilege who silence us in fear of losing their power. But I know that, despite the fact my lived experiences are often disgusting and sordid, they are truly erudite in their message. The feelings, strength and beliefs that have emerged from my experiences cannot be downplayed, they belong to me and they stand alongside the women who share similar lives – so I will continue to participate and listen and learn and *try* to raise my voice whenever I can, but it is shaky. My voice is an awkward and entangled web of verbosity – it doesn't sound clever, but it is definitely loud.

It – is – here.

So, fuck all that. No one taught me to speak nice, like most people out there I can only speak in the language of my streets. And it was only someone of privilege who decided that politics was to be conducted in a voice different to ours. That snobbery, that mockery. It is designed to keep us quiet. It is designed to keep us in our place. To keep us accepting zero hours and low wages and social cleansing.

It's OK to speak out about the injustices of society without coming up with a solution to the problem. Solutions are a team effort.

And it's OK to get flustered when entering into debate with a pompous man at a dinner party who is set in his horrid beliefs, who will shout you down and sneer because he has always been *allowed* to feel important – it is OK to feel unsure and stammer your way through your argument. Because whenever someone attempts to silence me I always remember this: being able to survive in the conditions in which women like us are forced to live, means that we are resourceful and powerful in a way they'll never be able to fathom. We fight to find a sense of worth whilst living in the most undignified of situations. When life collapses down on us we'll go to any lengths to keep our children safe, we'll sink to our knees to feed them and steal the glue required to stick back together their severed self-esteem. We are formidable creatures and, when we nurture our individual power for collective use, then it will be channelled positively to create change. I'm certain of that.

How many unheard voices are out there just like mine?

Mine is just one of many sordid little tales of what life is really like in modern Britain. There are millions of us who have been silenced, millions of us who have been left to rot.

Imagine if we all spoke up together.

NOTES ON WRITING *SKINT ESTATE*

Skint Estate was written between November 2018 and March 2019 in the following locations:

The Cockpit Estate, Marden
Glenmore Road, Belsize Park
Tunbridge Wells Hospital
Zona de Tolerancia, Cancun City

With these songs on repeat:

'The French Inhaler' – Warren Zevon
'Yes' – Manic Street Preachers
'Nightclub Jitters' – The Replacements
'Three Martini Lunch' – Jesse Malin
'Spring' – Vivaldi
'Chinese Rocks' – Johnny Thunders & The Heartbreakers
'Ain't Got Me' – Paul Westerberg
'Killing of a Flash Boy' – Suede

'The Last' – The Replacements

'Orphan Girl' – Gillian Welch

'Post to Wire' – Richmond Fontaine

'Meeting Across the River' – Bruce Springsteen & the E Street
   Band

'Frankenstein'– New York Dolls

'Frightened' – The Fall

'The Fall of Saigon' (Original London Cast Recording)

'Judge Yr'self" – Manic Street Preachers

'Desperados Under the Eaves' – Warren Zevon

ABOUT THE AUTHOR

Cash Carraway is an award-winning playwright, author and screenwriter from London.

In 2018 she was nominated for a British Journalism Award and won 'Innovation of the Year' at the 2019 Drum Online Media Awards. *Skint Estate* is her first book.